Hatemail:
Anti-Semitism on
Picture Postcards

University of Nebraska Press
Lincoln

Hatemail: Anti-Semitism on Picture Postcards

Salo Aizenberg

Foreword by Michael Berenbaum

THE JEWISH PUBLICATION SOCIETY
PHILADELPHIA

Manufactured in the United States of America

Library of Congress Cataloging-in-Publication Data

Aizenberg, Salo, author.
    Hatemail : anti-Semitism on picture postcards / Salo Aizenberg ; foreword by Michael Berenbaum.
        pages cm
    "Published by the University of Nebraska Press as a Jewish Publication Society book."
    Includes bibliographical references and index.
    ISBN 978-0-8276-0949-5 (pbk.: alk. paper)
    1.   Antisemitism in art. 2.   Jews in art. 3.   Antisemitism—Europe—Pictorial works. 4.   Political postcards. 5.   Aizenberg, Salo—Art collections.   I. Title.
    NC1878.J4A39 2013
    305.892′400222—dc23
                                                                                                    2013017955

CONTENTS

FOREWORD

I began reading Salo Aizenberg's manuscript, *Hatemail,* deeply skeptical that it would be worthy of publication; by the end, I was deeply ashamed of my own skepticism. Permit me to tell you why.

I was speaking with a new college graduate about her job hunt and asked her to tell me her "elevator speech." Every fundraiser knows the term. If you are riding up the elevator with an important potential donor and only had the time between the first and twentieth floors to make your pitch, what would you say? How do you boil down the complexity of your case statement into a one-minute conversation that is impactful, interesting, and invites further consideration?

By coincidence, as I was reading Aizenberg's manuscript, I paused to have breakfast with an old friend, the head of one of the nation's largest greeting card companies, whose late father-in-law began the family fortune by selling what was then known as penny postcards. He reminded me that for a postcard to sell, it must do something similar to an "elevator speech." It must condense a complex range of visual impressions into one compelling shot; one picture that is worth a thousand words, one image that tells the story. For a caption on a postcard to work, its brevity must be impactful; very few words, carefully chosen, must do the work of many.

In my work with museums, I always remind the designers, curators, and historians that we also have to create an experience for the visitor who is travelling sixty-five miles an hour and will not spend the time that the exhibition deserves. The visitor pressed for time must be able to grasp the basic storyline in billboard fashion. Aizenberg creates just such an experience here. Open any page, to any postcard, and you quickly get the message. This book, with its powerful visuals and its brief explanations that contextualize these visuals, is a work to be treasured. It is also one to be dreaded and feared.

The hypothesis of *Hatemail* is original. Forget the endless orations of anti-Semites, the racist publications and quasi learned texts, political double speak, and the class warfare of the elite. If you want to understand anti-Semitism in a specific country and at a specified time, look at what people were sharing with one another, what they were willing to say openly for all to see without fear of consequences in notes to loved ones, cards to friends. Anti-Semitism is less problematic when said in hushed tones in the privacy of one's bedroom or with intimate friends in the living room, but it is far more dangerous when people are willing to share it openly. If you say something in the privacy of your home, those listening may understand that the view espoused, the hatred poured forth, is somehow inappropriate for public consumption. But if you share it on a postcard for postal carriers and neighbors to see, on postcards that are sold at stands that are produced for a mass market, then you are reaching another level entirely.

I admire the juxtaposition of what we can see and what we read. Aizenberg gives us an informed survey, country by country. We traverse the European continent: France and Germany, Great Britain, Poland, Hungary and the Ukraine, among others. We cross the Atlantic to the United States and journey down to North Africa. We find postcards that were sent from the resort areas of Karlsbad and Marienbad and their famous baths, where many diverse peoples came to get treatments and where Gentiles would encounter Jews, giving them a good amount of discomfort. (As I saw those images, I was reminded of the fact that while anti-Semitism was widespread in the United States, Jews vacationed among their own there; recall the once-thriving Jewish Catskills).

Aizenberg briefly covers anti-Israel postcards and those that can still be found circulating in the world of Islam, where anti-Semitism is most virulent today. He devotes an entire chapter to the Dreyfus trial and its aftermath in France, and another to the proliferation of scathing postcards in Nazi Germany. (The Nazis did not invent the image of the Jew that had been portrayed in German postcards, they merely followed the implications of those images to their most extreme—their most "final"—conclusion.)

Hatemail serves as a concise—and I was tempted to say painless, but seeing these images is quite painful—introduction to anti-Semitism in the years since postcards were invented and in their heyday, the sixty years between 1880 and 1940. Such cards were "eagerly disseminated, shared by the general population, delivered by government-operated post offices and later saved by collectors." There was no effort for the sender to "remain anonymous."

One must be grateful to Salo Aizenberg for his most impressive collection, but I wondered why he was so clearly drawn to this hateful material. The answer he gave was twofold: (1) These postcards represent actual documented history of anti-Semitism, and in a world where revisionists try to deny the Holocaust and the Jewish connection to Jerusalem, we need to preserve as much actual evidence that we can; and (2) his basic fascination with history.

And to understand this history, we must confront its dark side. As one sees image after image, one is struck by how grotesque they are, and uncomfortably familiar. Jewish faces are depicted with long noses; Jewish bodies with misshapen feet and distended stomachs. (It is no wonder that American Jewish historians consider the crowning of the beautiful Bess Meyerson as Miss America and the making of baseball star Hark Greenberg a national hero essential to ushering in the postwar decline of anti-Semitism in the United States.) In these postcards, both poor and rich Jew, Jewish Communist and uber-capitalist alike are depicted with disdain. Seeing these images in multiple languages, in diverse countries, over a span of six decades, one perceives that the motifs are eerily common, basic themes with only mild variations.

Those of us who were raised in post World War II America and who can live anywhere we desire, do anything we are capable of doing, and who seldom, if ever, experience any obstacles to our career or personal advancement because we are Jewish, those of us who were raised in a world where Israel is a reality, and where we, together with Theodore Herzl and the early Zionists, believed that the normalization of the Jewish condition would end the pernicious hatred that is anti-Semitism, are shocked to see how pervasive it was. And we can't help but question if it could someday be so again.

Aizenberg has performed a valuable service. By collecting such vicious relics of the past and sharing them with us, he reminds us that hatred and scorn can become insidious. He reminds us that motifs so deep in modern culture are not easily eradicated; motifs so widely disseminated can morph into new images and take on new forms in new media.

If only we could live in a world where these images and the sentiments behind them could have shared the fate of the vanishing postcard!

Michael Berenbaum
Los Angeles, California

Dedicated to Karine, Tal,
and Maayan

Many thanks to my parents for
their support and advice.

Special acknowledgment to
Markus Krah, Lite Sabin,
Hane Liebmann, Dr. Evelyn Wortsman,
and Annie Kleinhaus for their
assistance with translations.

Hatemail: Anti-Semitism on Picture Postcards

INTRODUCTION

We think of hate mail as a form of harassment in which a sender mails a recipient, typically an individual, a letter containing offensive or threatening remarks. The sender usually remains anonymous since the act may be illegal or invite a lawsuit. Today, hate mail is often perpetrated through the Internet on forums, blogs, and social websites. This book will examine an entirely different, more virulent type of hate mail that was distributed in vast quantities worldwide beginning in the late 1890s and lasting through the 1940s. It was conducted in the open with no effort by the sender to remain anonymous, and with the secure knowledge that the act would not result in any negative consequences. In fact, this hate mail was eagerly disseminated and shared by the population, knowingly delivered by government-operated post offices, and later saved by collectors. This hate mail came in the form of postcards that had images on one side that conveyed a clear message of disgust and abhorrence for a *specific* group of people, often framed in the form of "humor." I am referring to anti-Semitic postcards, whose target was Jewish people collectively.

Most people today associate the postcard with the short, innocuous missive we occasionally receive from parents or friends vacationing abroad. The postcard has become truly irrelevant, long ago replaced by phone calls, e-mail, Facebook, and Twitter. There was a time not so long ago, however, when the world was awash in postcards, with literally billions sent each year. They were part of the everyday fabric of life and an important tool for short and quick communication. Before looking at anti-Semitic postcards, it is important to know how postcards in general became the "text messaging" system of one hundred years ago.[1]

A BRIEF HISTORY OF
THE POSTCARD

The postcard was a revolutionary way for people to keep in touch. Prior to its development, postal authorities only allowed sealed letters. Like most new messaging tools, there was initial resistance to both the picture-less *postal card,* pre-stamped by the post office with one side left blank for the text, and to the more colorful *picture postcard;* postal authorities feared that a cheaper and shorter form of mailing would cannibalize the more profitable business of closed letters.

The postcard dates back to the 1860s in both the United States and Europe. In 1861, John P. Charlton of Philadelphia invented and copyrighted the preprinted postcard. His invention had a preprinted message on one side, which was usually an advertisement, and space for a stamp and an address on the other. Charlton quickly passed the rights to a certain H.L. Lipman, and the new postcards were imprinted with the phrase "Lipman's Postal Card." Although the copyright for this postcard was filed years earlier, the first known use was on October 25, 1870. The Europeans were no less in the postcard avant-garde. In October 1869, the Austro-Hungarian postal authority issued a prestamped postal card (*Correspondenz-Karte*) based on a recommendation by Dr. Emmanuel Herrman. A German named Heinrich von Stephan developed the same idea separately in 1865. In October 1, 1870, the Swiss and British postal authorities introduced their own prestamped cards. Figures A and B are examples of the first Austro-Hungarian and British postal cards.

In the same fortuitous year of 1870, a French stationer named M. Leon Bésnardeau produced the first picture postcard. Bésnardeau's card was illustrated with military and patriotic designs for use by the French army, then fighting the Franco-Prussian War. When the post office authorized these postcards, France unknowingly became the first nation to allow picture postcards to be sent. By 1872, nearly all countries in Europe had introduced government-issued cards, and the U.S. Post Office followed in 1873 (privately produced postal cards, such as the Lipman postcards, were already permitted). The low postage rates induced companies to buy large quantities for use as acknowledgments or price notices. Later, many companies added logos or small images promoting products, effectively transforming these government-issued cards into picture postcards. By the late 1880s, picture postcards had come into use in Europe; town and village views were the most common subjects.

The Paris Exhibition in June 1889, celebrating the public opening of the Eiffel Tower, was a milestone for postcards as well as for architecture. Few people at the time had been as high off the ground as the summit of that tower, and the opening event attracted worldwide attention. A French newspaper publicized a postcard with a small vignette of the tower that people could purchase and post from the top. This genius of a scheme proved widely popular. The year 1870 may be the official date for the birth of the picture postcard, but 1889 is the year it began to capture the imagination of the public. Figure C is an early example of an Eiffel Tower postcard. Other European countries quickly imitated the French innovation, and soon visitors could mail a picture postcard from the top of any summit. In the early 1890s, German postcard publishers developed a chromolithographic printing process, which allowed them to create high-quality, multicolor postcards, further accelerating postcard usage. Figure D depicts one of the earliest multicolor litho postcards. In the United States, the picture postcard made its debut at the World's Columbian Exposition in Chicago on May 1, 1893. Figure E shows one of the first American picture postcards.

FIGURE A. Austrian *Correspondenz-Karte* mailed from Prague to Vienna in 1871.

FIGURE B. Unused British postal card from 1870–1871.

FIGURE C. Early example of an Eiffel Tower postcard, mailed from Paris in June 1892.

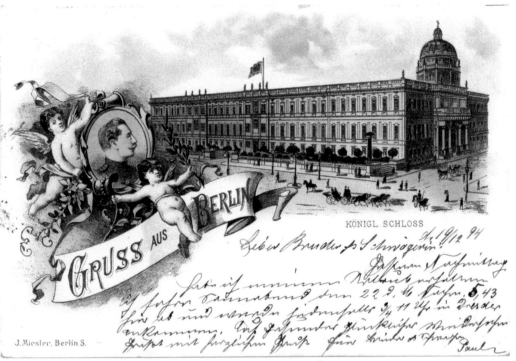

KÖNIGL. SCHLOSS

GRUSS AUS BERLIN

J. Miesler, Berlin S.

FIGURE D. Early example of a typical "Gruss Aus," or "Greetings From," litho postcard printed in Germany. This 1894 postcard depicts the Royal Palace in Berlin with an image of the Kaiser at left.

U.S. NAVAL EXHIBIT.

BATTLE SHIP "ILLINOIS."

OFFICIAL SOUVENIR POSTAL WORLD'S COLUMBIAN EXPOSITION.

FIGURE E. An example of one of the first picture postcards printed in the United States. The card was issued at the World's Columbian Exposition, which opened in Chicago on May 1, 1893. The card shows a full-scale model of a modern battleship, the *Illinois,* built for the U.S. Naval Exhibit.

THE GOLDEN ERA: A WINDOW ON THE WORLD

Over the remainder of the 1890s, picture postcard production expanded rapidly in both Europe and the United States, fueled by the development of photography and the printing trades. The years 1895 through 1898 saw an explosion in postcard usage and stimulated what is known as the Golden Era of postcards, which lasted unabated until World War I. An estimated 200 to 300 billion postcards were sold over this twenty year period, or 10 to 15 billion on average every year. In Great Britain alone, an estimated 2 billion postcards were purchased in 1906, or fifty for each of the country's 40 million residents. Similar statistics and descriptions of the "postcard craze" of the Golden Era abound. It is easy to understand how images and messages, both favorable and hateful, could be spread massively and quickly.

The manufacture of billions of postcards spawned an industry comprised of hundreds of companies employing many skilled workers. The Germans became the undisputed industry leaders during the Golden Era, supplying postcards for just about every country in the world, including the United States. German-made postcards were of the highest quality, including the litho types that are still highly sought after by collectors today—especially the *"Gruss Aus,"* or "Greetings From," multiview cards from every city in the world. Many young German printers emigrated to Great Britain and the United States to establish businesses, using skills they learned at home. But there was an underbelly to the success: the Germans were also the unrivaled leaders in the production of anti-Semitic postcards, not only in terms of quantity and quality, but also in the virulence of the messages and images.

Postcards of the Golden Era depicted every possible topic from the sublime to the ridiculous, from the serious to the raunchy: cities, villages, and landscapes (the most common themes); ethnicities and racism—not only against Jews, but also against blacks, Asians, and others; politics, royalty, wars, and special events; industry, technology, and transportation; fantasy, satire, art, comics, and nudity; holidays, greetings, and religion; and everything else from natural disasters to sports. Instead of television and the Internet, postcards were the window to the events and peoples of our world.

Golden Era cards were not merely a means of sending a message. Half of them were saved by collectors who helped spur the development of postcards; as they actively sought new and exciting images, the publishers made every effort to meet their demands. Collectors asked acquaintances to mail them postcards from their travels, as evidenced by the large number of surviving examples with the phrase "for your collection" written on the reverse. Postcard aficionados proudly placed their acquisitions in albums serving as do-it-yourself coffee table books that expressed their taste and expertise in any subject they fancied. Collecting postcards was revealingly described by the media as a classless craze that swept the world.

World War I created a new reason to publish postcards, resulting in tens of thousands of unique images printed by all nations involved in the conflict. But after the Great War, the popularity of postcards declined significantly and the Golden Era ended. Reasons included the development of the telephone, increased postal charges, greater use of photographs in other media, such as newspapers and magazines, as well as the economic difficulties of the postwar period. Germany, the leading postcard producer, was devastated by the war; the presses shut down. Only a few of the original printers returned to full-time postcard production in the 1920s. An epoch had come to a close. Postcards were still widely used in postwar times, but the quantity and diversity of the Golden Era would never again be replicated.

Fortunately, many Golden Era postcards survive to this day, providing us with an incredible visual window to a bygone world that cannot be met by any other medium. Motion pictures were in the earliest stages of development at this time, and there was no television. The development of photography went hand in hand with the growth of the postcard industry, and, indeed, a large proportion of postcards were based on the work of professional photographers. However, photographs were not commercially produced in the same volume as postcards, and they were not mailed around the world. Postcard publishers often commissioned photographers to produce images specifically for postcard production. Thus, many photos survive in postcard format only. Finally, most newspapers and printed media didn't use photographs prior to 1910. For all these reasons, the photographic record is neither as extensive as the postcard record nor as available to historians.

Postcards also offer significant benefits to the historian that photographs lack: detailed captions that explain the picture; written messages that provide a historical context; postal cancellations and stamps that offer useful data; and, often, a colorized image from a time when black and white photos were the standard. In addition, many postcards were based on artistic works or drawings developed specifically for the postcard, providing the historian with yet another visual medium. Political satire cartoons are an important example of such non-photographic elements. Nearly all of the postcards shown in this book are of the artistic or cartoon variety, but, in this case, they were used as weapons to display hatred toward Jews and all things Jewish.

SOME WORDS ON ANTI-SEMITISM

Before delving further into the topic of postcards, an introduction to anti-Semitism and its roots is in order.[2] Anti-Semitism refers to a belief or behavior hostile to Jews just because they are Jewish. An expansive definition was issued a few years ago by the European Monitoring Center on Racism and Xenophobia (EUMC):

> Anti-Semitism is a certain perception of Jews, which may be expressed as hatred toward Jews. Rhetorical and physical manifestations of anti-Semitism are directed toward Jewish and non-Jewish individuals and/or their property, toward Jewish community institutions and religious facilities. Such manifestations could also target the state of Israel, conceived as a Jewish collectivity. Anti-Semitism frequently charges Jews with conspiring to harm humanity, and it is often used to blame Jews for "why things go wrong." It is expressed in speech, writing, visual forms, and action, and employs sinister stereotypes and negative character traits.[3]

Anti-Semitism dates back to ancient times, when Jews were criticized for remaining separate from the pagan societies in which they lived. An early example can be found in the biblical book of Esther (3:8–9) when Haman, the advisor to the Persian king, advocates for the persecution and annihilation of Jews. The canard of Jews as an alien and disloyal people emerged in antiquity.

But Christianity provided the tragic kindling wood for millennia of anti-Semitism. In the first centuries after its rise, most Jews were unwilling to convert and accept Jesus as the Messiah. As Christianity grew to become the dominant faith, underscored by the Roman emperor's conversion in the fourth century CE, Jews became a tiny religious minority in a region where the church and state were the same. However, it was still understood that Christianity had its roots in Judaism, a contradiction that the newly dominant religion needed to address. To reconcile the contradiction, Christianity asserted that since the Jews rejected Jesus as the savior, they were no longer the chosen people of God, and now Christians were the "new Israel." Far worse was the charge that Jews were responsible for the death of Jesus, even though it was the Romans who ordered and carried out the crucifixion. All Jews, present and future, were held collectively responsible for this act. By the sixth century , this core root for Jewish hatred had become firmly established in Christian thought. With every reenactment of the story of Jesus over the centuries, millions of Christians were taught that the Jews had committed the worst crime in history. Shockingly, it was only in 1965 that the Roman Catholic Church issued a declaration stating that Jews could not be held responsible for Jesus's death, decrying acts of anti-Semitism. Even so, old canards linger. A 2009 poll showed that 23 percent of people surveyed in several European countries, including Germany, France, and the UK (and 48 percent in Poland alone), believed that Jews were responsible for the death of Christ. Many observers believe that Mel Gibson's highly popular 2004 film *The Passion of the Christ* perpetuated the charge of Jewish responsibility for Jesus's death, an opinion that was bolstered by Gibson's well-publicized anti-Semitic rant in 2006. The issue still resonates, evidenced by a widely broadcast statement by Pope Benedict XVI in March 2010 affirming that the Jews did not kill Jesus—as if this fact was still in dispute.[4]

The charge of deicide led to further discrimination, with Jews excluded from positions in government and many areas of economic and social activity. The separation eventually led to certain myths about Jews that literally demonized them, such as the belief that Jews had horns and tails and engaged in the ritual slaughter of Christians. This accusation of murder, known as a *blood libel,* was first made in England in 1144 to explain the mysterious death of a Christian boy. The blood libel, and its variations, would be a prominent feature of anti-Semitism throughout history, even in recent years. In August 2009, the Swedish newspaper *Aftonbladet,* with a circulation of well over one million readers, stated that the Israel Defense Forces harvested the organs of Palestinians—even though the editor-in-chief admitted that the newspaper had no evidence of this charge.[5] The exclusion of Jews from most professions and sectors of trade (including agriculture, since Jews were forbidden to own land in most of Europe) left only a handful of occupations in which Jews could earn a living, primarily commerce and money lending. This led to the most enduring negative stereotype against Jews, that of the money-hungry businessman and usurer. The stereotype of the greedy Jew evolved into accusations that Jews were unproductive parasites who took advantage

L'EBREO ERRANTE.
LE JUIF ERRANT

Ho oltraggiato Cristo ed ora vado errando senza tregua alla ricerca di una Pace... che non trovo.

J'ai outragé le Christ et maintenant j'erre sans cesse à la recherche d'une Paix introuvable.

FIGURE F. "The Wandering Jew," further captioned at the bottom in Italian and French: "I offend Christ and now I am wandering ceaselessly in search of a peace that cannot be found." This postcard makes clear that the suffering of the Jewish people, not only at the time of Jesus but also today and in the future, is a direct result of their transgressions against Jesus. Jews were supposedly condemned to wander the earth until the day of final judgment. The myth was "bolstered" by actual events that made it seem that Jews were moving from place to place—of course, as a result of persecution and expulsions. The Jew in the image is wearing a German *pickelhaube* military helmet, implying that the Jews are in league with Germany. This postcard was published in Italy during World War I, when Italy and Germany were enemies. Associating Jews with foreign forces (ironically, in this case, German) was a typical tactic frequently found in the anti-Semitic postcards of France during the Dreyfus Affair, as described in chapter 1. [Publisher: Società Editoriale Milanese, Milan; 1917.]

Kozacy rabuią
Die Kosaken plündern
Az artatlan hazátlanok
Kozáci pustoši

S. Adam pinx.

FIGURE G. "The Cossacks Plunder" is an artistic image of a Jewish family lamenting the burning of their home by mounted Cossacks engaging in a pogrom. The Cossacks were a Slavic group of people who lived in the area of the Ukraine and southern Russia. From time to time, armed bands of Cossacks would attack and plunder Jewish homes and property, such as during the Chmielnicki Uprising in the seventeenth century and the Kiev pogroms of 1919. [Publisher: Wydawnictwo Salonu Malarzý, Krakow, Poland; mailed by Austrian military field post office to Vienna in September 1917.]

of the labors of others. The corollary to this stereotype was that Jews were cheap. By the end of the Middle Ages, the alleged characteristics of Jews, both physical and behavioral, transformed the Jew into a dehumanized and mythical figure completely disconnected from reality.

Widespread, irrational hatred for Jews led to regular acts of violence. One prominent violent expression of anti-Semitism was the pogrom, or the organized destruction of Jewish communities. The pogrom arose out of the religious fervor of the Crusades, which began in 1096, when soldiers swept through Jewish villages in Europe looting and killing their inhabitants. Over the next five hundred years, hatred of Jews manifested itself in dramatic ways. A notable example was the expulsion of Jews from England ordered by King Edward I in 1290. Similar expulsions occurred in France in the 1390s as well as Spain and Portugal in the 1490s. During the Bubonic Plague in the fourteenth century, which ultimately killed about one-third of Western Europe's population, Jews were blamed and persecuted for poisoning wells and spreading the disease. With Jews seen as responsible for the horrible wave of deaths (the multitude of Jews who died of the plague was ignored), virtually every Jewish community in Europe was attacked. The situation for Jews did not improve in subsequent centuries; Jews were subject to continued persecutions, expulsions, exclusions, and special requirements, such as being forced to live in a ghetto. The Protestant Reformation in the sixteenth century did

little to change attitudes toward Jews. On the contrary, Martin Luther, the founder of the Protestant Reformation and one of the most prominent anti-Semites in history, effectively called for the slaying of all Jews. Pogroms continued well into the twentieth century, such as the July 1946 pogrom in Kielce, Poland, which resulted in the death of about forty Jews.

In the eighteenth and nineteenth centuries, the condition of Jews began to improve in many parts of Europe as the idea of universal human rights and equality of individuals began to emerge. Several nations granted emancipation to the Jews, ostensibly providing full civil rights and citizenship and allowing Jews to enter professions previously denied to them. Even so, high levels of discrimination and ancient stereotypes were still prominent in daily life. An anti-Semitic myth that developed in this era was the concept of Jewish control of the world, combined with the old accusation of their disloyalty to their home nations. This concept was most prominently disseminated in Russia around 1905 through the publication of the so-called *Protocols of the Elders of Zion,* which purported to be a document stolen from a secret Jewish organization that sought world domination. Although an obvious forgery, with much of the text copied from earlier French writings, the document still continues to be endorsed by many Muslim leaders. For example, in 2002, Egyptian state-owned media released a forty-one-part television series called *A Knight Without a Horse* based on the *Protocols.* The Egyptian infor-

FIGURE H. "Germany for Germans." This 1902 postcard evokes a long history of Jewish expulsions from European countries and cities throughout the Middle Ages and thereafter. A strong medieval soldier character, a representation of the German nation, is seen holding up a sword in a threatening manner and pointing at the Jews to leave. A sign at the far right points to the destination: "To Palestine." A large caravan of Jews is seen fleeing in panic into the horizon at right. In the background at the far left is the Hermann Monument, which commemorates a decisive Germanic victory over the Romans and represents the "values" of the German nation, which, of course, excludes Jews. The image makes it quite clear what many Germans wanted at the time: to kick the Jews out and live in a country comprised of only "pure" Germans. Their goals were realized a few decades later. It is ironic that dozens of Muslim nations and their supporters today want the opposite: for the Jews to leave the Holy Land. In May 2010, Helen Thomas, a prominent White House reporter, remarked that Jews should "get the hell out of Palestine" and "go home" to "Poland and Germany." It is doubtful that she has ever seen this postcard.[6] [Publisher: Illegible; mailed within Germany in July 1902.]

mation minister rejected calls by the U.S. State Department to prevent the broadcast.[7] Around the same time as the *Protocols* was published, one of the most prominent anti-Semitic events in modern history occurred: the Dreyfus Affair, in which a French Jewish army captain was falsely accused of being a spy. This incident was a stark reminder that anti-Semitism remained a powerful force, even in the enlightened societies of Europe. Forty years later, one-third of worldwide Jewry was murdered in the Holocaust.

Although Jews were generally considered to be better off living under Muslim rule versus Christian rule during the Middle Ages and the Ottoman era, they were still heavily discriminated against. Both Jews and Christians were regarded as *dhimmis,* or non-Muslim subjects deserving of protection, but only as second-class citizens with Muslims considered superior. Jews were subject to certain rules, such as restrictions on dress and outward expressions of religion, their testimony was not valid in court, and they were required to pay special taxes. Classical anti-Semitism was prevalent; for example, a famous blood libel in Damascus, Syria, in 1840 led to the arrest, torture, or death of several Jews. In the last century, the attitude of Muslims toward Jews has dramatically changed with more virulent hatred and increased violence directed at Jews. Today, all of the major themes of classical Christian anti-Semitism have been fully adopted by Muslim nations and their media, including a perverse new one—the comparison of Jews and Israelis to Nazis.

In addition to the evolution of Muslim anti-Semitism, in the last thirty years, a new form of anti-Semitism has arisen globally with a focus on Zionism and Israel as a proxy for hostility to Jews. A key reason for the rise of the new anti-Semitism is the fact that traditional, overt anti-Semitism has become unacceptable in mainstream democracies (it is still perfectly acceptable in Muslim nations). The new anti-Semitism is, by design, more subtle, thereby more frequently avoiding condemnation. The EUMC, whose definition of anti-Semitism was cited earlier, offers examples of how anti-Zionist and anti-Israel criticism becomes anti-Semitic, regardless of the motive: "denying the Jewish people their right to self determination; applying double standards [to Israel] by requiring of it behavior not expected or demanded of any other democratic nation; using symbols and images associated with classic anti-Semitism to characterize Israel or Israelis; drawing comparisons of contemporary Israeli policy to that of the Nazis; holding Jews collectively responsible for the actions of the state of Israel."[8] One feature of contemporary anti-Semitism that continues an old stereotype is the concept of "Jewish Power," or the idea that Jewish lobbies and shadowy groups control the levers of economies and governments.

WHY POSTCARDS AND ANTI-SEMITISM?

have explained why postcards provide a unique method of studying history—at the simplest level, they provide us with a way to see images of places and events from a century ago. But postcards become an even more powerful tool when used to understand social phenomena like anti-Semitism. As I've noted, the postcard was a quick form of communication that was used frequently by the average person living in Europe and the United States around the turn of the twentieth century. Although the written message was the most important aspect of the communication, publishers printed images on the obverse side that would appeal to the sender as well as the collector, offering a second reason to purchase the card. The fact that anti-Semitism was chosen by so many publishers reveals two points: first, the general public demanded and was willing to spend money on postcards that had messages derogatory to Jews; and second, the anti-Semitic image was not something shocking or unusual, but an accepted, everyday concept that was part of the fabric of society. Clear evidence of the routine and ingrained nature of the anti-Jewish depiction is the similarly routine and banal messages usually written on the reverse. In most cases, the message did not make any reference to the image, which was a view like any other; to the sender, it was no different from mailing a card with a picture of a local landscape. In some cases, the message did refer to the image with the sender pointing out the anti-Semitic "comedy" to the recipient. It provided the recipient with a small laugh, much like jokes that are passed around by e-mail today. Sinister or heinous implications were not considered.

Postcards were thus unique since they represented, perhaps, the only form of "casual" anti-Semitism that was practiced daily by average folk. Anti-Semitism was, of course, disseminated in numerous other ways that are well documented: newspaper articles and cartoons, books, pamphlets, speeches, blood libels, pogroms, and so on. But the key distinction from all of these other forms is that the anti-Semitism was either perpetrated by leaders and prominent intellectuals (e.g., journalists, authors, and politicians) or groups of people who could be considered radical (e.g., a lynch mob or an anti-Semitic association), not the general population through exercising a basic and common task—sending a short communication. Sending this type of postcard would be similar to an e-mail today containing a short anti-Semitic quip as a footer appended to the message. Anti-Semitism on postcards was therefore a chilling form of day-to-day hatred occurring millions of times per annum, and subtly delivered across the population by the postal system, enhanced by collectors. The longevity of the collectors' work makes a book like this possible. But the objective is now completely different.

The ordinary and pervasive nature of this hate mail supports the position presented by Daniel Goldhagen in his controversial 1996 book *Hitler's Willing Executioners*. The key thesis of the book is that one of the aspects that made the Holocaust possible was the fact that anti-Semitism was an ingrained and widespread part of German culture. The Nazi leadership did not have to force the destruction of Jews onto the German population; people saw it as a natural outcome of the cultural hatred for Jews that had been widely prevalent for many centuries. Quite simply, Germany was a nation that embraced anti-Semitism and was thus in agreement with the "Final Solution," even if only a small portion of the population actually implemented it. Germany was the lead producer and sender of anti-Semitic postcards. Although it is not possible to calculate figures, the numbers were enormous based on the overall scale of postcard usage during the Golden Era. The vast majority were discarded at the time, just like mail today (two world wars also destroyed a large number), but a large quantity survived as evidence.

I don't believe that it is a coincidence that German anti-Semitic postcards outclassed other nations in the virulence of their hatred. It makes sense based on the acts committed against Jews that were so easily accepted in the 1930s and 1940s. In contrast, American and British anti-Semitic postcards were significantly more benign, usually depicting "humorous" images of greedy, large-nosed Jews, but not Jews as demonic or Jews being expelled and persecuted. This matches how Jews were treated in these two countries—they were discriminated against, often quite visibly but never to the level of organized violence or state-sponsored discrimination. Anti-Semitic postcards were

FIGURE I. This 1900 postcard is a stark example of how ordinary people, in this case a German, practiced "day-to-day" anti-Semitism by purchasing and mailing a postcard. The image shows a group of stereotypical, large-nosed Jews, "Israelites," encamped around a directional sign that points "to Frankfurt am Main" (commonly known simply as "Frankfurt") in Germany. The poem tells the story:

Moses parted from his people
He was buried in a cave,
And from a fiery cloud above
The God of Israel declared:
'Moses aggrieved you already
For as long as 40 years,
Hence I made a resolution
To provide you a sweet reward:
Go forth to the German land
Master there the people, rule it.
On the banks of the river Main
Go set up your residence.'

The text mockingly implies that instead of leading the Jews to the promised land of Israel, Moses, who wasted forty years wandering the desert, was told to bring his people to Germany. The anti-Semitic punch line is that the Jews were also instructed to "master" the German people and "rule" the country, alluding to the myth of Jewish power and control. This postcard, which was the second of a series of three cards, was published by the Hotel Kölner Hof in Frankfurt, which publicly and proudly prohibited Jews from entering its establishment. The hotel even served beer to guests in mugs inscribed with the words "Kauft nicht bei Juden," or "Don't buy from Jews."[9] The hotel was a prolific publisher of anti-Semitic postcards that were sold to guests and visitors (see figures 2-23 and 3-23 for other examples). The guest who purchased and mailed this postcard clearly endorsed the anti-Jewish message, writing on the front: "Last night I was with [illegible] and thought of you. I am sending you warm greetings from this *Judenstadt* [Jew City] 'New-Jerusalem.' Your brother-in-law Otto Müller [also signed Elizabeth]." Frankfurt was sometimes referred to in anti-Semitic fashion as the "New Jerusalem on the Jordan River of Frankfurt," implying that Jews had so overrun the city it had become like Jerusalem of the Holy Land (the Main River of Frankfurt is shown in the panel at bottom). The Nazis used the same terminology to refer to the city decades later. [Publisher: Hotel Kölner Hof, Frankfurt; mailed from Frankfurt to Magdeburg in October 1900.]

FIGURE J. The picture side of this German postcard from 1914 (not shown) depicts an artistic image of three medieval German soldiers; the image is not anti-Semitic. However, the person who purchased this postcard and mailed it decided that, along with a written message, he or she was going to paste an anti-Semitic label above the message to make clear that they did not care for Jews. The quote by Johann Wolfgang von Goethe, considered by many to be the most important German writer, says: "The Israelite nation has never been worth much, as it has been a thousand times reproached by its leaders, judges, principal men, and prophets; it possesses few of the virtues and most of the flaws of other nations." The deliberate action of transforming a regular postcard into an anti-Semitic one by adding this label is evidence that anti-Semitism was not just perpetrated by political leaders, journalists, and rabble-rousers, but proactively practiced by ordinary Germans through the mailing of postcards—this was truly hate mail. [Publisher: Not provided; mailed within Germany in April 1914.]

(and, in Muslim nations today, still are) a litmus test and a neglected historical record for the cultural pervasiveness and virulence of anti-Semitism in a society.

Unfortunately, even though the Holocaust is now more than sixty-five years in the past and Germany today ranks as one of Israel's main supporters,[10] anti-Semitism and threats to the destruction of the Jewish people remain in full force, arising primarily from the Muslim nations and their numerous sympathizers. The leading propagator of anti-Semitism today is the Iranian regime, most visibly its president, Mahmoud Ahmadinejad. In October 2005, President Ahmadinejad famously stated that "Israel must be wiped off the map." Officials from Iran and its proxies in Gaza and Lebanon (Hamas and Hezbollah) regularly spew the worst kinds of anti-Semitic language.[11] In Western nations, hints of underlying anti-Semitism regularly creep into our daily lives, from statements by actor Mel Gibson, journalist Helen Thomas, and Christian Dior designer John Galliano, to nasty anti-Israel articles and statements that reflect double-standards that can only be explained by anti-Semitism. Anti-Semitism is sadly as relevant as ever, and it is therefore important to continue to study and understand this hatred; postcards provide another tool in this effort.

Postcards are also relevant to the study of anti-Semitism because they provide a tangible history that cannot be refuted. This is critical today since a key aspect of "modern" anti-Semitism is the attempt to rewrite or erase Jewish history. In a television program called *Jerusalem—History and Culture,* aired by the Palestinian Authority in August 2009, a university lecturer argued that the Jews invented their connection to Jerusalem and that Jews are engaging in "an attack on history, theft of culture, falsification of facts, and Judaization of the place."[12] There are numerous other examples of arguments that Jews have no connection to the Holy Land, Jerusalem, or the Temple Mount.[13] A second area of revisionist history is Holocaust denial. In December 2006, the Iranian leadership, in charge of the seventeenth most populous country in the world, hosted a Holocaust denial conference, inviting prominent anti-Semitic authors and deniers to attend.[14] In my first book, *Postcards from the Holy Land, A Pictorial History of the Ottoman Era, 1880–1918,* the postcard evidence clearly demonstrates the Jewish ties to the region and the Jews' presence during the Ottoman Era (ironically, in most cases, these postcards were published in Germany). In this book, anti-Semitic postcards document the anti-Semitism that was the precursor to the Holocaust.

OVERVIEW OF THE ANTI-SEMITIC POSTCARD

The first anti-Semitic postcards were issued in the 1890s at the same time that postcards in general were becoming popular. In fact, there was a convergence between the start of the Golden Era and the Dreyfus Affair. In this famous incident that began in 1894, Alfred Dreyfus, a patriotic French army captain, was falsely accused of passing military secrets to the German military attaché in Paris. Even though there was no visible motive and all the evidence was circumstantial, the blame was laid on Dreyfus for one reason: his Jewish heritage. Dreyfus was convicted in 1895 in a sham trial that featured "secret" evidence that Dreyfus's lawyer was not allowed to examine; the army invoked national security as a reason to keep the documents hidden. Even after the army became aware of the real spy and the fact that some of the evidence against Dreyfus had been forged, Dreyfus was reconvicted in a second trial held in 1899 (after Dreyfus had spent four years in harsh prison conditions on Devil's Island). Fortunately, Dreyfus was pardoned by the French president ten days after his second conviction, but he was still not exonerated. Only in 1906 did the court declare Dreyfus completely innocent.

The Dreyfus Affair reached deep into French politics and society, splitting the nation between those who supported nationalism, the Church, and a military that spared no effort to continue the cover-up, and intellectuals, progressives, and a small handful of brave politicians and army officials who wanted to learn the truth and promote an equal society. Underneath the drama was the unmistakable anti-Semitic nature of the affair and its influence on the fate of the entire nation. The Dreyfus Affair was also important as one of the factors that influenced Theodor Herzl, the founder of the Zionist Movement, to recognize that anti-Semitism could not be eliminated and that the Jews needed their own homeland. The affair still resonates, with new books written each year about the incident and its relevance to current events. The Dreyfus Affair was the perfect subject for postcards at the time, since it included all types of sensational events, such as political scandals, forgeries, a suicide, arrests, and, of course, anti-Semitism. All of these subjects are depicted on numerous postcards as featured in chapter 1.

The postcards shown in this book cover multiple nations, every stereotype, and every form of hatred. They depict Jewish men, women, and children with large noses, grotesque feet, deformed bodies, ugly faces, and poor hygiene; money-hungry Jews; rich, crafty, cheap, and cunning Jews; Jews in control of the world; Jews as animals and demons; and Jews as cheaters. They show Jews being ridiculed, mocked, attacked, excluded, and expelled. The reader will not be spared the full extent of the hatred; I believe many will be shocked with what is shown in this book. Even readers who have previously studied anti-Semitism and its messages might be surprised to realize the evil that could be placed on a simple postcard and widely used around the world by "regular" people living in what were considered to be enlightened democracies. Germany, France (including its North African territories that had significant Jewish populations), Great Britain, and the United States were the leaders. Austria, Hungary, and Poland were also key participants. Fewer examples are found in other nations, not necessarily because anti-Semitism was weaker, but because postcards were published in much fewer numbers in these locations. Each country's postcards had a distinct style of anti-Semitism.

As mentioned, Germany ranked first in anti-Semitic postcards, producing images that immediately cut to the heart of the matter: Jews are filthy animals that deserve to be persecuted, expelled, and excluded from society. French postcards were a close second in their vileness. Images of Jews in control of the world or as evil or ugly money grabbers are the main motifs in French anti-Semitic postcards. Those from other nations, especially Great Britain and the United States, were sold almost exclusively as "humorous" souvenirs—but the anti-Semitism was still palpable. British anti-Semitic postcards generally avoided the worst forms of imagery, instead focusing on large-nosed Jews as conniving and money-hungry. American anti-Semitic postcards are the least virulent, focusing almost entirely on Jews as greedy. American postcards also ridiculed the physical features on Jews, drawing not only large noses, but also large hands and awkward mannerisms.

The postcards in this book all come from my personal collection, which I have been amassing for the last ten years. The more than 250 examples depicted here are only a small sample of the many thousands of different types that were printed, but they will take the reader through the many permutations of hatred for Jews and help us to better understand a phenomenon which still exists throughout the world today. The reader will then be able to more effectively identify and combat anti-Semitism—especially when anti-Semitism today is often more subtle and disguised in euphemisms (e.g., the "Israel Lobby"). The first chapter will introduce the emergence of the anti-Semitic postcard during the Dreyfus Affair; the second chapter will describe the various stereotypes and themes found in anti-Semitic postcards from all countries. Chapters 3 through 6 will survey the postcards of the countries that were the leading publishers of such postcards in the order of their vileness, Germany being the most and the United States the least. Chapter 7 offers examples from several other countries. Chapter 8 continues the study of German postcards, highlighting a particular type of card that depicts a Jew known as "The Little Cohn." Chapter 9 also focuses on a subset of cards, in this case from the spa towns of Karlsbad and Marienbad, which are located today in the Czech Republic. The last two chapters will examine postcards from the Nazi era and modern anti-Israel types. The reader will not be surprised that the Nazis published these types of cards, but it is useful to understand how several decades of German anti-Semitic postcards culminated in the 1930s. Anti-Israel postcards show a newer form of anti-Semitism. Ironically, Nazi motifs are often used in these cards to depict Jews as evil and murderous.

CHAPTER 1

THE DREYFUS AFFAIR AND THE BIRTH OF THE ANTI-SEMITIC POSTCARD

As described in the introduction, the Dreyfus Affair and the emergence of the Golden Era of the postcard created the perfect conditions for the birth of the anti-Semitic postcard. Although there were anti-Semitic postcards published in Germany around the same time as the Dreyfus Affair, it was this incident that made international headlines and fueled the production of thousands of different postcards, including numerous anti-Semitic types.

Documents, public and private, genuine and forged, were the key catalysts that moved the Dreyfus Affair forward through all of its lurid twists and turns, as will be summarized in this chapter. The case began with the discovery of a torn memorandum exposing the fact that the French military had a spy in their midst, a story leaked to the anti-Semitic press helped press the case against Dreyfus, forged and secret documents were used to falsely convict Dreyfus, and a scathing letter published in a newspaper was critical in the reopening of the case. Postcards also served as important documentation that affected the outcome of the affair. Public opinion was critical in influencing government and court action, and postcards helped shape attitudes, both for and, by a large majority, against Dreyfus.[1] There were many hundreds, if not thousands, of Dreyfus-related postcards published in the 1890s, mostly in the 1897–1900 period as the Golden Era was entering its peak. The "anti-Dreyfusard" postcards depicted Captain Dreyfus as a large-nosed, money-hungry miscreant still in league with the German enemy. The "Dreyfusard" postcards showed Dreyfus simply as a French army captain (the fact that he was Jewish was not shown) and supported the various brave politicians, journalists, and lawyers who championed the truth. Both types of cards will be highlighted in this chapter.

The backdrop to the Dreyfus Affair was the German defeat of the French in the Franco-Prussian War of 1870–1871. Twenty years later, France was still licking its wounds from the devastating loss, and the nation remained fearful of Germany's growing strength. The revelation that French military secrets were being passed to the Germans created a sense of panic and paranoia. At the same time, anti-Semitism experienced a strong resurgence in France, led by its principal propagator, Edouard Drumont. Drumont fanned the flames of Judeophobia in 1886 with the publication of *La France Juive* (Jewish France), a virulent text that asserted that the nation was in the clutches of Jews, calling for their expulsion. Drumont was not just a fringe radical. His book was a best seller; with more than 100,000 copies sold in its first year, it became the most widely read book in France. In 1892, Drumont launched a newspaper called *La Libre Parole* (the Free Word), an anti-Semitic daily with a circulation of 200,000, which blamed all ills on the Jews. Drumont parlayed his newspaper fame into politics; he was elected as a member of Parliament in 1898.[2]

FIGURE 1-1. Edouard Drumont (1844–1917) is bordered by the newspaper he controlled, *La Libre Parole* (the Free Word). Drumont was a rabid anti-Semite who constantly railed against Dreyfus, his supporters, and anyone who even hinted their support for the Jewish officer. The initial story of Dreyfus's alleged espionage was first published on October 29, 1894, in *La Libre Parole*. The paper not only announced that a Jewish officer had been arrested, but claimed certainty of his guilt. Drumont was one of the leading anti-Dreyfusards and was influential in swaying public opinion against the Jewish officer. [Publisher: S.I.P., France; circa 1900.]

On ne croirait pas à te voir,
Que tu descends en droite ligne
D'un Youpin portant on sautoir
Une besace remplie de Vermine!

Depuis, la besace s'est remplie
De nos écus, le vieux filou!
Mais pour empêcher qu'on oublie
Il reste ton nez, face de grigou!

Drumont.

FIGURE 1-2. A Jewish man at the left is shown in ragged clothes and torn shoes; he has a generally ugly appearance. The anti-Semitic poem at right was written by Drumont: "It is hard to believe looking at you, that you are descended from the line of a *Youpin* [a derogatory word for a Jew, similar to 'kike'] carrying a bag filled with vermin, since the bag was filled with our coins, by this old crook. But your nose is there to prevent us from forgetting, you skinflint [defined as a miser and a swindler]." Was Drumont ostracized for his views? On the contrary, Drumont was elected to parliament in 1898 and his anti-Semitic book, *La France Juive,* continued to be published in France into the 1940s. [Publisher: Not provided; circa 1899.]

SUMMARY OF THE AFFAIR

Hundreds of books have been written about the Dreyfus Affair (e.g., in June 2010, the *New York Times* reviewed one of the latest books on the subject: a 560-page tome called *Dreyfus: Politics, Emotion, and the Scandal of the Century*) and a detailed study of the incident can be easily found elsewhere. I will thus offer a summary that will highlight some of the sensational twists and turns of the case, and provide context for the picture postcards.

The affair began in September 1894 when a cleaning lady (working for French counter-intelligence) stole a letter from the wastepaper basket of Maximilian Von Schwartzkoppen, the military attaché at the German embassy in Paris, and took it to the French intelligence office. The unsigned letter, which became known as the *bordereau* (detailed memorandum), revealed that a French military officer was spying for the Germans. Suspicion quickly fell on Captain Alfred Dreyfus, an artillery officer, primarily because he was Jewish. The head of French military counter-intelligence, Colonel Jean-Conrad Sandherr, happened to be a known anti-Semite. Handwriting experts concluded that Dreyfus authored the *bordereau* even though two out of the five examining experts disagreed with the finding. Although this one piece of evidence was obviously flimsy and there was no motive cited for his alleged treason, Dreyfus was arrested in October 1894.

The matter remained an internal military affair and may have possibly ended without fanfare; however, a subordinate of Colonel Sandherr and another known anti-Semite, Major Hubert-Joseph Henry, leaked the story to Drumont's *La Libre Parole*. The arrest of the "Jewish officer A. Dreyfus" was published the next day, with the article stating that there was "absolute proof that he had sold our secrets to Germany." The military office now had no choice but to pursue the matter to its end since the press and the public had already condemned Dreyfus; the officers in charge of the investigation did not want to be next in the crosshairs of the aggressive anti-Semitic press.

The trial began on December 19, 1894, and lasted four days. The secretive proceedings relied mainly upon the testimony of the handwriting experts. To overcome the weakness of the evidence, Major Henry provided the judges with a fabricated file that identified Dreyfus as a traitor. Dreyfus's defense lawyer was not allowed to review the file in the name of national security. The military court was fully persuaded by the "evidence" and pronounced Dreyfus guilty of high treason on December 22. On January 5, Dreyfus was paraded publicly in the courtyard of the military academy and stripped of his badges and buttons. The nearby crowd called out, "Death to the Jews!" In March 1895, Dreyfus arrived at Devil's Island in French Guyana to serve his life sentence in horrible conditions.

The affair might have ended with Dreyfus spending the rest of his life in captivity; however, the real spy, still at large, continued to pass secrets to Schwartzkoppen. In March 1896, the new head of counter-intelligence, Colonel Georges Picquart (who succeeded Sandherr) obtained another note from Schwartzkoppen's wastepaper basket; this time the retrieved document implicated a certain Major Ferdinand Walsin Esterhazy. Picquart did not assume that the new document and the *bordereau* were connected and simply believed that he had found a new traitor. Picquart began to quietly investigate Esterhazy and was stunned to find that his handwriting matched that of the original *bordereau*. Picquart brought the new evidence to his superiors, but they had no intention of reopening the Dreyfus case. Admitting to this error would have brought great embarrassment to the military leadership; therefore, the new evidence was buried. In order to further obscure the evidence that Picquart had uncovered, Major Henry (the same one who fabricated the file against Dreyfus in 1894) produced another forged document known as the *faux Henry* that named Dreyfus as the spy. In a twist right out of a television thriller, the forger Henry commissioned was found hanged in his room a few months later in circumstances that still remain unclear. Even though it was clear that Picquart would face an uphill battle, he remained convinced of Dreyfus's innocence and would not let the matter fade; consequently, Picquart was relieved of his position and sent to a posting abroad in December 1896.

Over the next months, the Dreyfus family, led by the captain's wife and brother, continued their attempts to exonerate Dreyfus and to show that Esterhazy was the actual spy. The Dreyfus family had been made aware of certain evidence against Esterhazy as well as the fact that Dreyfus was convicted with evidence that was held in secret. A new military hearing was finally held in January 1898 to discuss the Esterhazy matter, but the deck was stacked against Dreyfus's supporters. Most of the key evidence against Esterhazy remained secret and the hearing ended with the unanimous acquittal of Esterhazy. The military was determined to protect Esterhazy and ensure that the original verdict against Dreyfus could not be reversed. The ruling seemingly ended any possible reexamination of the wrongful conviction of Dreyfus, but public opinion soon changed the course of the affair.

A few days after the Esterhazy hearing, a novelist named Emile Zola published in the Paris newspaper *L'Aurore* an open letter to the president titled "J'Accuse" (I Accuse). In this letter, Zola stated that Dreyfus was convicted on false evidence, and he accused specific military officers of perpetrating the fraud. Zola added that the court knowingly acquitted the guilty party, Esterhazy. The letter also asserted that anti-Semitism was a key factor in the campaign against Dreyfus. The letter proved to be a sensation. Unfortunately for Zola, the accusations were too strong for the military to accept; Zola was brought to trial for libel in February 1898. Zola was convicted, but the verdict was overturned on a technicality leading to a second trial. Zola lost his case again, but rather than serve his one-year jail sentence and pay a fine, Zola hastily fled to England.

Fortunately, the article resonated among the public and led to calls over the next months for a "Revision" of the Dreyfus case. The controversy deeply divided French society. The military, most politicians, and the Catholic Church, along with the anti-Semitic press and its sympathizers, collectively known as "anti-Dreyfusards," allied against the Revision; Socialist politicians and certain intellectuals supportive of the Revision were called "Dreyfusards." In July 1898, the newly appointed minister of war, Godefroy Cavaignac, decided that he was going to muzzle the Dreyfusards and end the controversy once and for all by producing the original proof against Dreyfus. Standing before the National Assembly to discuss the matter, Cavaignac unwittingly presented the secret dossier from the original trial, as well as the *faux Henry,* which was read aloud for the first time. Cavaignac's demonstration was enthusiastically received by the assembly and the press declared the Dreyfus case a "buried matter." However, the next day Picquart openly challenged Cavaignac, asserting that the documents were, in fact, forged. Cavaignac publicly stood by the evidence and refused to reconsider Dreyfus's conviction. Picquart was punished again; this time he was arrested on the charge of passing military documents to civilians.

In spite of Cavaignac's stated position, the doubts expressed by Picquart and others about the authenticity of the documents left him with some doubt, and he chose to investigate further. Cavaignac ordered an officer to reexamine the documents, and the new inspection concluded that the document had, in fact, been forged by Colonel Henry. Henry was called in for questioning, and he eventually confessed to the forgery and perjuries in the Dreyfus trial. Henry was sent to prison, where he subsequently committed suicide. On the same day, Esterhazy fled from Paris to London, realizing that he risked arrest. Initially, the anti-Dreyfusards were overwhelmed with the new revelations, but they created the absurd theory that Henry's act was a "patriotic forgery" since the real evidence could not be revealed to the public without divulging military secrets. This stance was widely accepted and military leaders (including Cavaignac) refused to see a reason for a retrial. However, citing the new evidence, Prime Minister Henri Brisson requested that the court reconsider a retrial, and the court agreed. Brisson's bold move was met by the anti-Dreyfusards with fury and accusations of a campaign against the army, eventually leading to the resignation of Brisson and his cabinet. Nevertheless, the court's acceptance of the review still stood; after many months of deliberations, on June 3, 1899, the court annulled Dreyfus's sentence and ordered a new court martial to be held at Rennes. Dreyfus was transferred back to France in July 1899 following five years of harsh confinement and held at a military prison to await the new trial.

With all of the information that had come to light in the previous months, it was assumed by the public and international observers that the Rennes trial would be a mere formality that would lead to Dreyfus's exoneration. After all, that same July, prior to the start of the new trial, Esterhazy, from safety in England, publicly admitted that he was the author of the *bordereau* under orders from his superiors. Unfortunately, the army still had no intention of allowing its error to be recognized.

The new trial began on August 7, 1899, and immediately became bogged down in endless testimony and deliberation that avoided the core issues. Conveniently, for the anti-Dreyfusards, Esterhazy's admission was considered null and void. On August 14, Dreyfus's lawyer, Fernand Labori, was shot and severely wounded and could not attend the hearing for a week. After a month-long trial, on September 9, Dreyfus was stunningly found guilty of treason once again, but this time with what the court called "extenuating circumstances." The verdict caused an international uproar and the intense pressure led President Loubet to pardon Dreyfus ten days later on the condition that Dreyfus withdraw his appeal. After the exhaustion of his incarceration, Dreyfus accepted the pardon, even though he still was not actually considered innocent. Another seven years would pass before Dreyfus was fully vindicated. In 1903, a new government ordered a review of the 1899 court martial, and in July 1906, Dreyfus was granted a full pardon and an award of the Cross of the Legion of Honor. Simultaneously, the court identified Esterhazy and Henry as the real culprits.

AFTERMATH OF THE AFFAIR

The Dreyfus Affair still resonates. Three examples offered below demonstrate how the affair influences current events even though it ended over a century ago. First, in February 1994, the head of the French army's history section published a study that cast doubt on Dreyfus's innocence, stating that "Dreyfus's innocence is the thesis now generally accepted by historians," implying that it was unproven and open to research and interpretation. The study glossed over the army's cover up and instead noted that the affair resulted in "the dismantling of French military intelligence and a reduction of funds for the armed forces at a time of German rearming." Amazingly, this echoed the century-old argument by the anti-Dreyfusards that a new trial and acquittal for Dreyfus, even if technically justified, would undermine the strength of the army. The French defense minister was furious when he read the study, which still managed to be published in the army magazine *Actualite,* and promptly dismissed the historian. Another historian discussing the publication of the study noted, "Unfortunately, it confirms the persistence of the old anti-Dreyfusard mentality, conserved and transmitted for over a century."[3]

Second, in September 2009, Yale University Press published a book by Louis Begley titled *Why the Dreyfus Affair Matters.* Begley made a connection between the abuses of the French government and military and the actions of the last Bush administration in the war on terror (e.g., the issue of the detainees at Guantanamo Bay, Cuba). A key element of the thesis was the abuse of civil liberties countered by claims of national security. While I have

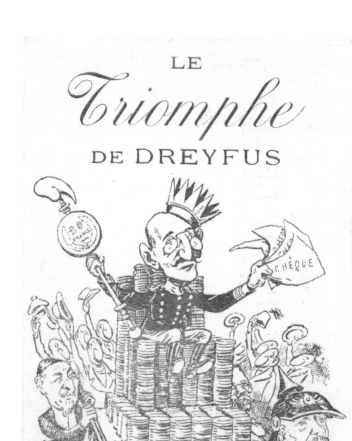

FIGURE 1-3. "The Triumph of Dreyfus," published after the officer's pardon in 1899, was a typical anti-Semitic postcard of the Dreyfus era. Dreyfus is shown with a large nose (even though he did not have one) and exaggerated ears, riding on top of a pile of money and holding checks, thereby asserting that Dreyfus committed espionage for money. Dreyfus, as the king of money here, is being carried by a German soldier, a religious Jew (*back left*), and Joseph Reinach (*front left*), a Jewish politician who supported Dreyfus. Reinach wrote a series of articles about the case, specifically highlighting its anti-Semitic elements. The postcard implies that Dreyfus and his Jewish carriers are in league with the Germans and thus should not have been pardoned. [Publisher: Edition Francaise (A.M.L.), Paris; 1900]

not analyzed the merits of Begley's argument or claims against Bush's actions, the author clearly believed that the Dreyfus Affair was an important antecedent to the actions of a U.S. president many decades later and that lessons could be drawn from the original event.

The third example demonstrates that the spirit of the Dreyfus case and its overt anti-Semitism remain alive into the second decade of the twenty-first century. A story in the Israeli media published in July 2010 stated that Carmen Weinstein, the nearly eighty-year-old head of the small Jewish community in Egypt, was sentenced to three years in jail for defrauding an Egyptian businessman. The court indicated that Weinstein had sold land belonging to the Jewish community, but after receiving payment, refused to transfer ownership or refund the money. Echoing the tactics used in the Dreyfus trial, Weinstein was never informed of the "trial" and, thus, could not defend herself. The media in Egypt and other Arab countries used the incident to launch attacks against Weinstein and Jews in general, similar to Drumont and the anti-Semitic French media. The article noted that the Egyptian media had reported previous attempts by third parties, including Egyptian members of Parliament, to fraudulently sell Jewish property in Egypt using forged documents and fake powers of attorney. These events led to various lawsuits and accusations involving these politicians. The same land was at the core of the case against Weinstein. This case has the same ingredients as the Dreyfus Affair: false accusations, forged documents, secret trials, and political intrigue thickly smeared with anti-Semitism.[4] In this case, Egypt and the Muslim world replaced France as the key perpetrators of anti-Semitism.

In conclusion, the Dreyfus Affair demonstrates how anti-Semitism can transform a seemingly civilized society into one that is shockingly crude—just like the delivery of anti-Semitic postcards reduces an advanced communication system (the post office) into an institution that disseminates hatred. Although France in the late nineteenth century was, in most ways, a modern Western nation, it was still one where a book that argued for the expulsion of Jews was a best seller. France was reeling from its defeat by the Germans, and in that time of fear, Jews were a convenient scapegoat. Like the anti-Semitic postcards that documented it, the Dreyfus Affair foreshadowed the Holocaust. Germany, too, was an advanced Western nation that lost all standards of civilization in its drive to destroy the Jewish people. One positive outcome of this anti-Semitic affair was its impact on Theodor Herzl, the founder of the Zionist movement. Herzl was apparently shocked by the events of the Dreyfus Affair and its obvious anti-Semitic nature. It was one of the factors that led Herzl to believe that the Jews would not be secure without a homeland.

FIGURE 1-4. This colorful and detailed postcard is titled "Souvenir of the Process of the High Court 1899–1900." It shows Dreyfus and his supporters dancing in celebration of the pardon, while two anti-Dreyfusards (*upper right*) leave France in exile and another stands behind bars. Dreyfus, at far left, is depicted wearing the German *pickelhaube* military helmet, insinuating that he was in league with the enemy. Dreyfus and the only other Jew depicted in the postcard, Joseph Reinach (*lower left wearing the yellow hat*), are holding bags of money, suggesting Jewish greed. Pierre Waldeck-Rousseau, at bottom center, was a politician who initiated the Dreyfus pardon and amnesty laws that ended prosecutions related to the affair. Émile Loubet, waving a yellow hat, was the president who signed the pardon on September 19, 1899. Alexandre Millerand, pouring the red wine, was a Socialist politician (and, from 1920–1924, the president) who supported the retrial. On the anti-Dreyfusard side were André Buffet, Paul Déroulède, and Jules Guérin. In 1899, all three were arrested for conspiracy in an unsuccessful attempt to overthrow the republic. Déroulède and Buffet were exiled, and Guérin, a rabid anti-Semite (profiled in figure 1-7), was jailed. While Déroulède, Buffet, and Guérin were not active players in the Dreyfus Affair, the postcard's publisher considered the trio true patriots, in contrast to the rejoicing, money-hungry Jews and their traitorous enablers. [Publisher: Not provided; signed Les Norwin's; 1900.]

FIGURE 1-5. This 1900s-era postcard depicts Emile Zola lifting up an ugly "baby" Dreyfus, who is holding a glass of the green drink known as absinthe. Absinthe is an alcoholic beverage made with a mixture of wormwood herb, green anise, and sweet fennel. The drink, highly popular in France in the late nineteenth and early twentieth centuries, supposedly had powerful psychoactive and hallucinogenic properties, although there is no evidence that it was more powerful than other spirits. By 1915, absinthe was banned in most European countries due to these alleged effects; these bans were overturned in the 1990s, and the drink has experienced a revival. The implication of this postcard is that Emile Zola was delusional as a result of drinking the "Absinthe Dreyfus," demonstrated by his famous letter supporting the Jewish officer and accusing the military of fraud. Captain Dreyfus is shown in typical anti-Semitic caricature. [Publisher: Not provided; circa 1900.]

FIGURE 1-6. This postcard depicts a stereotypical Eastern European Jew with an enlarged hooked nose, long beard, and hunched posture. The caption says: "Jaurès: humanity is not a Jewish newspaper." The postcard is critical of Jean-Léon Jaurès (1859–1914), a politician who became the leader of the French Socialist Party in 1902 and remains an important historical figure of the French Left. Jaurès was a committed anti-militarist who tried to use diplomacy to prevent what evolved into World War I. He was assassinated by a French nationalist in 1914, prior to the outbreak of war. During the Dreyfus Affair, Jaurès was the editor of the socialist newspaper *La Petite République*, and he wrote a series of articles strongly supporting Dreyfus and shedding new light on the trial. Jaurès also came out against anti-Semitism, although only after considerable evolution in his thinking. The anti-Dreyfusards railed against Jaurès and portray him as a Jew in this postcard (he did happen to wear a thick beard and mustache). The message suggested that Jaurès's newspaper was a Jewish one and that the positive traits of "humanity" could not be found in such a publication.[5] [Publisher: Not provided; circa 1900.]

FIGURE 1-7. Portrait of Jules Guérin, signed by Guérin himself (*at center*) on August 15, 1899. Guérin was a self-declared anti-Semite and one of the most outspoken anti-Dreyfusards. He founded the aptly named *Ligue antisémitique de France* (Anti-Semitic League of France) in 1897 with a membership of about 5,000. Guérin also published a weekly newspaper named *L'Anti-Juif* (The Anti-Jew), which published, among other things, the address of every Jewish tradesman in Paris and cartoons depicting "the flight of the Jews along the boulevards and their panic and agony—and their massacre."[6] Guérin joined forces with Paul Déroulède and André Buffet in their attempted conspiracy against the state (as described in figure 1-4), but when a warrant for his arrest was issued, Guérin and a number of his followers barricaded themselves in his newspaper's offices on Rue de Chabrol, in what was famously called the Siege of Fort Chabrol. In order to avoid bloodshed, the government cordoned off the building; after a 37-day siege, Guérin finally surrendered. He was sentenced to ten years' imprisonment. [Publisher: Not provided; mailed within Paris in May 1900.]

FIGURE 1-8. An image of Jules Guérin's Fort Chabrol, headquarters of his anti-Semitic newspaper. The sign in front of his building says "Grand Occident de France," that was the name of the right-wing anti-Semitic organization which was originally called the Ligue Antisémitique de France. The sign also says "AntiJuif" to make the purpose of the organization clear to passersby. These signs were unremarkable in the center of Paris 100 years ago. [Publisher: Not provided; 1900.]

THE MUSEUM OF HORRORS

These three postcards depicted (figures 1-9, 1-10, 1-11) are part of a set adapted from fifty-one hand-colored posters titled *Musée Des Horreus* ("museum of horrors" or "freak show"), which depicted key supporters of Dreyfus, from politicians to journalists, as animals such as pigs and horses. The drawings were created for the opening of the Paris World's Fair in April 1900, after Dreyfus was pardoned, by an artist operating under the pseudonym V. Lenepveu. The posters were eventually banned, but the images, still in circulation, were mailed across the world through postcards. These images are a prime example of the virulent and personal attacks the Dreyfus affair elicited.

FIGURE 1-9. Card No. 1 of the Musée des Horreurs series depicts Joseph Reinach, a Jewish politician and supporter of Dreyfus, as an ugly rat, with a caption calling the creature a "Jew Ball." Reinach's stance, and of course the fact that he was a Jew, enraged the anti-Dreyfusards. Drumont called Reinach "the false Frenchman, the classic German Jew, the typical invasive Jew."[7] Depicting Jews as animals was a common method of dehumanizing Jews, and rats were among the most favorite creatures used; one example is in the Nazi anti-Semitic movie *The Eternal Jew*. The film stated: "Where rats turn up, they spread diseases and carry extermination into the land. They are cunning, cowardly, and cruel; they travel in large packs, exactly the way the Jews infect the races of the world."[8] See figure 4-4 for another portrayal of a Jew as a rat.

FIGURE 1-10. Card No. 4 of the series is an image of Emile Zola, the author who wrote a public letter accusing the military of falsely convicting Dreyfus, as "The King of the Pigs" sitting on a trough filled with his own books. Zola is shown painting a map of France from a bowl captioned "Caca International" (International Dung), asserting that by supporting Dreyfus, Zola tarnished the nation. The term "international" implied that foreign forces, or the stereotypical worldwide Jewish conspiracy, were behind it all. The far right section of the map highlights the Alsace region, which was ceded to Germany in the Franco-Prussian War of 1871. The meaning is clear: it was the fault of traitors like Dreyfus and Zola that the French nation lost to Germany.

FIGURE 1-11. Card No. 7 of the series shows the head of the chief rabbi of France at the time of the Dreyfus Affair, Zadoc Kahn, attached to the body of a fox. The title of the postcard, "Kabosch d'Ane," has a double meaning. The first meaning is "head of a donkey," a further insult to Rabbi Kahn; the second is a play on words whereby the part of the first word that is spelled *bosch* was a derogatory word for a German. Dreyfus was accused of being in league with the hated Germans, and so his supporters were considered German sympathizers as well. Kahn spoke out against the growing anti-Semitism in France in the late 1880s and 1890s and denounced Drumont's *La Libre Parole* for its campaign against Jewish army officers. Kahn officiated at the wedding of Captain Alfred Dreyfus in 1890. During the trials, Kahn actively supported the Dreyfus family and testified in court in support of Dreyfus's good character. The postcard shows the rabbi cutting off the tail of a cow, suggesting that by supporting Dreyfus, he was amputating part of France. The poster at right indicates the prices for the "sacrifices" against France that Kahn was willing to make in return for money.

STERNFELD'S SET OF 12 "DREYFUSARD" POSTCARDS

This set of twelve postcards, published by G. Sternfeld in late 1898, recounts certain key events and highlights some of the major players in the Dreyfus affair from October 1897 to October 1898. In the fall of 1897, Dreyfus was still imprisoned on Devil's Island following his conviction in 1894, and there was an ongoing campaign by Dreyfus's family and his supporters, the Dreyfusards, to obtain a Revision, or retrial of the case. In September 1898, the court finally decided to consider a Revision, although it would be another nine months before the retrial actually began. In contrast to the anti-Semitic postcards that vilify and dehumanize Dreyfus and his few supporters, these postcards take the pro-Dreyfus side, which is not surprising since they were published by a Jewish-owned company.

FIGURE 1-12. Card No. 1 of the series. The first postcard of the series introduces the Dreyfus Affair and the attempt to secure the Revision. The French Republic is represented by a blindfolded woman who is being led away from the Revision (this word is printed above the rising sun at left) by the church and the army, the two key anti-Dreyfusard institutions.

FIGURE 1-13. Card No. 2 of the series. The publisher continues to introduce the affair by showing a portrait of Captain Dreyfus and a drawing of his confinement in chains. Note the normal and realistic representations of Dreyfus, in contrast to the common anti-Semitic depiction of the Jewish officer with a large nose, surrounded by money, and wearing a German military helmet.

FIGURE 1-14. Card No. 3 of the series. Here we are shown the real traitor, Maj. Ferdinand Walsin Esterhazy. By the time these postcards were published, it was clear to objective observers that Esterhazy was the actual spy, but the evidence did not convince the obtuse court to clear Dreyfus. When Esterhazy was first suspected, he realized that he may be arrested and convicted, so in order to protect himself and deflect scrutiny, Esterhazy invented an incident where an unknown "veiled lady" gave him a document, as imagined in the drawing, which could compromise certain senior diplomats. Esterhazy was acquitted in January 1898.

FIGURE 1-15. Card No. 4 of the series. This postcard depicts Godefroy Cavaignac, who was appointed the minister of war in July 1898. He immediately embroiled himself in the affair with an attempt to publicly announce the hidden evidence against Dreyfus in the hope of ending the matter. Cavaignac presented the secret documents in Parliament, and his speech was later posted publicly; the image at left shows people reading the speech. The next day, Colonel Picquart (shown in card No. 8 of the series) announced that the documents presented by Cavaignac had in fact been forged, a revelation which led to a reexamination of the evidence. Even after Cavaignac realized that Picquart was correct, he refused to acknowledge that it proved Dreyfus's innocence.

FIGURE 1-16. Card No. 5 of the series. At the left are representations of various anti-Dreyfusard factions jeering at Emile Zola (who is not actually shown in the postcard), who, following the acquittal of Esterhazy, published his famous letter accusing the military and the government of falsely convicting Dreyfus. Zola was subsequently found guilty of libel and fled to London to avoid serving a jail sentence. The anti-Dreyfusards are (*from left to right*): the army, the church, and a man and woman of the general public. The portrait at the right is of Henri Rochefort, an anti-Dreyfusard and owner and editor of the newspaper *L'Intransigeant*, which, like Drumont's newspaper, was rabidly anti-Semitic. The postcard also shows several images of newspapers which played a major role in swaying both public opinion and government action in the Dreyfus Affair.

FIGURE 1-17. Card No. 6 of the series. The next postcard highlights the key players in the trial of Emile Zola, shown at center. At the left is a portrait of Fernand Labori, the lawyer who defended Zola in the 1898 trials (shown in the circle at the right) and, later, Dreyfus in his second trial. During Dreyfus's second trial, Labori survived an assassination attempt (his attacker was never identified) and missed a week of the trial. The portrait at top depicts Georges Clemenceau, an ardent Dreyfusard and journalist who, as owner and editor of *L'Aurore*, published and supported Zola's letter. Clemenceau was also a politician who later served two terms as prime minister of France, first from 1906 to 1909, and then again from 1917 to 1920.

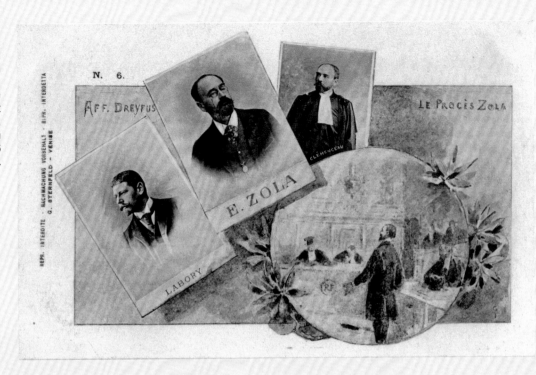

FIGURE 1-18. Card No. 7 of the series. This postcard honors Auguste Scheurer-Kestner, a member of parliament and one of the very few politicians who vocally supported Dreyfus. Scheurer-Kestner was made aware of Esterhazy's guilt by information provided to him by a friend of Colonel Picquart (shown in card No. 8 of the series). With this evidence, Scheurer-Kestner publicly pressed for a legitimate investigation of Dreyfus. The publisher attributes the initial idea of the Revision to Scheurer-Kestner. He was quickly vilified for his stance but stood firm and testified in favor of Zola during the author's trial. He died from cancer on September 19, 1899, the same day of Dreyfus's pardon.

FIGURE 1-19. Card No. 8 of the series. Col. Georges Picquart, one of the few military figures to support Dreyfus, is portrayed at the center. At the left and right are drawings of his deposition and the text of his defense in front of the court. In March 1896, as the new head of military counterintelligence, Picquart discovered that Esterhazy was the real traitor. When Picquart brought the evidence to his superiors, he was immediately warned to drop the matter. Picquart refused and was promptly relieved from his position and posted to Tunisia. Picquart nevertheless continued to testify against Esterhazy, and he was later arrested and jailed for the charge of improperly communicating secret documents. Picquart was finally cleared when Dreyfus was pardoned; when Clemenceau became prime minister, Picquart was appointed minister of war. He died in 1914 as a result of a riding accident.

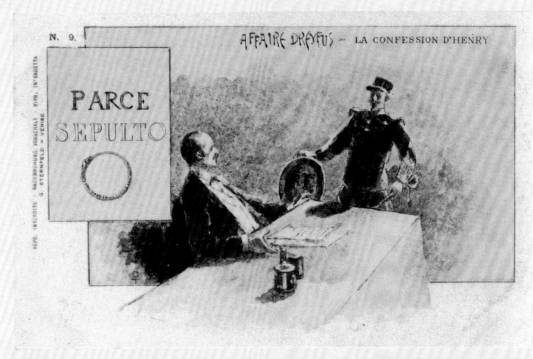

FIGURE 1-20. Card No. 9 of the series. This drawing imagines Colonel Henry's confession in August 1898, acknowledging that he indeed forged documents that implicated Dreyfus. Henry was sent to prison, but fatally cut his throat with a razor the next day. Although it seemed certain that this confession (as well as Esterhazy's later confession) would prove Dreyfus's innocence, the judges in Dreyfus's second trial did not see it that way. The Latin phrase *parce sepulto* means "spare the buried," implying forgiveness for those who have died. Given Henry's confession and suicide, the publisher perhaps believed some measure of forgiveness was warranted.

FIGURE 1-21. Card No. 10 of the series. Esterhazy is shown for the second time in the series, but, in this case, after Henry's suicide and Esterhazy's quick escape to London in September 1898. Esterhazy publicly confessed to his crimes, but was able to earn income through his writings while safe in England. The image depicts Esterhazy being paid for revealing what he knew, ironically using the same bags of money that were so often used in anti-Semitic postcards to portray greedy Jews. He lived in England until his death in 1923, never facing justice in France.

FIGURE 1-22. Card No. 11 of the series. The second to last postcard in the series refers to Alphonse Bard, who was appointed by the court as a rapporteur to investigate the Dreyfus Case to determine if a Revision was appropriate. Bard argued in favor of Dreyfus before the court in October 1898, which eventually led to the annulment of Dreyfus's original sentence and approval for a retrial. The Latin phrase *cedant arma togae* means "let arms yield to the gown," implying that, in this instance, military power (arms) gave way to civil power (the gown) since Bard, a representative of the court, overcame the wishes of the French army to maintain Dreyfus's guilt.

FIGURE 1-23. Card No. 12 of the series. The final postcard is a tribute to the Dreyfusard heroes of 1897–1898: Picquart, Scheurer-Kestner, Zola, Labori, and Bard. Although at the time this set of postcards was published it appeared likely that Dreyfus would be granted a Revision, nearly another year passed before the court decided to dismiss the original verdict and retry the case. Those who bought these postcards were surely still closely following the affair, unsure of how it would end.

CHAPTER 2

THE MAIN STEREOTYPES AND CANARDS

Chapter 1 introduced us to the anti-Semitic postcard and some of its typical themes. As the Golden Era of the postcard emerged in the late 1890s, anti-Semitic postcards began to proliferate in numerous countries, primarily in Germany, Austria-Hungary, Poland, France, Great Britain, and the United States; not coincidentally, these countries had some of the largest Jewish populations. Although each country published its own brand of anti-Semitic postcard, and an observer can often tell which country published a certain card just by examining the image, many of the common anti-Semitic stereotypes and canards are reflected universally. This chapter will explore these main themes.

The most obvious stereotype is the large and hooked nose, which was the primary method of identifying the Jewish character in the postcard. The next most common subject matter was the falsehood that Jews were greedy and pursued money above all else. Other stereotypes portrayed were the awkward and deformed Jewish body, including the hands and the feet; portrayals of Jews as animals and the devil; the unsuitability of the Jew for military service; expulsion and exclusion of Jews from nations and society; Jews in control of economies and worldwide levers of power; mocking of Jewish religion and ritual; and a lesser known motif: that of the Jew unnecessarily carrying an umbrella. The combined power of these negative images was to portray the Jew as inhuman and totally unsuitable to live among regular society. Once we understand the various anti-Semitic themes, we can better examine and evaluate the thousands of anti-Semitic postcards that were published in the Golden Era and are published today in some Muslim countries.

THE LARGE AND
HOOKED NOSE

The most common characteristic of the Jew in anti-Semitic postcards is the large, protruding, and often hooked nose. The precise origin of the stereotype is unknown, but is generally traced back to medieval times, as early as the ninth century CE. By the eighteenth and nineteenth centuries, the Jewish nose was the rule in nearly all representations of Jews. This feature was used simply to identify the subject of the image as Jewish, and as an object of ridicule, often in contrast with a non-Jew who had a "normal" nose. The exaggerated nose was part of the usual view of the Jew as physically deformed, awkward, primitive, and ugly, a broader topic explored further below. The hooked nose was also a representation of the Jew's diabolical and cunning nature. According to Christian tradition, the devil had a misshapen nose, as did the Jews. Physiognomists, scientists who claimed a person's character could be assessed by features of their outer appearance, asserted that the nose was an indication of all the negative traits associated with Jews. The nose stereotype was ubiquitous, from the relatively benign American and British postcards to the more virulent German and French types.

Studies have shown that the "Jewish" nose has no basis in reality and Jews are no more likely to have an enlarged nose than other segments of the population. Maurice Fishberg, author of *The Jews: A Study of Race and Environment,* conducted a study in 1911 of nearly 3,000 Jews in New York City, finding that only 14 percent had hooked noses. Comparable results were found in similar surveys in Europe. At the same time, the hooked nose was often found in non-Jewish populations in varying percentages in different regions, sometimes at a very high rate, such as 31 percent of Germans in Bavaria. North American Indians were also noted as often having a "Jewish" nose. Anthropologists today dismiss the stereotype of the Jewish nose, but it remains popular in the imagination of both Jews and non-Jews.[1]

Today, at least in the United States, the "Jewish" nose is not usually perceived as anti-Semitic; in fact, it has, at times, become a distinguishing point of pride. For example, in August 2010, Lea Michele, the star actress of the hit television series *Glee* (whose father is Jewish) stated that she has always been "proud of my body, my Jewish nose and all that," and admired Barbara Streisand "who has a Jewish nose" for not getting a nose job.[2] At worst, its usage in the United States today is considered to be mild ethnic humor in bad taste, as demonstrated in October 2007 when actress Halle Berry apologized for joking about the "Jewish" nose on the *Tonight Show with Jay Leno.*[3]

The vile anti-Semitic connotations of the hooked Jewish nose have been kept alive in the Muslim world where they remain part of the fabric of gross anti-Semitic imagery. However, one hundred years ago, at the time when the anti-Semitic postcards shown below were published, the attitude toward Jews and the meaning of the Jew's nose were far more negative. It is in this context that these postcards must be assessed.

FIGURE 2-1. American postcard depicting a Jewish man with an enormous nose. The man also speaks with a Yiddish accent that is being mocked, saying "vell" instead of "well." The sender of the postcard picks up on the play on words between "nose" and "knows," telling the recipient in the written message on front that "you know we are on our way." [Publisher: Glad Mitt Series by F.J. Haffner, No. 5472, Denver, Colorado; mailed from Denver to Colorado Springs in December 1911.]

FIGURE 2-2. American postcard depicting a Jewish girl named Irma Kohn unable to properly use the telephone because her enormous nose blocks her from speaking into the mouthpiece. The poem offers another play on words, replacing "nose'r" for "no sir." [Publisher: J.I. Austen Co., Chicago; circa 1905.]

FIGURE 2-3. "Say!" declares the enormous-nosed Jew to the gentile who appears nonplussed by the presence of this ugly person in front of him. The only purpose of this American postcard is to make fun of the stereotypical Jewish nose as well as the large lips, which were also a common feature of the "ugly" Jew. The message at center, written to a patient at the Battle Creek Sanitarium, one of the most famous in the world at that time, makes no reference to the image. [Publisher: F.S. Backus; mailed from Fort Scott, Kansas, to Battle Creek, Michigan, in December 1906.]

"DO YOU BELONG TO THE YOUNG MEN'S
CHRISTIAN ASSOCIATION?"

FIGURE 2-4. British postcard showing a Christian woman asking an obviously Jewish man, as identified primarily by his unusually large nose, if he belongs to the YMCA. The question is meant to be ironic and humorous. The artist makes sure to depict the Christian woman's nose as particularly flat in contrast. Also, note the man's shining jewel, a common depiction of the "moneyed" Jew, and his awkward and bent stance, another classic Jewish stereotype explored later in this chapter. [Publisher: Bamforth & Co. Ltd., Holmfirth; mailed within the United States in February 1915.]

FIGURE 2-5. This French postcard depicts a "Baptized Polishman," or a Polish Jew who has converted to Christianity. The man is dressed in proper French clothing and appears like a Frenchman, except that his profile in both the mirror and the shadow reveal his exaggerated nose. The caption states: "You have renounced the faith of your fathers but you keep your profile! Still be careful of the pruning shears!" This sinister postcard implies that the Jew has attempted to cover up his true nature by converting and dressing properly, but his Jewish origin cannot be hidden, just like his "Jewish" nose. The warning about the pruning shears refers mockingly to the tool used in the Jewish ritual of circumcision (ridiculing Jewish practices is yet another anti-Semitic tactic explored later in this chapter). Note the difference in tone between this French card and the previous American and British postcards, which were intended to be humorous. In general, French and German postcards were much more serious and virulent in their anti-Semitic message compared to American and British cards. [Publisher: Not provided, France; circa 1901.]

289. TONKIN. — Baie d'Along   Chenal de l'Hamelin. - Le Juif.

P. Dieulefils, Hanoï

FIGURE 2-6. The Jewish nose stereotype was so pervasive and ingrained throughout the world that a rock formation in a marine channel in French Indochina was named "The Jew" due to its features that appear like a head with a protruding nose. The Chenal de l'Hamelin is a sea channel in Ha Long Bay in the Gulf of Tonkin, Vietnam, which has been listed as a UNESCO World Heritage Site. The bay has more than 3,000 islets, most of which are made out of limestone. Many are named for their shapes, such as Voi Islet (elephant) and Ga Choi Islet (fighting cock), and, in this case, a "Jewish" nose. I have found no information about the current name for this rock formation. [Publisher: P. Dieulefils, Hanoi; mailed from French Indochina to France in June 1920.]

WEALTH, GREED, AND CHEATING

While the nose is the most prevalent physical stereotype associated with Jews, the most common characteristic attributed to Jews is their wealth, greed, and role as conniving and ruthless bankers, haggling businessmen, usurers, and cheats. The corollary to the stereotype is that since Jews always seek more money, they are cheap when it comes to spending. The negative association with excessive wealth and its power is one of the oldest anti-Semitic motifs, and it remains strong to this day. Recent surveys show that nearly 35 percent of all respondents in Europe believe that "Jews have too much power in the business world." Similar surveys in the United States show that 12–18 percent of respondents subscribe to negative stereotypes related to Jews and money. Although its usage is considered highly off-color, it is well known in the United States that "Jewed" or "to Jew down" is ethnic slang for cheapness or stinginess.[4]

The origin of the stereotype is sometimes attributed to an episode where Jesus visited the temple in Jerusalem and lashed out against merchants and moneychangers, Jewish ones according to some interpretations. The key verses from the New Testament (Matthew 21:12–13) are as follows: "And Jesus went into the temple of God, and cast out all them that sold and bought in the temple, and overthrew the tables of the moneychangers, and the seats of them that sold doves, And said unto them, 'It is written, My house shall be called the house of prayer; but ye have made it a den of thieves.'" Based on these sentences, Jews have always been associated with money and thievery.

The practical origin of the stereotype is from medieval Europe when Jews were excluded from most traditional trade professions and from owning land, which meant that agriculture was also off limits. For example, the Jews of southern Europe who had pioneered techniques for making glass and paper were eventually restricted from these trades and replaced by Christians. Only a handful of occupations were available to Jews, primarily commerce and money-lending. With only these options available, Jews took up these professions and succeeded. Jews were soon both needed and resented for their role in the commercial activities of a given city or nation, which only served to fuel existing animosity and anti-Semitism. As Heinrich Heine (1797–1856), a well-known German poet (and a Jew who later converted to Christianity) explained: "The Jews, excluded from the possession of land and the acquisition of property by handicraft, had as their only resources commerce and money-dealing, both of which the Church prohibited to the faithful. Thus the Jews were legally condemned to become rich and despised, and to be murdered."[5]

As Heine alluded, money-lending at the time was burdened with the issue of usury, whereby some interpreted the Bible to have prohibited the charging of interest. In the twelfth century, the Church condemned the charging of interest, but the decree resulted in the economic problem of how to obtain investment capital. In response to the dilemma, the Church specifically relied on Jews to become suppliers of capital. By the later Middle Ages, the restrictions against charging interest were eliminated and Christians soon took over leadership in banking, although several prominent Jewish banking houses remained. But the negative associations of Jews, money, and usury had been firmly and permanently established. The most well-known example of this stereotype from this time period is the character Shylock from Shakespeare's the *Merchant of Venice,* as described in figure 5-1.

In the nineteenth and twentieth centuries, this canard was perpetuated by many well-known figures. For example, Karl Marx, the father of socialism, stated that "money is the zealous one God of Israel, beside which no other God may stand."[6] Henry Ford, the founder of the Ford Motor Company, claimed in his four-volume anti-Semitic work from the 1920s titled *The International Jew* that "the Jew is the only and original international capitalist." Similar examples abound. Of course, it was not a surprise to hear these age-old themes echoed in a speech by Iranian president Mahmoud Ahmadinejad in front of the UN General Assembly on September 23, 2008: "The dignity, integrity, and rights of the American and European people are being played with by a small but deceitful number of people called Zionists. Although they are a miniscule minority, they have been dominating an important portion of the financial and monetary centers as well as the political

Le nouveau Juif-errant.

FIGURE 2-7. "The new wandering Jew" (see figure F for an explanation of the "old" wandering Jew) travels between the banks of Paris and Berlin stealing bags of money numbered "50,000." The masses of people below helplessly watch the giant caricature of a Jew walking away with their cash. Note the French publisher of this postcard: Librairie Antisémite. The publisher made it clear that it specialized in anti-Jewish publications, from books to postcards. Some of Drumont's writings, such as an 1899 work called *Le Juifs Contre La France* (the Jews against France), were printed by the Librairie Antisémite. Additional postcards from this set are shown in figures 4-6 to 4-8. [Publisher: Librairie Antisémite, Paris, France; 1st Series, No. 5; circa 1900.]

FIGURE 2-8. This American postcard depicts a large-nosed Jew offering to lend money at 10 percent interest *per month*. Note the contrast between the Jew's nose and the tiny pug nose of the non-Jew, who is clearly dismayed about the high interest rate. [Publisher: Not provided, United States; 1905.]

decision-making centers of some European countries and the U.S. in a deceitful, complex, and furtive manner." More surprising was that Ahmadinejad's speech (which was laden with additional anti-Semitic lines) was applauded by the audience and the president of the UN General Assembly, Father Miguel D'Escoto Brockmann, thanked Ahmadinejad for his "excellent" speech.[7] All that was missing was the distribution to all delegates of a commemorative postcard depicting a money-hungry Jew.

These perceptions sometimes still appear in the mainstream press in the West. An article in *Time* magazine from September 2010 titled "Why Israel Doesn't Care About Peace" explained that "as three Presidents, a King and their own Prime Minister gather at the White House to begin a fresh round of talks on peace between Israel and the Palestinians, the truth is, Israelis are no longer preoccupied with the matter. They're otherwise engaged; they're making money." While perhaps not intending to invoke anti-Semitic myths, the article infuses the age-old stereotype of Jews placing a disproportionate and inappropriate importance on money. One observer for the National Review took a less apologetic view stating that the *Time* article "is probably the most anti-Semitic essay I have ever read in a mainstream publication."[8]

A more curious manifestation of this canard comes out of China. Like many others, the Chinese believe that Jews are unusually adept at business, but instead of viewing it negatively and threatening, this skill is deemed to be an admirable trait that needs to be studied and mimicked. A December 2010 article in *Newsweek* titled "Selling the Talmud as a Business Guide" explains how books purporting to reveal the business secrets of the Jews hidden in the Talmud are popular in China. Although coming from the perspective of respect, the Chinese beliefs simply perpetuate falsehoods which are ultimately harmful.[9]

The postcards from the Golden Era reflected all angles of the Jews and their love for money. These images portrayed Jews as merchants, pawnbrokers, and second hand dealers; they are shown wearing jewels, cheating customers, acting cheap, embracing bags of money, charging high interest rates, haggling with customers, cheating for gain, and more. The majority of anti-Semitic postcards from all countries reflected these themes in one way or another, even if the central message of the postcard was not about money. Below are several examples that focus on money, greed, and cheapness alone; the reader will see this theme repeated over and over throughout this book.

FIGURE 2-9. An American postcard that shows a bag of money transforming into a "capitalist," clearly identified by his exaggerated hooked nose as Jewish. Here the Jew is literally made out of money. [Publisher: Not provided, United States; circa 1901.]

Hast Schulden Du, so geh' mit leichtem Herzen
Und lass' den Gläubigern die Schmerzen!

Gesetzl. gesch.

1048

FIGURE 2-10. The Jews at left, one holding a paper labeled *wechsel* (exchange) and another with one labeled *konto* (ledger), ring a bell as if trying to get the attention of a man resting under a tree. The caption says: "If you owe [money], don't have a heavy heart about it / And leave the pain to the one you owe the money to." It seems that the greedy money-lending Jews are pursuing debts from non-Jewish Germans. This late 1890s-era German postcard advises the debtors to ignore their obligations, implying that Jews are exploitative bankers that do not deserve repayment. Throughout history, anti-Semitic acts were often carried out not only for ideological and racist reasons, but also for economic gain. For example, when France expelled its Jewish population in 1182, all Christian debts were cancelled; the message in this postcard is rooted in actual events. [Publisher: Not provided, Germany; circa 1898.]

"MEESTER EISELBAUM, I LOUFE YOUR REBECCA
ALREADY YET, VIL YOU GIF HER TO ME?"

"GIF HER TO YOU, DO YOU VANT TO RUIN ME?
I NEVER GIF NODINGS AWAY."

FIGURE 2-11. This British postcard shows two Jewish men; the one at the left asks Mr. Eiselbaum if he can marry the latter's daughter, Rebecca. Mr. Eiselbaum replies with only greed in mind, making clear that he considers his daughter's marriage as merely an opportunity to earn money. Anti-Semitic postcards often portrayed Jews willing to commit callous and heinous acts for the sake of money. This card also makes fun of the Yiddish-accented English spoken by Eastern European immigrants, a common theme in anti-Semitic postcards. [Publisher: Bamforth & Co. Ltd., Holmfirth; mailed within the United States in December 1912.]

FIGURE 2-12. A "Yiddish" couple in love, but as this image insinuates, for Jews the primary object of affection is cash. The lovers stand happily posing with bags of money, with the man pawing the bags in one hand while holding his woman with the other. The faint caption on top says, "Yiddish Love." As was typically the case, the message on the back makes no note of the image: "Dear Verna: Yes they are having dances at the lake, I meant to have written before. From Helen." What was going through the minds of Verna and Helen when they saw this postcard? [Publisher: Not provided; mailed from Lake Gary, Florida, to Binghamton, New York, in May 1913.]

FIGURE 2-13. This 1930s-era postcard from Morocco, created at a time when the country was a French protectorate, depicts a Jewish vendor at the left, trying to sell the object in blue to the Arab customer. The vendor says, in Jewish-accented French: "With this you will be able to cook, make music and all that you want!" The customer understandably eyes the object with suspicion. The suggestion here is that the Jew will make wildly false claims to make a sale. The artist, P. Neri, drew hundreds of images that were adapted into postcards throughout the 1920s and 1930s, most caricaturing the non-French population of Arabs and Jews. Several additional examples are shown in chapter 7. [Publisher:Collections P. Neri, Casablanca; circa 1930.]

FIGURE 2-14. The Jewish pawnbroker taking advantage of the desperate non-Jewish customer is a common motif of American postcards in particular. In this example, "Cohen," depicted with large nose and awkward body, pawns a watch from a customer who appears stunned after "passing" his time away, implying that the Jew is taking advantage of this person's financial misfortune by offering an unfairly low price. Pawnshops existed in ancient times and are still widespread in the United States and Europe. (*Pawn Stars,* a television show about a pawnshop, was one of the top shows on U.S. cable television in 2011.) Pawnshops are identified with the symbol of the three balls (*see top of the window*), which is usually attributed to the non-Jewish Medici banking family in fifteenth-century Italy. Although Jews were normally associated with the pawn business, it was non-Jews, particularly from Italy, who dominated the industry in the Middle Ages. The subject of Jewish pawnbrokers is explored further in chapter 6. [Publisher: CA Co.; mailed from Eau Claire, Wisconsin, to Neenah, Wisconsin, in April 1906.]

THE ROTHSCHILD BROTHERS

One of the archetypes of Jewish wealth and greed was the Rothschild banking family, which was seen as the leading force of an international Jewish conspiracy to control the world economy. The family was also accused of financing wars, such as the French Revolution and the Napoleonic Wars, not caring which side won but only seeking to profit. The family's banking business was founded by Mayer Amschel Rothschild (1744–1812) in Frankfurt, Germany. Mayer's five sons expanded the business throughout Europe in the nineteenth century by opening branch offices in several countries: Salomon in Vienna, Nathan in London, Carl in Naples, Jacob in Paris, and Amschel in Frankfurt. The banking family had strong connections with key leaders and nobility, and established itself as one of the leading finance houses in Europe. Rothschild descendants continue to operate investment banking firms throughout Europe. Many anti-Semitic postcards caricatured the Rothschild family and portrayed it as the embodiment of the Jewish lust for money. A quick Google search shows that conspiracy theories regarding the alleged power of the Rothschild family remain widespread into the twenty-first century.

FIGURE 2-15. "Die 5 Frankfurter" (The five Frankfurters) refers to the five Rothschild brothers that opened bank offices throughout Europe in the nineteenth century. The images in this unusual postcard are caricatures of the brothers. The ugly-nosed Jews are not shown as financiers, but as persons of influence in German society, suggesting that not only do Jews control banking, but they also have insidiously infiltrated all areas of German society. At the top is "Sally Cohn," a lieutenant in the "Flatfoot" infantry regiment, referring to the stereotype that Jews had abnormally flat feet; next to him is "Dr. Itzig Bär" (*bär* means "bear"), professor at the Jewish University of Frankfurt; at the center is "Moses Stern," a student of Hebrew; at the lower left is "Aron Solomon," the mayor; and at the lower right is "Hirsch Levy," postmaster. Just to be certain that the viewer clearly understood that these reviled men are Jewish, the artist added a Star of David and the Hebrew word for "kosher." [Publisher: Hotel Kölner Hof, Frankfurt; mailed from Magdeburg to Dessau in December 1900.]

FIGURE 2-16. This Austrian postcard titled "Die fünf Frankfurter" (The five Frankfurters) is similar to the previous postcard. The brothers are shown here with smug expressions, indicating satisfaction with their wealth and power. [Publisher: Leo Stainer, Innsbruck; circa 1905.]

FIGURE 2-17. "Rothschild King of Nickel" is the title of this French postcard, which attributes control of the French monetary system to this banking family; a portrait of a Rothschild appears at top. On the corners of the postcard are drawings of the 25-centime coin, made out of nickel, that was in use from 1903–1904. The weight (seven grams) and size of the coin (twenty four millimeters in diameter) are also provided. At center is a group performing the "Dance of the Nickels." [Publisher: Édition Française (A.M.L.) Paris; mailed within France in 1903.]

THE AWKWARD AND DEFORMED BODY

After the hooked nose and the money/greed stereotypes, the awkward and deficient body of the Jew is the next most notable theme of anti-Semitic postcards. The representation of Jews as primitive and ugly was not limited to the hooked nose, but extended to every aspect of the body. The Jew was portrayed with multiple deformations, such as a hunched-over torso, a crooked posture, an underdeveloped musculature, bowed legs, large hands, and misshapen feet that led to an uncoordinated gait. The assertion was simple: Jews, as a race, were diseased and degenerate. It was also another way of presenting Jews as different from normal society; the misshapen Jew was often shown standing next to a noticeably stout Gentile. Congenitally deformed hands, feet, and bodies also meant that Jews were unable to serve in the military, and, therefore, were unworthy of being an integral part of the nation, another theme explored below. In fact, only one step further was necessary in the dehumanization of Jews: to simply portray them as animals, which is precisely what is shown in the next section. Once the Jew had been physically reduced to the level of a creature, it became much easier to treat the Jew as one. Several examples of the "Jewish body" are shown in the postcards below, but the reader will notice these features throughout this book.

FIGURE 2-18. The Jew at left is standing in an almost physically impossible posture, appearing bent in all directions. The two Jews have come to the spa town of Karlsbad (located in today's Czech Republic) to enjoy its curative waters, but instead are shown having intestinal problems. The one at the left has not been able to reach the toilet in time and has defecated in his pants. The text says: "Greetings from Karlsbad / Do you feel any effect? / I'm crying [oy vay], I'm breaking, / Below the frock / Everything stinks already." Note that the last three lines of the rhyme end with "ores," an allusion to Yiddish, which the writer mocks. The word for "breaking" is *kapores,* which also refers to the Jewish Yom Kippur ritual of beating or breaking a chicken. Also note the unusually large hand of the man at left. This German-published postcard not only mocks the Jew's physical appearance, but also his language and inability to control bodily functions. The anti-Semitic postcards from the spa towns of Karlsbad and Marienbad are explored in chapter 9. [Publisher: Ottmar Zieher, Munich; mailed from Karlsbad to Virje, Croatia, in June 1907.]

FIGURE 2-19. A postcard from 1930s-era French North Africa (Algeria) showing, at the right, a grotesque-looking Jew pushing his cart of wares. The customer appears perturbed at the price quoted by the Jewish vendor, who is shown pointing his very sharp finger. Note the Jew's hunched posture, enormous feet, and ragged clothing. The caption says, "Department store just like in Paris!" This same artist drew the image in figure 2-13. [Publisher: Compagnie Des Arts Photomecaniques, Schiltigheim-Paris; circa 1930.]

FIGURE 2-20. Although males were most often depicted in anti-Semitic postcards, women and children were also shown as awkward and ugly. Like this portrayal from a 1905 American postcard and in figure 2-23, Jewish women were depicted with large, shapeless bodies and grotesque facial features, such as thick lips and warts—exactly the opposite of the aesthetic ideal of an attractive woman. Here the woman drops her grocery basket and dogs and a bird immediately pounce on the fallen goods. Animals taunting and harassing Jews was yet another common depiction in anti-Semitic postcards, as seen in figures 3-26, 4-15, 7-9, and 7-10. This postcard, which is part of a series of cards from the same publisher (see figures 2-40 and 6-11 to 6-13), also makes fun of the woman's Yiddish language, providing a handy English translation. [Publisher: J.A. & A.A.; mailed from Vermont in September 1905.]

FIGURE 2-21. Unusually large and deformed hands and feet were a specific physical characteristic portrayed in anti-Semitic postcards. Jews were also ridiculed for the way they talked, supposedly with active and annoying movements of their hands. In this British postcard a group of Jews standing in front of the stock exchange (an obvious expression of the money stereotype) is shown with enormous hands in active conversation. The caption simply says, "Hands"; the sender also makes note of this feature, mockingly writing, "Kind gentle hands / Jack." Large hands also symbolized thievery, as such hands are better able to greedily grab large quantities of objects. The artist who drew this image, Tom Browne, was one of the first comic postcard artists in Great Britain, beginning his work in 1897. His art was depicted on numerous postcards until his death in 1910 at age thirty-nine. Like many of his contemporaries (see figures 5-9 and 5-12), Browne reflected British society's widespread prejudices against Jews at that time. [Publisher: Davidson Bros.' Pictorial Post Cards, from Originals by Tom Browne, Great Britain; circa 1907.]

FIGURE 2-22. Two Jews with ugly and awkward appearances are shown taking to each other "mit de hand," Yiddish-sounding English for "with the hands." To further mock Judaism, the American publisher wrote the word "kosher" in Hebrew at the center. The meaning of the written message at top, "This is the best I could do Bill," is unclear; perhaps the sender was supposed to send a certain type of postcard to the recipient. A note about the outfits worn by these men is worthwhile since they are a common feature of how Jews were depicted on postcards. Black suits and coats became the distinctive dress of Hasidic groups in Eastern Europe in the eighteenth and nineteenth centuries, self-marking themselves as different not only from other people but also from other Jews. Black was also considered by Hasidim to be an unattractive color; therefore, wearing black was a mark of modesty. Although other Jewish groups from the same period, such as Sephardic Jews from North Africa, did not dress in this way at all, the black coats and hats emerged as the stereotypical way of portraying all Jews. It is still true to this day; when an American newspaper decides to print a photo of a Jewish celebration, it will typically feature the more visually interesting Hasidic Jews, even though most American and Israeli Jews do not identify in this way. [Publisher: J.P.C.C.O., New York; mailed from Far Rockaway, New York, to Long Island City, New York, in August 1907.]

FIGURE 2-23. Two elderly Jews, a husband and wife, it appears, discuss their ugly legs and feet. The only purpose of this British postcard is to portray Jews as grotesque and misshapen. Although the focus is on Abraham's legs and feet, both are drawn as particularly horrid. In addition to being part of the overall awkward and ugly "Jewish body," the large and flat foot was also an analogy to the cloven-foot devil. In German thought at the time, flat feet were considered a key difference between Jews and pure Germans. The message on the reverse ignores the image on the front: "All well, will write tomorrow, March 16/1905." [Publisher: Empire Series, London; Series No. 431; mailed within Canada in March 1905.]

FIGURE 2-24. The secular and wealthy Jew represented the second major "character" of anti-Semitic postcards, after the more common Eastern European Jew with long black coat, beard, and sidelocks. These Jews appear to have successfully assimilated into society, but anti-Semitic postcards convey the message that the true character of the Jew cannot be hidden and they will always remain separate. Their awkward appearance and deformed bodies persist, but in a different form, as shown in this hand-drawn postcard on the obverse side of an official U.S. postal card (this side was most commonly used for the written message). The talented artist drew this Jew with an unusually large and protruding nose, thick lips, large hands, an obese body, and tiny legs. The jewel at center shines prominently, a common symbol used to portray Jewish love for money. See figure 4-1 for another hand-drawn anti-Semitic postcard. [Publisher: Official postal card from the U.S. Postal Service; mailed within Kingston, New York, in February 1904.]

JEWS AS ANIMALS

The next stage in the dehumanization of Jews was to compare them to animals, such as lions, rats, birds, and insects. Equating humans with beasts builds on a long tradition. The concept of physiognomy assumed that similarities between the face and figure of a person and a specific animal pointed to certain character traits. Since a person's external appearance was a mirror of his inner traits, a man who looked like a certain animal had the character traits ascribed to that animal. During the Renaissance, re-nowned Italian scholar Giambattista della Porta (1535–1615) wrote a work on the subject called *De Humana Physiognomia,* complete with sketches comparing human and animal features. His work was highly influential among scientists and artists, and it influenced scientific thinking into the nineteenth century. Postcard publishers eagerly printed visually striking portrayals of Jews as wild animals. Several examples are shown below. Also see figures 2-38, 3-23, and 3-30 for additional examples.

FIGURE 2-25. A particularly graphic and vile anti-Semitic postcard from Germany that depicts various animals with stereotypical Jewish faces caged in a zoo. The publisher plays on the meaning of common Jewish names which are written in German above each animal's cage. (*From right to left*) Familie Löwy (the family of lions); Bär for bear; Wolf, which has the same meaning in English; and Hirsch for deer. Even the parrot at the top right has an exaggerated nose, as if also "Jewish." The mocking of double-meaning Jewish names was a common theme in German anti-Semitic cards, a topic further discussed in chapter 3. The sign at the bottom says: "New! Large Menagerie / paraded [in a manner meant to humiliate] by the German 'Michel' [a typical German name]." The depiction of Jews behind bars in this 1890s-era postcard is an eerie foreshadowing of the ghettos of World War II. [Publisher: Not provided; circa 1898.]

FIGURE 2-26. "Greetings from Russian Poland," referring to Polish territory that was under Russian rule until Poland gained independence after World War I. Fritz Ferdinand Preiss (see his signature on the man's jacket), the artist and publisher of this postcard, had a simple anti-Semitic message: Russian-Polish Jews were analogous to the Russian-Polish louse at right. Note the detailed drawing of the grotesque insect—the dehumanization of the Jew in this image is stark. Fritz Ferdinand Preiss (1882–1943) was a famous German sculptor particularly known for his ivory statues and figurines. Preiss is regarded as one of the leading ivory carvers of the Art Déco scene in the 1920s, and his statues are highly sought after by collectors today. Recent auctions of his works at leading worldwide auction houses, such as Christie's, have sold for over $50,000. Preiss's paintings and drawings are less well known and not widely sold. It is unlikely that Preiss collectors are aware of his virulent anti-Semitic drawings from the World War I period. Another example of Preiss's bigoted art is shown in figure 7-7.[10] [Publisher: F. Preiss, Berlin; 1915.]

FIGURE 2-27. Going one step beyond the typical portrayal of the Jew as an animal, this postcard depicts him as a devil-like creature. This cynical French example displays "The Six Pretenders of France," with images of the king, the emperor, the Church, the Jews, the Freemasons, and the army. The Jew is shown with pointed ears and facial features that appear demonic. The association of the Jews with the Devil originates in the early medieval period when Christianity had to resolve the refusal of Jews to submit to the truth of Christianity. Their answer was to assert that the Jew was virtually inhuman, a creature of the devil who is Satan's weapon against believers in Christ. Several verses in the New Testament also support this view; the Gospel of John states that the devil is the father of the Jews (8:44) and Revelation calls a Jewish house of worship a "synagogue of Satan" (2:9). These notions would be reflected in European art and literature for many generations, well into the twentieth century. [Publisher: Not provided; circa 1900.]

FIGURE 2-28. The Jew in this postcard is drawn as a devil-like abomination in the form of a spider. The text reads: "Just as the poisonous evil spider / Falls over your husband, / You drain it of its last bit of / Spirit and life, you empty out the moneybag." The image shows a man on his knees with a face in a fearsome expression, his hair standing up, and his hands in a gesture as if pleading for his life. His attacker, according to the poem, is the Jewish wife, disguised as a horrible poisonous spider with long distorted legs and a hairy body. The spider has a stereotypical Jewish face with demonic features: a hooked nose, sharp teeth, and a forked tongue ready to drain the man of his spirit and life—as well as his money. The creature is seen taking the coins from the moneybag laying near the man. [Publisher: Not provided; circa 1905.]

FIGURE 2-29. This American postcard does not depict a Jew as an animal, but compares him to an elk. The elk asks the Jew if he is one too, implying that a Jew can somehow be confused for this animal. This image alludes to the stereotype that Jews have horns on their heads, an old myth that still had its believers into the twentieth century. Its roots can be traced to a second century CE translation of the Hebrew Bible into Greek by Aquila Ponticus. In Exodus 34:29, Moses is described as descending from Mount Sinai with his face shining. The Hebrew word for "shone" in the text, *karan*, was mispronounced as *keren* which means "horn"—so instead of a shine emanating from his face or head, it was mistranslated as horns. This error was carried into later translations, and the myth gained further legitimacy in 1515 when Michelangelo fashioned his famous sculpture of Moses with two horns on his head. The horns played well into the demonic imagery used to portray Jews. The sender acknowledges the content on the front, writing in the message, "How does this strike you!" [Publisher: J.S. Wilson; mailed within the United States in July 1907.]

EXPULSION AND EXCLUSION

The expulsion of Jews from cities and countries throughout Europe was a common action taken by nations and their leaders in reaction to their intolerance and hatred for Jews. Expulsions are recorded as early as 1182 from France (and again in the 1390s), from England in 1290, and, most famously, during the Inquisitions in Spain and Portugal in the late fifteenth century. Expulsions occurred on a smaller scale as well; in only one of many dozens of examples, the city of Regensburg, Germany, expelled its five hundred Jews and burned the Jewish quarter to the ground in 1519, blaming its economic troubles on the Jews. By the mid-sixteenth century, most of Southern and Central Europe had evicted its Jews at some point in its history.[11] At various times, Jews were allowed to return by sympathetic leaders or because of the economic benefit that they brought to the country. The expulsions were not merely an expression of hatred; they were sometimes based purely on financial factors, whereby the motive for the expulsion was a desire to cancel debts owed to Jews or simply to confiscate their property.

By the seventeenth century, the era of expulsions was mostly over, and, with the rise of the Age of Enlightenment, Jews began to obtain emancipation (recognition of rights as equal citizens) in many countries, beginning with France in 1791. Although emancipation, in principle, was supposed to abolish discriminatory laws against Jews, the reality was quite different. In practice, Jews were excluded from many key facets of society, such as the right to hold an officer's rank in the military or hold jobs in civil service. Private institutions implemented their own exclusions, which were allowed by law, often prohibiting Jews from entering establishments, such as hotels and clubs. Emancipation also did not alter the desire by a large segment of the population to get rid of the Jews in their country. Increasingly virulent anti-Semitic attitudes in the second half of the nineteenth century led to the publication of books and pamphlets calling for the removal of the Jewish population. Postcards from several nations similarly reflected this fantasy, which would finally be realized in the Holocaust. The postcards below provide examples of Jewish expulsion, followed by examples of exclusion.

FIGURE 2-30. This 1898 postcard from Germany titled "The Future" shows a caravan of Jews exiting Germany and walking in the direction of a sign that says "To Palestine." Two German soldiers can be seen in the rear, one pointing at the Jews to leave. The colorful image portrays various stereotypical Jews, such as the awkward Eastern European Jew (the one in front still carries his wares in a box that says "for sale"), the bow-legged, large-nosed boy (*lower right corner*) reading a Talmud as he walks, and the wealthy, secular Jew with jewels and gold. A previous owner of this postcard who lived in Israel shortly after the founding of the state in 1948, decided to mock this image of exile. He/she pasted a 1952 stamp of Chaim Weizmann (1874–1952), an early Zionist leader and the first president of Israel, on the front of the card and obtained a Tel Aviv–Jaffa cancellation from the post office (the card was not actually mailed). Ironically, today a widespread campaign of delegitimization of Israel calls for the Jews to leave the Holy Land. [Publisher: München Odinstarte, Germany; circa 1898.]

FIGURE 2-31. "Unique Polish Export" refers to the long line of Jews leaving Poland for France by the hand of the Polish man with the whip. Like the German postcard above, this image reflects a yearning for the Jews to leave the country. This 1920s-era postcard foreshadowed the complete destruction of Polish Jewry in the Holocaust and thereafter. Prior to World War II, Poland had the largest Jewish population in Europe, with approximately 3.5 million persons (every tenth Pole was Jewish). More than 3 million were murdered in the Holocaust, and most of the survivors were forced out in postwar pogroms and a 1968 anti-Jewish purge. There are only about 10,000 Jews in Poland today.[12] [Publisher: Nákl knihkupectví Novotný a Bartošek; 1920s era.]

FIGURE 2-32. "Greetings from [Hotel & Restaurant] Kölner Hof in Frankfurt" shows a Jew at the left (holding umbrella) attempting to enter the hotel. The guard points to a sign which reads: "Juden ist der Eintritt verboten" (Jews forbidden to enter). Several people on the street and on the trolley watch the scene. This hotel prided itself on being a Jew-free establishment, as described in figure I (also see figure 3-23 for another example from this notorious hotel). A guest purchased and mailed this postcard, writing: "I arrived here well. Parents aren't here yet, but hope that they will still come today. My parents arrived at 8 o'clock." It is apparent that the exclusion of Jews was of little note or concern to this guest, reflecting the general attitude of the nation at the time. The postcard further disparaged Jews by referring to Frankfurt as "Neu-Jerusalem am Fränkischen Jordan" [New Jerusalem on the Frankish Jordan], implying that Frankfurt was infested with Jews such that it had become like Jerusalem. The image at the lower left is of the local opera house, and at the right is the train station with text saying: "Main train station right exit."[13] [Publisher: Hotel Kölner Hof, Frankfurt; mailed from Frankfurt to Wuerzburg in April 1897.]

BROADMOOR BY THE SEA   MIAMI BEACH, FLA.

THE BROADMOOR HOTEL
On The Ocean at 75th St.
Miami Beach, Fla.
North Beach's Newest and Finest Modern Fire-
proof Hotel — Restricted Clientele — Dining
Room — Patio Bar — Private Beach — Solarium
— European Plan.

FIGURE 2-33. It wasn't only in Germany where Jews were excluded from certain hotels. Incidents where Jews were prohibited from entering hotels in the United States are recorded as early as the 1870s. In the 1920s, anti-Semitic attitudes were on the rise in the United States, leading to widespread restrictions at educational institutions, clubs, hotels, and even certain neighborhoods. Harvard, Yale, Princeton, and numerous other schools instituted restrictive quotas on the number of Jews allowed admission, regardless of merit. Developers of residential properties refused to sell plots and new homes to Jews. Harsher restrictions were implemented at private clubs and hotels, with a complete exclusion of Jews in many cases. Hotels advertised this openly, promoting terms such as "restricted," "exclusively for Gentiles," or "no Hebrews allowed." This attractive late 1940s-era postcard for the Broadmoor Hotel in Miami Beach, Florida, appears innocent enough on the picture side. However, on the reverse, at the top left (see partial scan of the back of the postcard), the hotel listed among its "amenities" that it only allowed a "restricted clientele," which was clearly understood to mean no Jews and no blacks. Additional examples of these American postcards and the subject of restrictions on Jews in the United States are discussed further in chapter 6. [Publisher: Colourpicture, Cambridge, Massachusetts; mailed from Miami Beach to New Jersey in March 1947.]

JEWS IN CONTROL

The myth of Jewish control of national and worldwide levers of power, both political and economic, rose to prominence at the turn of the twentieth century with the publication of the *Protocols of the Elders of Zion* by the Russian secret police. The twenty-four sections of this forged booklet outline the confidential plans of a Jewish cabal to attain total world domination. This anti-Semitic charge quickly became popular since it fed into existing stereotypes of Jewish wealth, disloyalty to their home nation, and evil acts, such as the ritual murder of Christian children. Henry Ford endorsed this canard, sponsoring the printing of the *Protocols* in the United States from 1920 to 1922, and arriving at the same conclusion in his book *The International Jew.*

Although the *Protocols* and Ford's publications have been discredited (except in the Muslim world where the forgery is still sold at newsstands), the concept of disproportionate Jewish control of politics, wars, the economy, and the media is still pervasive in many circles today. In July 2010, Oliver Stone, one of the most prominent Hollywood directors, stated that the American focus on the Holocaust stems from "Jewish domination of the media." Commenting on Jewish political control, Stone added that "Israel has fucked up United States foreign policy for years."[14] A 2007 best-selling book in China titled *Currency Wars* singled out the cause of various events such as the 1997 Asian Financial Crisis: historical control of money issuance by the Rothschild banking empire.[15] In 2003, Malaysian Prime Minister Mahathir Mohamad told a summit of world leaders that "Jews rule the world by proxy" and they "invented socialism, communism, human rights, and democracy" to gain control of powerful countries.[16]

In the United States, Jewish conspiracy theories are generally considered fringe concepts; however, a 2007 book called *The Israel Lobby and U.S. Foreign Policy* by Harvard University and University of Chicago professors Stephen Walt and John Mearsheimer perpetuated this myth by claiming that U.S. foreign policy was being harmfully influenced by a nebulous "Israel lobby," which has "unmatched power." An analysis of the gross errors and falsehoods in this book is beyond the scope of this chapter and better covered by other scholars.[17] Jeff Robbins, writing for the *Wall Street Journal,* sums up his assessment: "Walt and Mearsheimer have repackaged the 'the Jews-run-the-country' stuff which has long been the bread and butter of anti-Semites."[18] Michael Gerson, commenting for the *Washington Post,* concluded that "every generation has seen accusations that Jews have dual loyalties, promote war, and secretly control political structures. These academics may not follow their claims all the way to anti-Semitism. But this is the way it begins. This is the way it always begins." The postcards from a century ago propagated and perpetuated the falsehood of Jewish control in whatever political event or situation was prominent at the time. Several examples are shown below.

FIGURE 2-34. A giant devil-like Jew with clawed hands and feet grips the globe as if in control. Note the coins and paper money falling below. The caption says: "Their homeland." This French postcard succinctly summarizes the assertion that Jews dominate the world in a parasitic fashion. This postcard is part of the same series as the card shown in figure 2-7 published by Librairie Antisémite. [Publisher: Librairie Antisémite, Paris, France; 1st Series, No. 2; circa 1900.]

FIGURE 2-35. This unusual postcard printed in Germany during World War I shows the Russian tsar, Nicholas II, pleading on his knees to seek help from the Jews. By the time this postcard was published, the Russian Revolution of 1917 had forced the tsar to abdicate (he was later executed) and the Romanov dynasty collapsed. The implication here is that somehow the Jews possess ultimate control and the only place the tsar can now turn at the moment of his demise is to the Jews. The card says at top: "To my beloved Jews! / Help me—Help me—Help me / when you whip me that will be your reward." The tsar then confesses to the evils that he perpetrated against the Jews in the hopes of mercy. The text inside the box at the left ironically says: "Here are all the good deeds of the House of Romanov! / We arranged for the pogroms, we carried out the Beilis process [a 1911–1913 blood libel case in Kiev],[19] we didn't tolerate foreign Jews in Russia, and so on and so on. / Now help me—forbidden [or impossible]!"[20] The paradox of the Jews in control yet unable to stop pogroms and blood libels, does not seem to put an end to this anti-Semitic canard. [Publisher: BAF, Germany; World War I era, circa 1917.]

Nikita hadikölcsönt vesz fel!

GRAFIKAI INTÉZET R.T. BUDAPEST.

FIGURE 2-36. The charge that powerful Jews finance and generate wars is an old anti-Semitic lie and a subset of the stereotype of Jewish control. This World War I–era postcard published in Hungary shows a Jew in his pawnshop (*Zalogok*) taking a crown and scepter from a customer who is portrayed as King Nicholas of Montenegro (1841–1921). In October 1912, Montenegro, along with Bulgaria, Greece, and Serbia, attacked the Ottoman Empire in what is known as the First Balkan War to completely free itself from Turkish control and gain additional territory. In this image, King Nicholas is pawning his prized possessions to the Jew (with sidelocks, skullcap, and hooked nose) in exchange for cash to pay for the war. The caption says: "Nikita [nickname for Nicholas] takes a loan for war." Even in recent times, hints of this claim can be heard. For example, in March 2003, Congressman James P. Moran of Virginia said that "if it were not for the strong support of the Jewish community for this war in Iraq, we would not be doing this. The leaders of the Jewish community are influential enough that they could change the direction of where this is going, and I think they should." Both Republicans and Democrats strongly condemned Moran, and the congressman apologized, calling his statements "insensitive."[21] [Publisher: Tákacs És Bálint, Budapest; mailed from Budapest in February 1915.]

Führer der deutschen Arbeiter

FIGURE 2-37. "Leader of the German Worker" refers to the Jew at right who has the German laborer hooked by his nose. The Jew here is not portrayed as the typical Eastern European Jew, but as a modern secular Jew, still with a bulbous nose and short stature—in sharp contrast to the tall, powerful German carrying a hammer. Here the Jew exploits labor and economies. [Publisher: Bau Nordbayern vom Deutsche, Marktbreit; circa 1920.]

MOCKING PROHIBITIONS
AGAINST EATING PORK

In addition to ridiculing the physical appearance of Jews and perpetuating the canard that Jews possessed greedy, evil personalities, anti-Semitic postcards also scorned Jewish practices and rituals. Kosher dietary restrictions, especially Jewish aversion to pork, were particularly targeted for ridicule. Jews have historically had a specific abhorrence to the pig, with the Bible prohibiting Israelites from eating its meat (Leviticus 11:7 and Deuteronomy 16:8). This restriction was quite noticeable to the general population as far back as ancient times, since until the recent past, pork was the only type of meat regularly available for eating. Most other animals, such as cattle, sheep, and goats, were kept primarily as work animals or for milk and wool. During the Hellenistic period in the Holy Land (333–63 BCE), King Antiochus tested the loyalty of Jews by asking them to eat pork. With consumption of pork set as a marker between being a pious Jew or a Hellenist, pork became not just simply a forbidden meat, but a powerful symbol of Jewish identity.[22] Sixteenth- and seventeenth-century Spanish inquisitors used the same ancient test to determine whether a Jew had renounced his or her Judaism.

With this background in mind, anti-Semitic imagery from as far back as the thirteenth century mocked this Jewish prohibition and deliberately showed Jews in contact with a *Judensau*, German for "Jewish sow," or an adult female swine. Pictures and carvings of Jews surrounding, suckling, or having intercourse with a sow became widely disseminated as a blatant symbol of hatred aimed at dehumanizing Jews. Sculptures of *Judensau* can still be found today in diverse Christian sites of worship, such as the Notre Dame church in Aarschot, the Basel Cathedral in Switzerland, the Metz Cathedral in France, and the famous Wittenberg town church in Germany where Martin Luther preached and wrote one of his two infamous anti-Jewish tracts.

E.B.&C.i.B. 9090.

F. EYPRIEDT DÜSSELDORF.

Gruss aus

Sieh die Karte freundlich an!
Knüpft sich doch der Wunsch daran,
Dass ein jedes dieser Drei
Dir ein rechtes Glücksschwein sei.

FIGURE 2-38. This German "Greetings From" postcard from 1899 shows three Jews with the heads of pigs chatting on a bench. The four lines at left say: "Look kindly at this card! / As it comes with hope, / That each of these three / May be a lucky charm for you." The text is a play on the German word *Glücksschewein,* which literally means "lucky pig," but is used as a term for "lucky charm." Portraying Jews not just as animals, but specifically as pigs, was a potent anti-Semitic affront given Jews' avoidance of pork. This aversion had a history of being twisted to insult Jews. In one example, William Blake (1757–1827), the famous English poet, interpreted the incident of the Gaderene swine (Matthew 8:28–34) to suggest that Jesus made the Jews look like pigs.[23] More recently, in 2010, the BBC reported that a network of more than forty Islamic schools in Great Britain was teaching from a Saudi Arabian curriculum that taught that Jews "looked like monkeys and pigs."[24] [Publisher: E.B & C.i.B., Germany; mailed within Germany in April 1899.]

Oh, what a face.
What do you care?
Turn it around
And have your share.

FIGURE 2-39. This novelty postcard in its upright position shows a stereotypical Jew; but when turned over (*right*), it appears as the head of a pig. The caption mockingly urges the Jew to have his share of pork. Given the history of how Jews were persecuted by being forced to eat pork, the suggestion in this postcard was particularly offensive. [Publisher: Not provided; circa 1910.]

FIGURE 2-40. A Jewish man sits at a table ready to eat a plate of pork with a sign in Yiddish that says "You Can Eat Pork." The man winks; the postcard implies that that this Jew is knowingly violating prohibitions against eating ham. This postcard, which is titled "A Kosher Note," is part of a set ridiculing Jews and their Yiddish accents, as described in figures 6-11 to 6-13. The popular awareness of the Jewish prohibition against pork perversely led to the belief by Gentiles that Jews gluttonously ate pork in private, even though they were forbidden to do so. Thomas Bridges (1710–1775), a British writer, explained in his novel *Adventures of Bank-Note* that if Jews ate less pork, the price would come down, allowing poor Christians to eat more of the meat. This American postcard clearly alludes to the supposedly covert Jewish hungering for *chaser* (Yiddish for "pig").[25] [Publisher: J.A. & A.A.; mailed from Phoenix, Arizona, to Oklahoma City, Oklahoma, in December 1905.]

FIGURE 2-41. "Trade and Traffic!" (the words rhyme in German) shows an Eastern European Jewish peddler attempting to sell trinkets to two peasant women. The women are portrayed as pretty and innocent Germans, while the Jew, who is always associated with trade and commerce, holds up his wares with a smirk on his face, as if he has the upper hand in the transaction. Note the pig behind the Jew—this is not a coincidence, but a deliberate mocking of the Jewish distaste for pork. The handwritten message from a German soldier stationed in Germany in 1916 makes no reference to the image: "27.9.16. Dear Gerti, I received your letter from the 21st. Why do you write such reproaches? I can't write any sooner till I come in possession of the packages. Hopefully we will see each other soon. Regards to the children, the parents, and Joseph. Sebastian." Did the soldier deliberately pick an anti-Semitic postcard to deliver his frustrated message, or was this the only one available at his base? [Publisher: Wenau-Postkarte; mailed from German military field post office in September 1916.]

FIGURE 2-42. This World War I–era postcard from Austria shows a military officer and his assistant happening upon two Jews, one of whom is waving his hat while standing next to three pigs. The officer brings his hand to his mouth in shock at this scene; he is clearly aware that Jews are prohibited from consuming pork. Besides mocking the Jewish dislike for swine, the artist may be suggesting that Jews secretly raise and eat pigs. The soldier here then stumbles onto this unexpected scene. [Publisher: B.K.W.I., Austria; circa 1916.]

THE UNSUITABILITY OF JEWS IN THE MILITARY

Discrimination against Jews in the military was another form of anti-Semitism practiced widely in Europe, and, of course, reflected in the postcard record. The Dreyfus Affair is the most prominent example, whereby the French military immediately assumed that a Jewish officer was a spy leaking secrets, even though the evidence clearly pointed elsewhere. In Germany, discrimination against Jews in the army was law, as they were prohibited from the officer corps. They were thus excluded from what was considered to be the pinnacle of respectability in German society. As one observer noted, "There was no Dreyfus Affair in Germany because there was no Dreyfus."[26] Similarly, in Russia, Jews were barred from becoming military officers under the May Laws of 1882. The exclusion of Jews from leadership in the military rested on two principles. The first was the canard that Jews were unfit for military service because of their deformed bodies and small statures. The second was a belief that Jews were ultimately disloyal to their home countries. While the practice was muted in America and never became law, Jews also faced discrimination in the U.S. military, especially in World War I. The postcards below focus on the concept of Jewish unsuitability for the military. Also see figure 8-10 for another example.

FIGURE 2-43. "Israel im Heere!" ("Israel [a Jew] in the Army!"), exclaim the three surprised officers while examining the papers of one of the new draftees entering army training (*kriegscourse*). Note the awkward appearance of the bow-legged and wimpy Jew wearing an oversized and inappropriate *pickelhaub* helmet. In the back are several stout trainees marching. The insinuation is that the Jew could not possibly belong to the "German" institution of the military. This postcard was one of a series of anti-Semitic cards published by the Hotel Löwen in Müllheim, Germany, and sold to guests. [Publisher: Hotel Löwen, Müllheim; circa 1902.]

The Sergeant-Major (meeting new recruit): "I've seen Hielanders frae Glesga, I've seen Hielanders frae England, I've seen Hielanders frae Cork, but, haggis me, this is the first time I've seen a Hielander frae Jee-rusalem!"

FIGURE 2-44. This British postcard mirrors the same theme as the previous German postcard. The sergeant-major is surprised to see a Jewish recruit joining the prestigious Scottish Highlanders. Once again, the Jew is portrayed in an awkward fashion, with slumped shoulders, an oversized hat, and an unusually large nose. [Publisher: Bamforth & Co. Ltd., Holmfirth, England; Series No. 1204; mailed within the United States in October 1910.]

JEWS CARRYING UMBRELLAS

An interesting and lesser-known stereotype common in many anti-Semitic postcards from every country is the image of the Jew carrying an umbrella, often one that is red. What is obvious in these depictions is that it is not raining and no one else in the scene is carrying an umbrella. I have not found scholarly references to the umbrella as an object associated with Jews, but the umbrella-carrying Jew does appear in literary works from which we can understand the meaning of the object. The image is so widespread in anti-Semitic postcards from the Golden Era that an analysis of this motif is worthwhile.

Dan Miron, in his book *The Image of the Shtetl*, explains that in a story by Sholom Aleichem (a leading Yiddish author who lived from 1859–1916), the narrator observes the Jews of an imaginary town called "Kasrilevke" carrying unusually large and awkward umbrellas:

> The narrator observes that such umbrellas are rarely seen actually protecting their owners from rain. This, he explains, is either because they would not open or because when they do open, they never fold up, and then with the first wind they might turn into parachutes, carrying their owners away into the cloudy sky to great distances "almost like an airplane." The fanciful hyperbole, as merry as it is, conveys a sense of up-rootedness, of a dizzying suspension of the law of gravity that is far from being funny. . . . These images emphasize the essence of the exile experience as the core of the historical individual or mass departure from the shtetl. This experience means dispersion, alienation, loss of one's connection with terra firma, whether it is enacted, or rather reenacted, as a repetition of an ancient expulsion.[27]

It seems that the artists and publishers of anti-Semitic postcards were aware of this imagery and used the umbrella to further identify and classify the Jew, thereby adding to the sense that Jews were not permanent residents. Jews needed to carry umbrellas, even if it was not raining, since they never knew where they would be and they might not have a chance to go back to their homes to get an umbrella. Carrying an unneeded umbrella was also another way to portray the Jew as different, someone who simply could not fit in with the norms of society. The frequent red color was probably meant to highlight the umbrella. Although the umbrella-carrying Jew has lost its relevance today, it was a subtle, but important stereotype a century ago. The postcards below are some of the many examples that the reader will see throughout this book.

FIGURE 2-45. "Greetings from Karlsbad" depicts three Jews in classic anti-Semitic fashion, with all the physical characteristics described in this chapter. All three also happen to have umbrellas. The numerous anti-Semitic postcards from Karlsbad are discussed in chapter 9. The banal message reads: "My dearest, Gratefully received your card, inform you herewith that I could not give your regards to the 'Little Child' since it had left for [illegible] four weeks ago already. Today I am by myself [illegible]. Greetings from the whole family. Special regards from [illegible]."[Publisher: Not provided; mailed from Karlsbad in September 1897.]

FIGURE 2-46. The key message in this American postcard is that Jewish love for money is an "Old Old Story." A stereotypical Jew, "J. Green," is seen carrying a gold brick while two onlookers snicker. But also note the Jew carrying an umbrella that seems unnecessary since the other two men are without one. The message ignores the image, saying: "I got a date for Sunday so don't come up Charl." [Publisher: Not provided; mailed from Boston, Massachusetts, to Lynn, Massachusetts, in May 1906.]

FIGURE 2-47. The two Jews in this German postcard slip on the snow while the children surrounding them mock and laugh at them. The Jews exclaim in Yiddish, "Oi Vei Ghevald," which means something like "good grief." The purpose of this postcard is to humiliate the strange-looking Jews who are outsiders that cannot act normally in society (e.g., walking on a snowy hill where children are sledding). Note the dropped umbrella; again, there is no apparent need for one in this scene. [Publisher: Not provided; circa 1900.]

FIGURE 2-48. A Moroccan postcard that is titled "Greed" or "Desire." The caption says: "While you take the bone, I'll take the umbrella." The two ugly and ragged Jews are so greedy that they want to take a bone from a dog and a red umbrella from a garbage pile even though one already holds three of them. While the focus of this postcard is to portray cheap Jews, the umbrella motif is a key feature. [Publisher: Collection P. Neri, Casablanca, Morocco; circa 1930.]

CHAPTER 3

POSTCARDS FROM GERMANY

Although France and the Dreyfus Affair introduced the anti-Semitic postcard to a worldwide audience, Germany was the undisputed leader in the field, publishing the most diverse, virulent, and largest quantities of such cards. The German postcards depicted every negative stereotype imaginable to promote hatred and assert that Jews did not belong: physical deformities, depictions as wild animals and demons, uncleanliness, cowardice, raunchiness, stupidity, thievery, and greed. German postcards then took the next step and announced what should be done to the Jews: humiliation and expulsion. The German postcards conveyed a revulsion that was unmatched by the anti-Semitic postcards of any other nation. The many examples shown below and elsewhere in this book highlight the creativity employed by postcard artists, writers, and publishers in creating images and situations to spread Judeophobia. The peak era for the anti-Semitic postcard in Germany closely followed the postcard's Golden Era from the late 1890s through World War I. After the devastation of World War I, Germany was not in a position to print large numbers of postcards, and the population was less interested in this discretionary purchase. The 1920s saw a marked decline in postcard usage. By the Nazi era in the 1930s, anti-Semitic postcards were revived and continued the tradition of Golden Era postcards, depicting the Jews as an evil cancer that had to be removed. Several Nazi-era postcards are shown in chapter 10.

The history of Jews in modern day Germany can be traced back to Roman times. Documentation attests to the presence of Jews in Cologne as early as 321 CE. By the eighth century, Jews were flourishing in several communities, such as in Mainz, Worms, and Speyer. Jews generally lived well during this period and Jewish culture flourished. Mainz attracted prominent rabbis and scholars in the tenth century to become one of the leading centers of Jewish thought and learning. The Crusades were a turning point for the Jews of Germany and other parts of Europe. The religious fanaticism that marked the Crusades meant that Jews were targets for assault since Jews were considered responsible for the crucifixion of Jesus. During the first Crusade in 1096, entire Jewish communities in Cologne, Mainz, Trier, and Worms were devastated, with many thousands killed. Each Crusade brought on a new onslaught, and the status of Jews permanently changed in Western Europe. Jews were now subject to typical anti-Semitic accusations and persecutions; for example, a blood libel in Fulda in 1235 led to the death of thirty-four Jews. Throughout the twelfth and thirteenth centuries, blood libels, expulsions from many cities (e.g., from Mecklenburg in 1225), and massacres occurred with regularity.

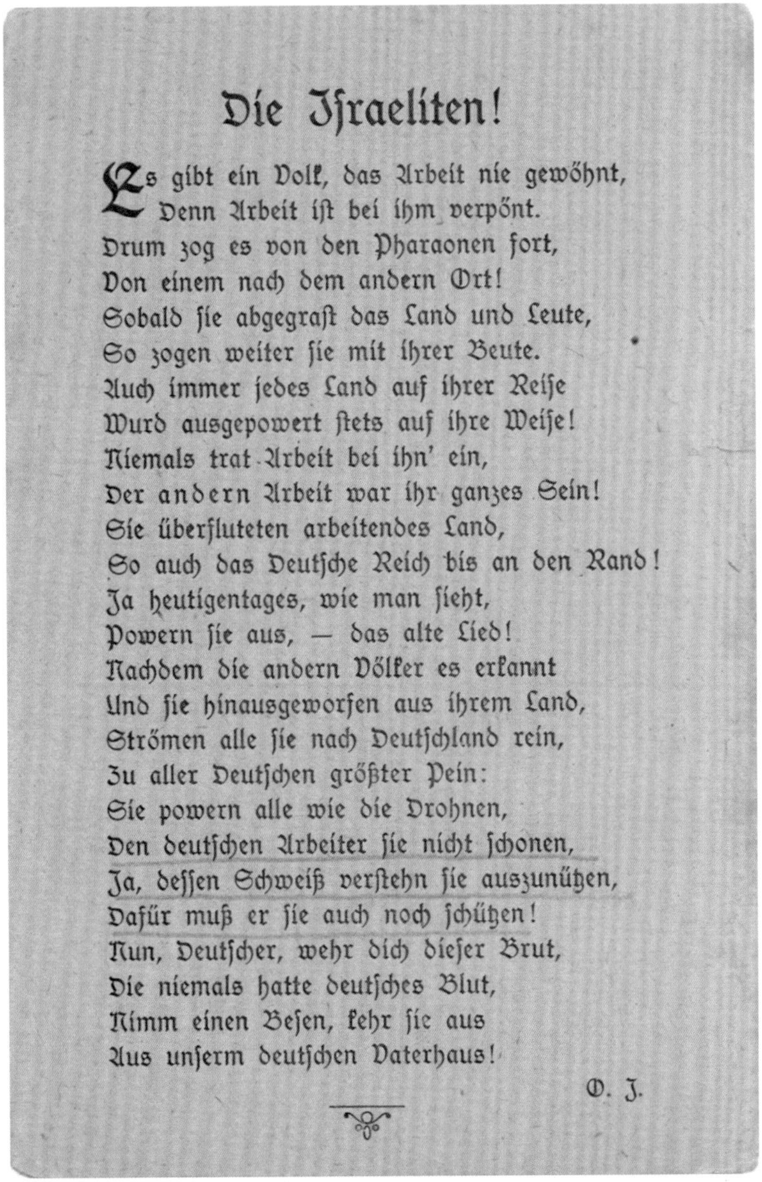

Die Israeliten!

Es gibt ein Volk, das Arbeit nie gewöhnt,
Denn Arbeit ist bei ihm verpönt.
Drum zog es von den Pharaonen fort,
Von einem nach dem andern Ort!
Sobald sie abgegrast das Land und Leute,
So zogen weiter sie mit ihrer Beute.
Auch immer jedes Land auf ihrer Reise
Wurd ausgepowert stets auf ihre Weise!
Niemals trat Arbeit bei ihn' ein,
Der andern Arbeit war ihr ganzes Sein!
Sie überfluteten arbeitendes Land,
So auch das Deutsche Reich bis an den Rand!
Ja heutigentages, wie man sieht,
Powern sie aus, — das alte Lied!
Nachdem die andern Völker es erkannt
Und sie hinausgeworfen aus ihrem Land,
Strömen alle sie nach Deutschland rein,
Zu aller Deutschen größter Pein:
Sie powern alle wie die Drohnen,
Den deutschen Arbeiter sie nicht schonen,
Ja, dessen Schweiß verstehn sie auszunützen,
Dafür muß er sie auch noch schützen!
Nun, Deutscher, wehr dich dieser Brut,
Die niemals hatte deutsches Blut,
Nimm einen Besen, kehr sie aus
Aus unserm deutschen Vaterhaus!

O. J.

FIGURE 3-1. This simple postcard from the pre–World War I era summarizes the anti-Semitic world view of the German nation at the time. What is especially interesting about this postcard is that it has no image, only text. There was no attempt by the publisher to provide entertainment by printing an interesting picture or a humorous caricature. Disseminating hatred for Jews was the only purpose, and there was clearly a market for this type of product in Germany. The poem, which was written in rhyme, reads as follows:

The Israelites!
There are a people, never got accustomed to working,
Since they frown upon work.
Hence it got away from the Pharaohs
To one new place after another!
As soon as they have grazed off land and people,
They moved on with their booty.
Each and every land along their route,
Was exploited and weakened this way!
Never ever did they taste work,
But lived off other people's work!
They flooded working countries,
Such as the German Reich, to the brink!
Indeed, nowadays, as one can see,
They exploit and weaken—same old, same old!
After the other peoples understood this
And threw them out of their lands,
They all streamed into Germany,
To the greatest pain of all Germans.
They exploit everyone, like drones,
Don't spare the German worker,
Whose sweat they know to exploit,
And on top of that, he has to protect them!
Now, German, resist this mob,
Which never had German blood.
Take a broom and swipe them out
Out of the house of our German fathers!

Many classic anti-Semitic themes are touched upon. Jews are portrayed as lazy parasites who exploit other people, moving from one nation to the next (the poem refers to immigration of Jews from Russia and Eastern Europe) and are now in Germany. The Jews, who do not have "German blood," take advantage of the pure German worker—note the injection of race into the anti-Semitic equation, not just religion, which was the traditional focus of Jew hatred. The text then complains that the German state, in fact, protects Jews, not realizing at the time that these protections would completely fall away two decades later. The conclusion is an eerie foreshadowing of exactly what happened in the Holocaust: Germany "swiped" the Jews out of the country. [Publisher: Deutschvölkische Buchhandlung, Berlin; circa 1910.]

The period of the Black Death in 1348–1349 and its unknown causes led to allegations that Jews poisoned Christian wells, triggering renewed deadly attacks against Jews. The persecution led to an exodus of Jews east into Poland, which eventually became the largest Jewish community in Europe. However, some of these migrations would reverse themselves when the Jews of Poland were subject to worsening persecutions in the seventeenth and eighteenth centuries. Jews became increasingly isolated from the Christian population as a result of ongoing persecutions and exclusion. One outcome of this isolation was the Jewish community's development of the Yiddish language, which combined German dialects and Hebrew—a language that would later be mocked in anti-Semitic postcards worldwide.

During the Reformation period in the sixteenth century, Jews continued to be oppressed. Martin Luther (1483–1546), a German-born priest who played the leading role in launching the Protestant Reformation, was a rabid anti-Semite who publicly and virulently denounced the Jews (see the Appendix for one of Luther's quotes on a postcard). His writings and teachings would be prominently featured in Nazi literature 400 years later. The situation for Jews was little changed in the sixteenth and seventeenth centuries. Beginning in 1772, the Kingdom of Poland was partitioned, with a portion going to Prussia, bringing a new population of Jews under German rule. Life began to improve for the Jews in the decades after the French Revolution, which spread new ideas of freedom to Western Europe. In 1812, Prussia became the first German state to grant citizenship to its Jews, although, like in France, Jews were still far from being equal. Even so, Jews lived mostly secure and prospered in nineteenth century Germany until a new wave of anti-Semitism emerged later in the century.

The Jews of the Second Reich (1871–1914) witnessed a revival of classic medieval anti-Semitism, but Jews were now also viewed negatively under the lens of growing nationalism and xenophobia. Jews were perceived as an alien people that could never be true Germans. Even if Jews converted to Christianity, which was enough to save Jews in the Spanish Inquisition, it would not remove their "Jewish blood." Now, it was not only about religion, but also about race. Jews were considered to be a separate species, sometimes compared to vermin that needed to be exterminated. One of the many scholars and intellectuals

FIGURE 3-2. "Fighting Hirsche" shows two *Ostjuden* in a street fight. The caption is a play on words, with the word *Hirsche* referring to both a common Jewish last name and the German word for deer. The Jews are depicted in typical awkward and crooked fashion. Their degenerate status is affirmed by the crude fighting for no apparent reason. The goal of this postcard was not hidden by its publisher, who is listed at the bottom as the Antisemitische Buchhandlung von Emil Keil, Berlin, or the anti-Semitic bookstore of Emil Keil in Berlin. [Publisher: Antisemitische Buchhandlung von Emil Keil, Berlin; mailed within Germany in December 1900.]

Der Mandelbaum und seine Früchte.

Einst und jetzt.

FIGURES 3-3 and 3-4. These two postcards from the same series depict the assimilated German Jew Mandelbaum, at the left with "his fruit" (even the children are depicted with large noses and awkward bow-legged bodies) and at the right, the same man seated. However, the second image makes clear that the assimilated Jew cannot escape his origin as an *Ostjude,* as depicted at the left. The caption says "Then and Now," showing the progression of this particular Jew in German society. The message is that even if dressed and acting like "real" Germans, the Jews' true identity cannot be hidden. A similar theme is depicted in the French postcard shown in figure 2-5. [Publisher: Not provided; circa 1900.]

who promoted this thesis was Eugen Dühring, an influential philosopher and economist. In one of his pamphlets titled *The Jewish Question as Racial, Moral and Cultural Question* (1881), he argued for the extermination of Jews since they were a foreign organism that had to be surgically removed from the German host body. Professor Heinrich Treitschke (1834–1896), a prominent German writer, historian, and politician, was another openly anti-Jewish figure who is credited with spreading and legitimizing anti-Semitism in academia. One of his quotes, "The Jews are our misfortune," was a common slogan used by the Nazis (the quote was memorialized in a postcard shown in the Appendix). The person who in 1879 coined the term "anti-Semitism," Wilhelm Marr (1819–1904), was a journalist who spread the message that Jews were a powerful people who were winning the battle against Germany and had to be repulsed immediately to save the German race.

A financial crash in 1873 combined with an influx of Jews from Eastern Europe converged to exacerbate anti-Semitism. Like the financial scandals in France in the 1880s and 1890s, Jews were singled out for blame even though many Jews were financially ruined in the crash as well. Around the same time, large number of Jews from Eastern Europe (known as *Ostjuden*, described in more detail below) began immigrating from Russia, Poland, and Galicia to escape pogroms and other persecutions; these lands were, in fact, more hostile to Jews at the time than Germany. The Eastern European Jews appeared and acted differently than the secular German Jews, and thus fed paranoia about a foreign element, like a virus, seeking to engulf Germany. As Klaus Fischer, a scholar on German anti-Semitism who wrote a book aptly titled *The History of an Obsession,* points out, "Prejudices against the *Ostjuden* . . . embodied the most virulent form of anti-Jewish hate: xenophobic nationalism and biological racism." Postcards of Jews as animals, including insects, conform to this new way that Jews were perceived.[1]

It is not certain that Germany in the late nineteenth century was more anti-Semitic than other countries in Europe, but Fischer noted, "Treitschke and like-minded Jew-haters were doing their best to make it so."[2] In the last two decades of the nineteenth century, anti-Semitic articles, books, societies, and speeches began to multiply, led by organizations with names such as the League of Anti-Semites. Even in this atmosphere, Jews thrived in German society and lived physically secure. Although vulgar Jew-hatred had become common and infiltrated all areas of life (e.g., in 1902, a hit song "Der Kleine Cohn" or "The Little Cohn" was based entirely on anti-Semitic themes, as described in chapter 8), there was no reason to believe, prior to World War I, that society would soon turn to extreme violence.

World War I presented Jews with an opportunity to prove their loyalty to their home nation, and 100,000 Jews served in the army (12,000 lost their lives). Unfortunately, Jewish eagerness to support the nation did little to stop growing anti-Jewish prejudice, which accelerated as the war began to turn against Germany. False rumors that Jews were avoiding frontline duty spread, and military leaders reacted by conducting a survey to assess Jewish participation in the war. The results were never published because it confirmed that Jews were, in fact, carrying the same level of responsibility as non-Jews; yet, the role of Jews as scapegoats for losses in the war had to be preserved. The economic depression in the postwar period provided another reason to blame Jews. As Fischer explains, during the period between 1919 and 1923, "The sort of annihilatory Judeophobia that would cause the Holocaust was born." The rise of the Nazis in 1933 elevated Jew-hatred to a new plateau that spread to the entire nation. Given the long history of anti-Semitism, especially in the previous sixty years, it was not hard for the public to accept this new form of Judeophobia. While there was clearly a pervasive atmosphere of anti-Jewish feelings, it would be wrong to say that the entire German people wanted to literally annihilate the Jews. But many Germans did lend a hand to this mass murder, and not many worked to undermine it. It was still the leadership of Hitler that put in motion the roundup and murder of Jews. The church of the Middle Ages had already paved the road for all the anti-Semitic beliefs that were assumed to be true in Nazi Germany. The Nazis, however, did not seek to convert or expel the Jews as a solution to the problem, but to solve it once and for all by exterminating them.

Postcards were just one of the many manifestations of German anti-Semitism in the 1890s–1930s era. As presented in the introduction, the widespread and daily usage of postcards proves that virulent anti-Semitism was not just the ideology of German politicians, philosophers, journalists, and other thought leaders. Postcards were a tool for the masses, those who eagerly purchased and mailed these "instant messages." The many examples shown below highlight the intensity of Jew-hatred during the prewar period.

"OSTJUDEN"

One of the leading Jewish "characters" that starred in many German anti-Semitic postcards, as well as postcards from other nations, was the Eastern European Jew or the *Ostjude.* The *Ostjude* was how most Jews were perceived in Germany. This concept developed during the first half of the nineteenth century and gained popular currency in the late nineteenth century as *Ostjuden* (the plural form of *Ostjude*) began to immigrate to Germany in large numbers. The Ostjude was clearly identified by his long black coat, beard, sidelocks[3], hat or skullcap, and black boots; his body was displayed as misshapen and crooked with an oversized nose and hands; his clothes were ill-fitting and often ragged; he was unkempt, sometimes shown with objects hanging out of his pockets; he was considered dirty, loud, and coarse. Correlated with the deformed body were the negative moral qualities of lewdness, dishonesty, and cowardice. *Ostjuden* were perceived as culturally

backward and degenerate, thus outside the mainstream of German society and norms. Even their language, Yiddish, which is a derivation of German, was regarded as an abomination. As a noted scholar on the subject explained, "The *Ostjuden* played a central role in the genesis, mythology, and disposition of pre–World War I German anti-Semitism. The East European Jews were symbolically and legally alien, a lethal combination. Visible and vulnerable, they made obvious and easy targets."[4] The images of *Ostjuden* on this page are taken from several anti-Semitic postcards.

Hatred for *Ostjuden* accelerated in the second half of the nineteenth century as the number of Jews immigrating from the East, particularly Russia, Poland, and Galicia (a region which comprised parts of modern day Poland

and Ukraine), increased due to rising pogroms and persecution. From 1884 through 1887, Germany enacted a series of official expulsions of Polish nationals, Jews and non-Jews alike. In every subsequent decade before World War I, there were several more local expulsions of *Ostjuden.* These Jews stood out sharply because of their distinct appearance, Yiddish language, and tight-knit communities. This fed into the idea that the Jews were an alien entity infecting the German nation. Even assimilated German Jews who wanted to fit into mainstream society looked down on the *Ostjuden.* But unfortunately for these secular German Jews, there was little difference in how various types of Jews were seen by Judeophobes. German postcards also target the well-dressed and assimilated Jew. The Nazis did not distinguish between classes of Jews.

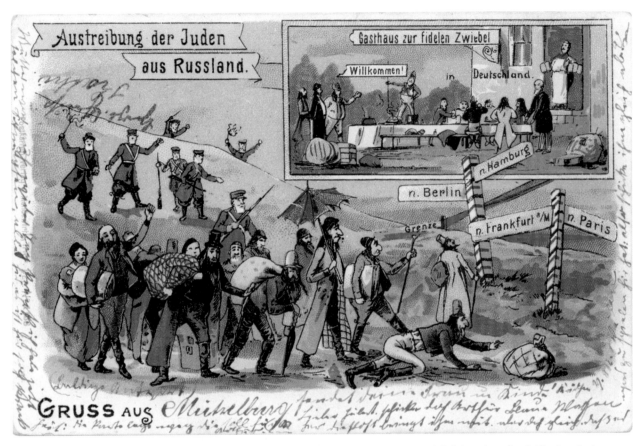

FIGURE 3-5. "Expulsion of Jews from Russia" portrays Russian gendarmes at the top left forcing a group of *Ostjuden* to leave Russia. The Jews fleeing are portrayed as a sorry group, with sacks of meager belongings, the one at the right crawling in exhaustion. Several hold walking canes, the staff of the wandering Jew (see figure F), and others carry umbrellas. The Jews stop at a sign indicating the direction of cities in Germany, including Berlin (the small sign under Berlin means "the border"), Hamburg, and Frankfurt as well as Paris, France. The yellow caption in the inset at top reads "Inn of the Jolly Onion," with a German exclaiming, "Welcome!" The Russians enacted anti-Jewish policies and pogrom violence in 1881, and over the next few decades that led to the migration of hundreds of thousands of Jews; in 1903, a bloody program in Kishinev spurred a new wave of emigration. Under the circumstances, Germany and France at the time were considered relatively liberal toward Jews and attracted many thousands (many also went to America and Palestine). This postcard reflects the expulsion of Jews from Russia and the feeling in Germany that the country was being overrun by *Ostjuden* by perhaps being too welcoming to these outsiders. [Publisher: Illegible; mailed within Germany in June 1902.]

FIGURE 3-6. This 1899 postcard is packed with anti-Semitic messages, and it is obvious that the artist and publisher devoted much thought to the various images and captions. The unifying theme is the German fantasy of the nature of the Jew and the desire for Jews to leave the country. In the top left circle, there are two *Ostjuden* holding or pointing to pouches of money and eagerly dealing with a well-dressed German man holding a cane. The caption at the top of the circle notes that these are Jews from the nineteenth century. At the center it says, "Anno 430," which refers to the number of years that, according to the Bible, the Israelites lived in Egypt (Exodus 12:40–41). The central image then shows not ancient Jewish wanderers, but a large group of nineteenth-century *Ostjuden* marching in a form of modern exodus. Under the caravan it says, "The Jews crossing the Red Sea," and to the far left is a sign pointing "To Palestine." This image represents the German fantasy: the expulsion of Jews from Germany to where they originally came from; leaving Germany after centuries of residence in the country would be akin to the Jews leaving Egypt. The reason why Jews must depart is because they are greedy usurers, as demonstrated at top left. The Exodus image also shows the contrast between the ancient Jews wandering the desert and what they have allegedly become in the nineteenth century. At far right are three Jews watching this exodus, but they are not meant to represent biblical leaders, such as Moses, Aaron, or Jacob. Instead, they are also stereotypical *Ostjuden,* and the yellow boxes with text have them speaking a form of gibberish, a distorted form of their Yiddish language. They are saying, "Now our people are crazy," and "Let's now make a Rabbi." The publisher designed this postcard to be used from any location, with only the words "Gruss Aus" or "Greetings From" printed with space for the sender to write in their location and a short message. [Publisher: Not provided; mailed within Germany in December 1899].

FIGURE 3-7. "Please, have a seat" is what the woman asks the guests of this inn. It is evening, the sun is seen setting through the window, and the innkeeper holds up a lantern. The sign below the window says "Place for the night for 'fair foreigners' 8 marks," and the location, Leipzig. The inn is already filled with guests; one is washing his feet in the "bath of the house." Two Jews have entered and seem to want to lodge overnight, but the guests clearly want them to leave. The woman points to a man lying on a straw mat, under which it says "JUDEN RRRAUS," or "Jews Out," a phrase which was used later by the Nazis when rounding up Jews for deportation. The guest at far right is ready to throw a boot at the unwanted interlopers. The Jews, in turn, try to entice the proprietor to let them stay, offering coins and diamonds. Although the Jews are shown as crooked and disgusting (note the dog pulling a raw bone from the pocket of the Jew at left), they are still paradoxically portrayed as wealthy, adorned with diamonds on every finger. Although assuming that all Jews carried diamonds as a matter of course is a gross exaggeration, there is a historic reason as to why many Jews did, in fact, horde precious stones and gold. Since Jews were forbidden since the Middle Ages from owning land and real estate or joining guilds and were subject to sudden expulsions from cities and countries, gold, jewelry, and diamonds were easy to carry, hide, and smuggle. These treasures saved lives and allowed Jews the possibility of settling in other lands. [Publisher: Karl Fickenscher, Leipzig; mailed from Leipzig within Germany in August 1918.]

FIGURE 3-8. The title of this unusual postcard says "God Salutes the Art of" with space for the sender to fill in a location (in this case it is written "Pottery Street"), and at top right, "Zwiebelfische," which means "Onion Fish." The image is of a printing shop. Four workers stand at special tables holding a variety of lead type equipment used at the time for printing, each identified by the name of the font or type. They all look back with irritation at the Jew below, one patronizingly saying, "putt putt" like "tsk tsk." The Jew, with skullcap, beard, and sidelocks, is kneeling and handling lead types called "Cicero Hebraisch," or "Hebrew Cicero," referring to Hebrew letters (Cicero in the printing context refers to a certain print type). The text at the lower left reveals the Jew's name: "Schlaum," or "Shlomo." The four lines read: "'Schlaum' did not invent work / haggling is much more to his taste / that's why at his kosher midday meal / there is no garlic but 'onion fish.'" The assertion is that the Jew does not work hard like the other four non-Jewish men, but would rather haggle, fighting for the last bit of money. The text is also a play on the word Zwiebelfische: "Z" in German printing jargon refers to a single letter that was accidentally set in a different type. The Jewish printer here is searching through a heap of letters to find the "Z" that got lost in a pile of Hebrew letters. The poem suggests that it was the Jew's poor work that caused the letter to be lost in the first place. At the same time, the Jew's meal is mockingly described as a "Z" for *Zwiebelfische*. The handwritten text of the sender does not refer to the anti-Semitic content: "Dear [illegible]! Please be advised that I am working since last Saturday. Please come to the 'Uviswald.' Jelmann will of course come along. You will have to inform the Schweitzer since I do not have his address. With best greetings, yours [illegible]." [Publisher: Gustav Bergmann, Leipzig; mailed within Leipzig in June 1908.]

FIGURE 3-9. This 1899 postcard is titled "The Electric Streetcar Is Coming" at a time when electric trams were still relatively new (the first ones appeared in the 1880s and expanded throughout Europe in the 1890s). At the center is a Jewish man who has fallen to the ground as a result of the passing streetcar. Next to him is a suitcase that has broken open revealing gold bars. It appears that the two men to the left and right of the fallen man are also Jewish (and perhaps the four men on the sidewalk), as identified by their large noses, black coats, and umbrella. The Jews are saying (see text at *bottom left*): "Oy Vay, why does the electric streetcar come in the midst of my doing business." The message conveyed is that while regular Germans are quietly riding the tram to Lindenau, the Jew is self-centered, concerned only about his business and his gold, and cannot behave normally in society that now has the conveniences of the electric tram. The Jew is also portrayed as a bungling idiot who gets knocked over (the same theme is shown in figure 5-4, a British postcard). [Publisher: Bruno Bürger & Ottillie, Lith.-Anst., Leipzig; mailed from Leipzig within Germany in September 1899.]

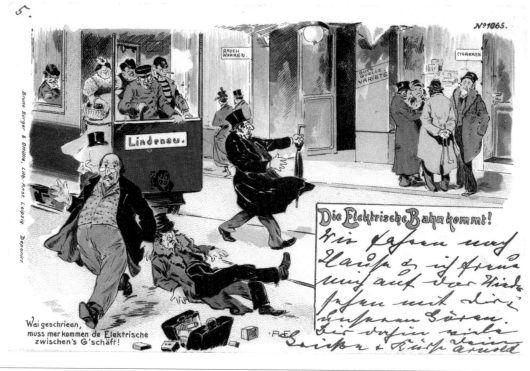

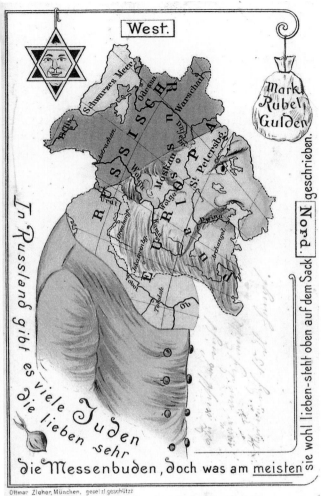

FIGURE 3-10. A map of Europe, with north to the right, in the shape of a Jewish face with an exaggerated hooked nose. The text at left and bottom reads: "In Russia there are many Jews who much love the booths at fairs, but what they certainly love best—that's written on the sack." The sack is shown at top right with the names of different currencies: marks, rubles, and gulden. The map includes the cities of Warsaw, Moscow, St. Petersburg, and Tbilisi. At top left is the Jewish Star of David. This postcard dwells on the anti-Semitic theme of the insidious spread of Jews across the land in search of money and profits. [Publisher: Ottmar Zieher, Munich; mailed within Germany in May 1904.]

FIGURE 3-11. This is one of the earliest anti-Semitic postcards, published and mailed in 1897. It is titled "Israel's Hunting Sport!" which refers to the Jewish mother's search for lice in her son's hair. Associating Jews with poor hygiene and dirtiness was a typical anti-Semitic theme, in this case implying that Jews were lice-infested. The handwritten message makes no reference to the subject: "Dear Alfred! I haven't had a sign of life from you for a while. I had the intention to write to you. Please let me know if it will be possible this year for you to visit me. Consider this my invitation. Kind regards." This postcard was like an "Evite" with an anti-Semitic theme page. [Publisher: Not provided; mailed within Germany in November 1897.]

FIGURE 3-12. This card depicts a stereotypical Eastern European Jew pulling a cow away from the herder and the milker. The caption is a German expression that means something akin to "when two quarrel the third one enjoys it." The point of this scene is that the greedy Jew is taking advantage of the hard work of the two German workers for his own selfish benefit. The artist who signed at bottom is Fritz Quidenus (1867–1913), a Czech-born painter and illustrator who settled in Munich in 1891. Quidenus was best known for his work in Mettlach stoneware for the prominent Villeroy & Boch china producer. Like many artists at the time who were well known for a certain type of art, Quidenus supplemented his income by drawing anti-Semitic caricatures for postcards (see figure 2-26 for another example). [Publisher: CA & Co., Germany; circa 1907.]

Wenn zwei sich streiten, freut sich der Dritte.

Du Gauner kommſt ſo ſchlau Dir vor,
Denkſt wohl, Du hauſt mich über's Ohr,
Doch hab ich ſelbſt 'ne feine Naſ',

Ich pfeif' Dir was!

D. W. 1902 Nr. 22.

FIGURE 3-13. A Jew with a top hat and long beard is approached by a German pointing to his head. The German says: "You crooks think you are so smart / Think that you can pull wool over my eyes / But I wasn't born yesterday either [literally written as "'I' have a good nose myself," which is a play on words related to the Jewish nose] / Get Lost!" This Jew is not an *Ostjuden,* but a secular "Germanized" Jew in contrast to the "pure" blond German. But the message that Jews are conniving thieves remained the same. [Publisher: D. W., Germany; 1902.]

Geiz ist die Wurzel alles Uebels.

FIGURES 3-14 and 3-15. Two views of the same money-hungry Jew. In the first example, the Jew sits on top of a large pile of money bags. The caption says: "Greed is the root of all evil." In the second example we are shown how the Jew obtains his money: by literally squeezing it out of a sweating man. These graphic postcards portray Jews as obsessed with money, climbing on bags and tables to grab cash. [Publisher: Not provided; circa 1910.]

FIGURES 3-16, 3-17, and 3-18. These three German postcards are part of a series that depict the actions of a pair of ugly and disgusting *Ostujden.* The two characters have all the typical negative physical features, including hooked noses, large and flat feet, misshapen bodies, ill-fitting clothes, and lack of hygiene. The first card is captioned, "Nothing further, perfection!"; the second says, "Siesta" or nap; the third shows the pair's "morning toilet." The three cards were all purchased by the same person and mailed simultaneously to the same recipient. The sender obviously knew that they were sending a series of anti-Semitic images, with short greetings written on each card. [Publisher: Not provided, Germany; mailed within Germany in February 1905.]

FIGURE 3-19. A grossly exaggerated caricature of a Jewish child holds a bunch of garlic, a condiment associated with Jews, and stands in front of an open keg on which it is written the Hebrew word "kosher." The publisher of this postcard was obviously aware of, and mocked, Jewish eating preferences and the prohibition on eating pork. The poem reads: "Leave me alone with the pork and radish, / And spare me the nonsense, / Something kosher with garlic and matzah, / Phew! look at that, what a treat." The Jew does not want pork and radish, instead preferring garlic and matzah. The title of the card loosely means "nonsense from the Munich child," referring to the ugly Jewish boy. [Publisher: Not provided; mailed within Germany in February 1900.]

FIGURE 3-20. Three Jewish gymnasts weakly and poorly perform while two German Gentiles in the back mockingly clap. The caption calls the Jews "Foreign Helpers," implying that they are aliens who do not belong in the society of the Gentile observers. The Jews' inability to fit in is demonstrated by their awkward and weak bodies, which reflect their overall character. Ridiculing Jews was so accepted by German society at that time that this postcard was unremarkable as the setting for a short romantic message written on the front: "Mirzi you are so pretty today I like you a lot." [Publisher: Not provided; circa 1900.]

Fremde Helfer.

O schieb, so lang du schieben kannst.

MALZ, SCHIEBER & Comp.
Möbel Transport
Ges. m.b.H.
München.

FIGURE 3-21. "Push as long as you can push," says the enormous-nosed Jew at the left to the group of Gentiles at the right. The Jew owns a furniture delivery company in Munich and watches as others labor. This image harps on the canard of the lazy and parasitical Jew who takes advantage of the work of others. [Publisher: Not provided; circa 1910.]

Russen gefällig? Billiges Angebot, wegen Auflösung des Hauses „Nicolaus Romanow"

FIGURE 3-22. This interesting postcard depicts a stereotypical Eastern European Jew with a bulbous nose, beard and sidelocks, long flat feet, umbrella, and tattered clothes. Note the bugs crawling on the ground and on the Jew's coat, similar to the imagery in figure 7-7. The Jew is holding a miniature version of Tsar Nicholas II in his palm as well as two Russian soldiers on his back. The caption says: "Care for a Russian? Cheap offer, due to the House of 'Nicolaus Romanov' going out of business." This card was published during World War I at the time of the Russian Revolution and the downfall of the House of Romanov. The tsar was executed by the Bolsheviks in 1918. The Orwellian allegation of this postcard is that powerful Jews caused the downfall of the tsar and the Jew now holds the Russian leader in the palm of his hands—the same theme can be seen in figure 2-35. [Publisher: Schaar & Dathe; mailed within Germany in June 1917.]

Die sieben Raben.

GRUSS aus dem KÖLNER HOF in Neu-Jerusalem.

Der Michel liegt in süßem Traum
Im Gras in stiller Ruh,
Die Raben oben auf dem Baum,
Mauscheln ihm heiler zu.

In Küch'u. Keller fraßen sie
Zu Haus ihm Alles leer
Und immer noch plagt Hunger sie,
Drum suchen sie noch mehr.

Wenn nicht bald eine starke Faust
Den Michel weckt vom Schlaf,
Dann wird, ich sehe es voraus
Er selbst zum Rabenfraß.

FIGURE 3-23. This is the third anti-Semitic postcard displayed in this book that was published by the notorious Hotel Kölner Hof in Frankfurt, as described in figures I and 2-32. "The Seven Ravens," with the heads of Jews, are shown perched on a branch while "Michel," the allegorical representation of the German nation (note the coat of arms on his shirt), sleeps at the left. The text explains the evil of the Jewish ravens and the danger that they pose to Germany:

GREETINGS FROM THE KÖLNER HOF IN NEW JERUSALEM.

'Michel' sleeps and has sweet dreams
All peaceful in the grass,
The Ravens high up in their tree,
Merrily [speak in their Jewish language][5] at him.

In the kitchen and basement they ate up
Whatever he had in his house
Yet they are still haunted by hunger,
And thus they still want more.

Unless a strong hand soon
Wakes up 'Michel' from his sleep,
He will, I foresee it
Himself become fodder for the Ravens.

The message on the front was written by someone who enthusiastically embraced anti-Semitism: "1,500 German women and men send you a thundering *Heil* from an anti-Semitic gathering [illegible] that proceeded splendidly. Yours, Berthold." The message continues vertically at right: "Heil to our Germandom!! Down with Jewry!" It seems that this postcard was sold at some anti-Semitic gathering that attracted over 1,000 participants.[6] [Publisher: Hotel Kölner Hof, Frankfurt; mailed from Magdeburg to Dessau in December 1900.]

Nebbich -

FIGURE 3-25. *Nebbich* is a Yiddish word that refers to a timid, meek, or ineffectual person. The drawing is of a bulbous-nosed Eastern European Jew made to look the part. The card is more remarkable for its written message on the reverse: "My dear Emmy! As promised you some time ago we sent as a substitute for the chocolate which you didn't receive hereby is a full package with real 'frankfurters' it will probably arrive tomorrow evening or on Wednesday morning. I hope it will serve its purpose. At the same time the picture on the reverse is a real 'Frankfurter' which might be unpalatable. Greetings, your [initials illegible]." The message is a play on words, as in the first usage, "Frankfurter" meant hotdogs, but in the second usage refers to an undesirable Jew from Frankfurt with all of the associated stereotypes. [Publisher: J. Harrap & Son, London; mailed from Frankfurt to Solingen, Germany, in June 1914.]

FIGURE 3-24. This unusual postcard is a surrealistic drawing of a Jew's grotesque face, like a picture-within-a-picture puzzle. "Gaudeamus Isidor!" is a play on the phrase *Gaudeamus Igitur,* which is the title of a Latin song meaning "Let Us Then Be Merry." It is most often sung at university graduation ceremonies and other university events, mostly in Europe. This creative artist mocked both the facial features of the Jew and his name. [Publisher: Not provided, Germany; circa 1920.]

MOCKING JEWISH NAMES

Figure 2-25 introduced the concept of mocking Jewish names that had the double meaning of an animal. The three postcards below are common examples of the many anti-Semitic postcards from Germany that employed this theme. The importance of the Jewish name as an identifying feature reached its pinnacle under the Nazis in 1939. Jews who did not have a name that was on an official list of recognizable Jewish names were required to adopt either "Israel" or "Sara" as an additional name so that they could be properly identified, branded, and stigmatized. The play on words that, on postcards, might have been considered nothing more than mild ethnic humor evolved into something much more serious: a tool to separate out Jews for deportation and extermination.

FIGURE 3-26. The unkempt and awkward Jew at center is harassed and ridiculed by two dogs and two boys. The caption says "Deer Caught," as if the Jew is a captured animal. The common Jewish surname *Hirsch* also means "deer" in German. The two dogs attack, ignoring the boys, indicating that the canines sense the "danger" posed by the Jew. The boys also throw snowballs at the frightened man, hitting his umbrella and hat and laughing at the scene. [Publisher: Regel & Krug, Leipzig; circa 1898.]

Gruss aus

Gefangene Löwen.

FIGURE 3-27. "Caught Lions" refers to the two Jews who have been stopped by a police officer. It is not specified what offense the Jews have committed, but the insinuation is that the Jews, in general, are "lions" who prey on the population against the interests of the German nation. The common Jewish surname *Löwen* means "lions" in German. Three children are shown mocking the Jews, one with his hand to his nose in a taunting gesture. Note the contrast between the bow-legged Jews and the stout German officer. [Publisher: Schaar & Dathe, Trier; circa 1900.]

N° 3009.

Gruss aus

Wölfe Schlitten überfallend.

FIGURE 3-28. The drawing in this postcard is the same as in figure 2-47. The same images were often used by several publishers and recycled in different versions of the same postcard. In this example, the caption says "Wolves Fall Over Sliding," playing on the common Jewish name "Wolf" to mock two Jews in a scene similar to the two previous postcards. [Publisher: Not provided; mailed within Austria in November 1899.]

THE BLOOD LIBEL AND THE KONITZ AFFAIR OF 1900

As discrimination against Jews grew throughout the centuries, certain myths regarding Jews and their practices emerged, such as the belief that Jews engaged in the ritual slaughter of Christians particularly to use their blood for the baking of the Passover matzah. This accusation of murder, known as *blood libel,* stemmed from the medieval superstition and Christian belief that the Jews were the spawn of the devil. Jews allegedly used such Christian blood to anoint rabbis, for circumcision, in curing eye ailments, in making amulets, in preventing epileptic seizures, and in concocting "magical" powders. The first recorded blood libel occurred during the twelfth century in Norwich, England, to explain the death of a local Christian boy. Children were believed to be the main target for predatory Jews since they were considered "innocent" compared to adult Christians who had forfeited their purity through subsequent sin.

The Christian invention of blood libel was particularly ironic because Jewish religious practice since biblical days forbade Jews from even tasting animal blood (Leviticus 17:10–11) and certainly prohibited the shedding of human blood (Genesis 9:4–6). Why blood? As one scholar explained, "In Judaic, Christian, and Germanic folklore immense power was ascribed to blood, especially human blood. Blood was more than the substance of life; it became the symbol of the living spirit." Blood was also painted on doorposts to ward off witches and demons.[7]

Blood libel became a common occurrence in the Middle Ages, and not only did it lead to the false accusation of an innocent Jew, but it was also used by the populace as an opportunity to persecute Jews through riots and pogroms. So many Jews were tried for ritual murder well into the eighteenth century that Cardinal Ganganelli (1705–1774), who later became Pope Clement XIV, was compelled to study all ritual-murder charges against Jews. All but two were rejected by the cardinal as false, and even these two have since been rejected by historians. Blood libel experienced resurgence in late nineteenth-century Germany, France, and Russia. Several cases are on record even into the twentieth century, and, remarkably, into the twenty-first century as well.

One of the most prominent recent examples is a 2009 article in the Swedish newspaper *Aftonbladet* accusing the Israel Defense Forces of harvesting the organs of Palestinians, as recounted in the introduction. The Israeli Foreign Ministry called the article anti-Semitic "hate porn." Similar accusations occur worldwide. In July 2010, a Russian court dismissed incitement charges against Svetlana Shestakova, a college professor who, during a series of lectures at Tyumen State Oil-Gas University, claimed that Jews ritually murder Christian children and use their blood to make matzah. In November 2010, prominent Dutch film director George Sluizer said that he saw former Israeli Prime Minister Ariel Sharon shoot two toddlers at close range in Lebanon during the 1982 war. Israeli officials called the claim "a modern blood libel."[8] Also in 2010, the Hamas-owned Al-Aqsa TV channel aired an address by Dr. Sallah Sultan, president of the American Center for Islamic Research, in which he stated that Jews kidnap Christians for matzah baking. In September 2011, Turkish Prime Minister Recep Tayyip Erdogan accused Israel during an interview on CNN of having killed "hundreds of thousands of Palestinians."[9] Blood libel accusations against Jews are rife in the Muslim world today.

The postcard on page 98 bears witness to an early twentieth-century blood libel that is known as the Konitz Affair. This incident led to the most severe outbreak of anti-Semitic violence in Wilhelmine, Germany. *Konitz* is the German name for Chojnice, a town that is now in Northern Poland. From 1871 through World War I, it was part of Germany, and then returned to Poland after the war. This postcard was issued and mailed while the murder investigation, with a Jew falsely accused, was still active. Thus it was not simply a souvenir—it was actually meant to spread the message that the authorities were seeking information about the case.

The Konitz Affair began on March 11, 1900, when Ernst Winter, an eighteen-year-old high school student, left his boarding house and did not return later that day. On March 13, the main portion of his body was discovered near the shores of Lake Mönchsee, its water still icy after a long winter. His right arm was found two days later in back of the small door of the Protestant cemetery, and his head was recovered a month later in a ditch at a nearby farm. Christian neighbors promptly rose against the Jewish inhabitants of Konitz with accusations of ritual murder. A Jew, Wolf Israelski, was arrested on the flimsy charge that two days before the discovery of the head, he had been seen walking with a sack on his back in which a round object was seen. He was kept in prison for five months, even though it was evident that the head had lain in ice far longer than two days prior to its discovery. His innocence was eventually proven in trial and Israelski was released; unfortunately, in the meantime, riots and violence directed against Jews in Konitz and surrounding towns erupted throughout that spring and summer. The matter came to the attention of the German Kaiser who, sensing a revolt not only against Jews, but also against state authority, ordered a battalion of Prussian solders into Konitz on June 12 to quell severe acts of violence and vandalism against the synagogue and Jewish homes. The troops remained for several months to maintain order.[10] Suspicion also fell on two local butchers due to

FIGURE 3-29. "Murder in Konitz. Twenty thousand Marks reward is promised by the Minister of the Interior to any private person who gives crucial information for the investigation of the murder of [high school student] Ernst Winter. The decision concerning the payment of the reward is reserved for the Minister. Marienwerder [a region in Germany], 27 April 1900. The Governor." The top center image is captioned, "Where the head was found on 15 April 1900"; at the right, "Where the right arm was found on 15 March 1900"; at the bottom, "Where the torso was found on 13 March 1900." The unexplained murder of a boy was pinned on a local Jew as a case of ritual murder and was used as an opportunity by the Christian population of the town and nearby areas to harass Jews.

the fact that the body seemed to have been "professionally" dismembered. One was a Christian named Gustav Hoffmann who, according to rumor, was upset that his daughter had been seen with the boy, and may have threatened him. There was no evidence for these allegations and the case against Hoffman was dropped. The second butcher to fall under suspicion was a Jew named Adolf Levy. Even though he had been previously investigated, his house had been thoroughly searched, and he had an irrefutable alibi, a group investigating the unsolved case convinced the authorities to reexamine Levy. He was arrested on October 6 (the same day that this postcard was mailed by a Konitz resident who surely knew what was happening) based on false testimony by a local man who claimed he saw Levy carrying a package, presumably containing Winter's body, to the lake on the date of the murder. Even though the testimony was unconvincing and the perjury eventually discovered, the government still tried Levy to avoid accusations that it was shielding Jews. The weak evidence was not enough to find Levy guilty of murder, but the rigged legal system still found a way to make sure Levy did not go free: he was instead convicted of perjury on the grounds that he lied when he stated that he was not acquainted with the murder victim. Levy was sentenced to four years in jail and had served for nearly three when the German emperor pardoned him. Ultimately, the real killer or motive behind the murder was never found, and remains unsolved to this day.

FIGURE 3-30. This particularly disgusting postcard evokes the theme of blood libel, as it depicts the Jewish "Löwy" family literally as carnivorous scavengers and lions. Like in figure 3-27, the common Jewish name Löwy was a play on the German word *Löwe*, which means lion. The large-nosed father and mother proudly watch their three children, also with stereotypical large noses, sharing a bone protruding out of a man's boot. The leg and boot represent Germany and the German people whom the Jews prey on for money and power.[11] [Publisher: Not provided; mailed within Germany in January 1900.]

THE POEMS OF FRIEDRICH AND ADOLF STOLTZE

Friedrich Stoltze (1816–1891) was born in Frankfurt, where he became a famous poet, writer, and journalist. He was best known for writing in what was termed the *Frankforterisch,* or the "Frankfurt dialect," peculiar to that region in Germany. In 1845, he was temporarily employed in the bank of Amschel Mayer Rothschild, founder of what would become the famous Rotshchild bank with branches throughout Europe. Stoltze went on to start the weekly newspaper *Frankfurt Lantern,* which became popular due to its anti-Prussian political stand. Stoltze remains known in his native city, above all, for having so faithfully bequeathed the heritage of the local dialect. Since 1978, Frankfurt has awarded a yearly prize bearing Stoltze's name to individuals who make a valuable cultural contribution to the city. Although Stoltze was not known for anti-Semitism and did not express himself in these terms, living in Frankfurt, a hub of Jewish life, he could not help but reflect many of the prejudices against Jews deeply ingrained in German culture at the time. At least two of his poems, "Der Profet Jonas" and "Levi un Rebbekkche," were specifically written to ridicule Jews and perpetuate ancient stereotypes. Both have been memorialized on anti-Semitic postcards. One example highlighting "Der Profet Jonas" is shown in figure 3-31.

Friedrich Stoltze had a son, Adolf (1842–1933), who followed in his father's footsteps to become a well-known journalist, writer, poet, and playwright. Adolf continued to write in the Frankfurt dialect made famous by his father. And, like his father, Adolf included in his works a poem that mocked Jews. Like Friedrich, Adolf was not particularly known to be an anti-Semite, but once again, due to the deep biases against Jews that were passed down generation to generation for many centuries in Europe, Adolf could not help but reflect these entrenched ideas. Adolf's poem, written in the late 1890s, is called "Der Regescherm," or "The Umbrella." The story is explained in figure 3-32.[12]

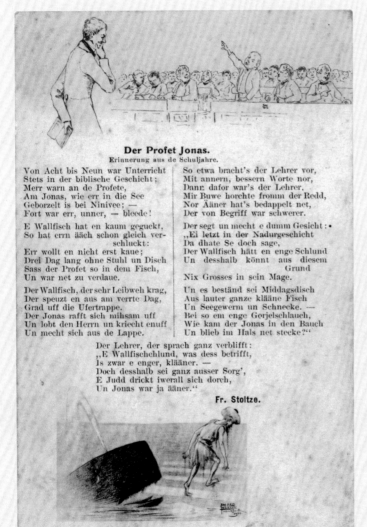

Der Profet Jonas.
Erinnerung aus de Schuljahre.

Von Acht bis Neun war Unterricht
Stets in der biblische Geschicht;
Merr warn an de Profete,
Am Jonas, wie err in die See
Geborzelt is bei Ninivee; —
Fort war err, unner, — bleede!

E Wallfisch hat en kaum geguckt,
So hat errn ääch schon gleich ver-
schluckt:
Err wollt en nicht erst kaue;
Drei Dag lang ohne Stuhl un Disch
Sass der Profet so in dem Fisch,
Un war net zu verdaue.

Der Wallfisch, der sehr Leibweh krag,
Der speuzt en aus am verrte Dag,
Grad uff die Ufertrappe.
Der Jonas rafft sich mihsam uff
Un lobt den Herrn un kriecht enuff
Un mecht sich aus de Lappe.

So etwa bracht's der Lehrer vor,
Mit annern, bessern Worte nor,
Dann dafor war's der Lehrer.
Mir Buwe horchte fromm der Redd,
Nor Ääner hat's bedappelt net,
Der von Begriff war schwerer.

Der segt un mecht e dumm Gesicht: •
„Ei letzt in der Nadurgeschicht
Da dhate Se doch sage,
Der Wallfisch hätt en enge Schlund
Un desshalb könnt aus diesem
Grund
Nix Grosses in sein Mage.

Un es beständ sei Middagsdisch
Aus lauter ganze klääne Fisch
Un Seegewerm un Schnecke. —
Bei so em enge Gorjelschlauch,
Wie kam der Jonas in den Bauch
Un blieb im Hals net stecke?"

Der Lehrer, der sprach ganz verblifft:
„E Wallfischchlund, was dess betrifft,
Is zwar e enger, klääner. —
Doch desshalb sei ganz ausser Sorg',
E Judd drickt iwerall sich dorch,
Un Jonas war ja ääner."

Fr. Stoltze.

FIGURE 3-31. *Der Profet Jonas,* or "The Prophet Jonah," uses the famous Biblical story in which Jonah is swallowed by a large fish (sometimes referred to as a whale) to explain how Jews manage to "squeeze through everywhere." The implication is that Jews are pushy, always haggle, use devious and dishonest methods, and find a way to take advantage of a situation for their benefit, at the expense of others if necessary. The postcard is subtitled "Memories of Schooldays" and shows a classroom at the top. The poem was written in rhyme in the Frankfurt dialect of German. The translation cannot properly reflect the rhyming. [Publisher: Hemr. Stoltze, Frankfurt; circa 1910.]

From eight to nine the lesson was
On Biblical history;
We were dealing with the Prophets,
Jonah, as he fell into the sea
At Niniveh;—
All gone in the water,—stupid!

No sooner had a whale seen him,
Then he swallowed him up;
He wouldn't even chew on him;
For three days the prophet sat in the whale
Without a chair and a table,
And was impossible to digest.

The whale which got severe belly pain,
Spat him out on the fourth day,
Right onto the stairs on the shore.
Jonah barely gets himself together
He praises the Lord, crawls up
And buzzes off.

That's how the teacher presented it,
Just in better words,
He was a teacher, after all.
Us boys, we listened devoutly,
Just one didn't get it,
He was slow on the uptake.

He said, with a dumb face:
"Just recently in biology
You told us
That the whale had a narrow gorge
And for that reason
Nothing big gets to his stomach.

And his lunch was made up
Of many very small fish
And sea worms and snails.—
If it has such a narrow gorge,
How did Jonah get down to the stomach
And didn't get stuck in the throat?"

The teacher was all surprised and said:
"As to the whale's gorge
Is tight and narrow, indeed.—
But don't worry,
A Jew squeezes through everywhere,
And Jonah was one of them."

Der Regescherm.

Herr Sali kam mit Frää un Kind
Derr in enn Lade hie
Un segt: „Ach gewwe Se ge-
                        schwind
Merr doch enn Parablie.

Enn, Scherm, gut, billig, leicht un
Es regend, 's is e Graus!   [fei,
Ich brauch enn ääch forn Sonne-
                        schei,
Drei Mark, die geww ich aus."

Der Hannel kam dann ääch zu Stann
Nach langer, schwerer Wahl.
Druff seggt zu seiner Frää der
                        Mann:
„Rebbeckche zahl emal !

Doch wie derr des sei Kläänes
                        heert,
Da fehrt des uff im Nu
Un hält der Mama ganz empeert
Die Rockdasch krampfhaft zu

Un kreischst: „Du gibst kää Geld
                        eraus,
Kään Fennig, sag ich dir!
Was leiht uns an dem Rege draus,
Merr sin im Trockne hier."

Druff segt die Frää: „Des mechst
                        de gut!
Der Kauffmann, uff mei Wort,
Lesst, wann mer nix bezahle dut,
Den Baba net mehr fort."

Da zieht die Krott mit bääde Ärm,
Die Mama nach der Dhier:
„Dann komm un nemm den Regescherm
Un lass den Baba hier!"   Adolf Stoltze.

FIGURE 3-32. "The Umbrella" recounts the tale of an upscale Jewish family who enters a store during a rainstorm to buy an umbrella. When it is time to pay, the child expresses extreme distress regarding the loss of money for the umbrella. The boy explains that it is not raining inside the store, and then suggests that he and his mother walk out with the umbrella, but leave the father as a substitute for payment. The poem powerfully dwells on the stereotype of the stingy Jew through the actions of a child, suggesting that the Jewish love for money and cheapness is learned at a young age. [Publisher: Not provided; circa 1910.]

Mr. Sali came with wife and child
He went into a store
And said: "Please give me quickly the umbrella.

An umbrella, good, cheap, and light,
It's raining, it's awful!
I also need one for the sun,
Three marks, I have to spend."

The deal was concluded
After a long, difficult selection.
After which the man said to his wife:
"Rebecca, pay him already!"

However, when the little one hears this,
He becomes upset
Forcefully holding her skirt pocket with all his might

And screams: "You're not going to spend any money,
Not a penny, I tell you!
What difference does the rain outside make to us,
We are inside, it is dry in here."

To which the wife says: "You did that well!
The storeowner, I swear,
If we don't pay anything here,
He won't let Papa out."

And so the brat pulls Mama,
With both arms to the door:
"So come and take the umbrella
And leave Papa here!"

AN EXPLOSIVE PACKAGE FOR JEWS

This unusual postcard from the late 1890s shows a group of stereotypical Jews at the left looking perplexed at a package that has been delivered by the mail carrier at the right. The caption reads "The mysterious package from Cologne." The parcel is addressed at top to *der Verein zur Abwher des Antisemitism* in Berlin," or the "Association for Combating Anti-Semitism." The sides of the package note the sender, Dr. Schwechten, and the date, 1896. What is inside this package? It turns out to be "explosive pamphlets" that were sent to these Jews by a well-known anti-Semite. Like a letter laced with anthrax or a delivery from the Unabomber, the goal was for the unsuspecting Jews to be injured or worse. The mailman waves goodbye with a smirk, as if he knows what he has just delivered.

The image in this postcard comes from an illustration from a reprinted edition of a thirty-four page anti-Semitic booklet called *"Das Lied vom Levi"* or "The Song of Levi." The booklet, written by Dr. Eduard Schwechten (1859–1919) in 1895, was created as a parody of a famous German poem from 1798 by Friedrich Schiller called "Das Lied von der Glocke" or "Song of the Bell." Schwechten's version was actually intended for children and tells about all the evils of the Jews: how they infiltrated Germany, live like parasites, control finance and commerce, and oppress the German population. The protagonist is a Jew named Levi. The conclusion has the Jews kicked out of Germany. The booklet was so inflammatory that it caught the attention of certain Jews who successfully obtained a ban on the book claiming that it incited class hatred. However, the German courts annulled the ban and the song spread unimpeded throughout the country.

The 1933 reprinting of the booklet, newly illustrated by Siegfried Horn with vile anti-Semitic images, including the one reproduced on this postcard, became widely popular. An introduction to this new edition by Dr. Hermann Bartmann noted that Dr. Schwechten was a visionary who had the foresight in the 1890s to recognize the malevolent spread of the Jews in Germany and to create a new anti-Jewish movement. The image in this postcard does not simply seek to harm Jews by what may be considered an act of terrorism, but rather it specifically taunts the very institution that was established in Germany to combat anti-Semitism. The Association for Combating Anti-Semitism (the actual German name for the organization was *Verein zur Abwher des Antisemitismus*) was founded in Berlin in 1890, prompted by legitimate fears that anti-Semitism was spreading with an aim to suspend civil equality for Jews. Unfortunately, and not surprisingly, the association, which was active until the 1930s, had little success in combating anti-Semitism; one scholar noted: "It is all too obvious that the history of the *Abwherverein* is no success-story in spite of forty-two years of existence." With a population that purchased and mailed large quantities of picture postcards like this one, it is not hard to understand why.

Das geheimnisvolle Paquet aus Köln

FIGURE 3-33. "The Mysterious Package from Cologne" contains explosives that are meant to harm the Jews at the left. They were sent by a Dr. Eduard Schwechten, a well-known anti-Semite. The circumstances behind this card are explained in the sidebar text. [Publisher: Not provided; circa 1899.]

THE ISLAND RESORT OF BORKUM

The island of Borkum is located on the North Sea coast of Germany. In the nineteenth century, the island became a popular tourist resort. By the turn of the century, it was one of the best-known vacation destinations in Germany (it was also famous for its anti-Semitism and total exclusion of Jews). In fact, the island was nicknamed "the only spot on Earth without a Jew." The town's outspoken anti-Semitism became further renowned through the "Borkum Song" with a finale that called for the Jews to "get out." The song was a hit (not unlike the hit single "The Little Cohn," described in chapter 8) and it became the usual practice in the island for the municipal band to play the melody at the end of each performance with the crowd joining in song. This postcard, which was published and mailed in large numbers (it is known to collectors as one of the most easily obtainable German anti-Semitic postcards), depicts a crowd of Germans joyfully singing the tune with hands raised and glasses filled, while the Jewish family at the right is turned away at the gate. The text under the rejected Jews reads: "I AM SORRY! But he who comes to you flat-footed,—he must get out!—get out!" The song is titled *Borkum Lied"* or simply the "Borkum Song." The translation is as follows:

We greet you with a merry song
Borkum's beautiful beach,
Where seagulls hover in the air,
And the green land wide extends!
Where on the dunes with thunder roars
The wild sea of the north.
[Where the lighthouse beams with pride up high
To guide the sailor on his way]
Hence loudly we will sing your praise,
All of us guests, from near and far,
With vigor shall sound the call:
Borkum hurray! Borkum hurray!

Admitted there are spas aplenty
In the German fatherland,
But none of them comes even close
To your glorious island strand;—
How your magic spell lets
My worried shy away!
[How my heart gets light and easy,

Happily I raise my eyes]
Hence loudly we will sing your praise,
All of us guests, from near and far,
With vigor shall sound the call:
Borkum hurray! Borkum hurray!

What rules on this green island is
Authentic German spirit,
Hence all of us kin and tribe
Flock happily to you.
On Borkum only Germanness rules,
German is the only banner.
[We keep pure the honor banner,
Of Germania forever]
But he who come to you flat-footed,
With hooked nose and curly hair,
He's got no place on your beaches
He must get out! He must get out!
"Get out!"

FIGURE 3-34. "Greetings from Borkum" shows a group of revelers at the left singing an anti-Semitic song while the Jews at the right are turned away from the social hall. The scene is explained in the sidebar text. [Publisher: E. Adami, Emden; mailed from Borkum to Brunswig in July 1910.]

The call for Jews to leave the resort was partially a reaction to the increasing numbers of Jews who participated in the German tourist industry, similar to the resort spas of Karlsbad and Marienbad described in chapter 9. As tourism increased, Christian Germans started to complain that Jews were disturbing their vacations. Hotel owners listened to their core client base and began to turn Jews away. This practice spread on the island, and soon Jews were not welcome anywhere in Borkum. In 1924, the island and the song caught the attention of politicians, and the Prussian socialist minister of the interior forbade the band to play the song. The regional chief magistrate published an ordinance enforcing the minister's decision. But the regional court contradicted this order by threatening a 100,000 goldmark fine to anyone who hindered the performance of the song. With the threat of arrest still possible, for a while the band stopped playing the anti-Semitic finale and so the crowd sang without musical accompaniment. By 1925, the matter was resolved and the band was once again able to play the complete melody. Around this time, anti-Semitic songs were adopted by several other resorts in Germany. It should be noted that the virulent anti-Semitism in Borkum and other resorts was not representative of the entire German tourist industry, and most Jews felt that they could go to the vast majority of hotels in the country. Even so, the mass Judeophobia of this resort island, supported by local politicians and memorialized in many thousands of postcards, is telling.[13]

These postcards were intended for tourists, and indeed, this example was sent by a vacationer to his parents in July 1910. The handwritten text on the back says: "Dear Parents, As we leave Borkum, I send you the 'Borkum Song.' Today, Friday morning, it rained a little, not for long. It is very hot here. One could get used to it, but it is not as beautiful as Norderney [another popular island in the North Sea]. We are leaving at noon. The hotel room was terrible; the whole night the window was clattering. Best wishes, also to [illegible], from [illegible]." The son was clearly proud to share this anti-Semitic song with his mother and father; it was probably a feeling that was passed down to him at an early age.

CHAPTER 4

POSTCARDS FROM FRANCE

Chapter 1 presented the birth of anti-Semitic postcards during the Dreyfus Affair, but the legacy of anti-Jewish postcards in France extends into the World War II era. This chapter will examine the diverse and virulent content of these postcards.

First, an overview of the history of the Jews of France. Today, the approximately 500,000-person Jewish community in France is an important one, ranking behind only Israel and the United States in population. Jews have lived in France since at least the Roman period, when Gaul was under Roman domination. The Jewish population in Gaul expanded from 132–135 CE when Jews fleeing the Holy Land after their failed revolt against Rome settled in the region. Under Roman rule, Jews enjoyed religious and commercial freedom under a tolerant Roman policy that demanded only loyalty to the state. In the fifth century, the Franks, a Germanic people, conquered parts of Gaul, and over the next three hundred years, they expanded the Frankish empire into what is now modern day France. Clovis I (466–511), the first king of the Franks, converted to Christianity, thus becoming an ally of the church. The Church's hostility toward the Jewish people led to the typical social prejudices and restrictions against them, such as prohibitions against holding public office and entering certain trades, and the imposition of special taxes. Even so, the Jews lived relatively well and secure under the Frankish kings into the ninth century.

The Treaty of Verdun in 843 split the Frankish empire into what would be the kernels of France, Germany, and parts of other European countries. Although there were many examples of persecutions in the new kingdom of France, for the most part, Jewish life continued peacefully and Jewish culture expanded, highlighted by the works of a French rabbi known as Rashi (1040–1105) who authored the first comprehensive commentaries on the Talmud and Hebrew Bible, works which remain a centerpiece of Jewish study to this day. The First and Second Crusades in 1096 and 1145 marked a turning point for the status of Jews in France who became subject to widespread, organized violence. France's first blood libel was perpetrated in 1171, and thirty-one Jews were burned at the stake as a result. King Phillip Augustus expelled the Jews in 1182 in an effort to confiscate their property and cancel debts owed to them, but the resulting loss of economic activity prompted the king to allow them to return in 1198. The climate remained aggressively anti-Jewish in the thirteenth and fourteenth centuries with local expulsion, blood libel, and confiscation of property being the norm. In 1306, the Jews were expelled en masse again, affecting an estimated 50,000 Jews—but once again, they were allowed to return a few years later due to economic considerations. As in most of Europe, the devastating Black Plague of 1348–1349 triggered accusations that the Jews were propogating the disease, and many Jews were put to death. In 1394, the Jews were expelled yet again, with the king citing complaints of usury and crimes committed against Christians. This expulsion removed most vestiges of Jewish life in France for the next two hundred years.

In the seventeenth century, Jews began to re-enter France, but continued to find themselves oppressed and subject to local expulsion. By the eve of the French Revolution in 1789, approximately 40,000 Jews lived in France. The French Revolution led to a new standing for Jews, as Napoleon granted them full citizenship in 1791. France was thus the first European nation to emancipate the Jews. However, even though technically Jews were entitled to full civic rights, in reality, their situation was little improved. Even still, Jews prospered economically and culturally during the nineteenth century until a new outbreak of anti-Semitism flared up in the late 1800s.

France, during much of the nineteenth century, was involved in a constant jockeying for power with other European nations, particularly Prussia. Growing tensions between France and Prussia eventually led to war in 1870. The German forces were superior, and France was soundly defeated. The devastating loss, which included the loss of territory, gave rise to paranoia regarding foreign influences in France, and Jews became an easy target for accusations of disloyalty to the state. Jewish immigration from Eastern Europe, and several financial scandals, such as the collapse of the Union Generale Bank and the Panama Canal affair, fueled further Judeophobia. Drumont's *La France Juive,* published in 1886, summarized all the hostilities that the French people held against Jews—the book became a best seller. French anti-Semitism in this period culminated with the Dreyfus Affair. From the end of the Dreyfus Affair at the turn of the century through the 1930s, conditions for the Jews improved again, and many Jews fought patriotically for France in World War I. In 1936, France elected its first Jewish prime minister, Léon Blum, who later survived imprisonment in Buchenwald and Dachau before he was rescued by the Allies in 1945. French anti-Semitism would resurface prominently again by the start of World War II, spiking upon the German invasion of France in 1940. The French Vichy government openly and actively collaborated with the Nazis to persecute and round up Jews; in the most prominent instance, in what is known as the Vel' d'Hiv Roundup, approximately 10,000 Jews were arrested and held for shipment to Auschwitz for extermination. It was not until 1995 that the French government, through a statement by its president, Jacques Chirac, acknowledged responsibility and apologized for its role in these events. For various reasons, including the division of France into two zones for much of the war and successful emigration to Spain and elsewhere, the Jews of France managed to survive the Holocaust better than the Jews of Eastern Europe. In all, approximately 25 percent of France's prewar Jewish population of 350,000 was deported to concentration camps.

Postwar France saw an influx of Jewish refugees, and over the next three decades the Jewish population tripled. The decline of French power in North Africa and the expulsion of Jews from Arab nations as a reaction to the Israeli victories in the 1948 War of Independence and the Six-Day War led to further increases in the Jewish population. Jews integrated successfully both socially and economically in postwar France. France voted for Israel's formation in 1948 and was its primary foreign supporter in the 1950s. Since the 1960s, anti-Israel attitudes have spilled into anti-Semitism, sometimes expressed by vandalism against Jewish property and institutions (e.g., in October 1980, a bomb exploded outside a Paris synagogue, killing four people). Overall, however, the Jewish community in postwar France has lived in prosperity and peace.

In recent years, tension has arisen as the growing Muslim population inside France has "imported" the popular and virulent anti-Semitism that is rampant in the Arab world. Some of this animosity is attributed to the Middle East conflict in which Jews everywhere are viewed as proxies for Israel. France's Muslim community stands at over 5 million, approximately ten times the size of the Jewish population. The French media has contributed to the deterioration of Israel in the eyes of the public and the Muslim community with its one-sided reporting against Israel.[1] Muslim violence against Jews in France culminated in the 2006 kidnapping, torture, and murder of a young French Jew, Ilan Halimi. The French leadership condemned this violence and has come out strongly against this resurgence in anti-Semitism. France still ranks relatively low in surveys of anti-Semitic attitudes with 20 percent of respondents believing common anti-Semitic stereotypes.

The anti-Semitic postcards from France mirror the negative attitudes against Jews held by French society in the late nineteenth century and through World War II. When ranking the level of virulence and hatred depicted in these postcards, they would place second to Germany. Given the open anti-Semitism exhibited by the Dreyfus Affair and the active collaboration by the Vichy government with the Nazis in World War II, this fact is not surprising. French anti-Semitic postcards go beyond simple stereotyping of greedy Jews with large noses; they depict Jews as demonic, in control of the levers of world power, and traitorous to the French nation. The postcards shown in this chapter will highlight all of these motifs, particularly figure 4-2, one of the most virulent anti-Semitic postcards ever published by any nation.

FIGURE 4-2. *(top of next page)* This colorful and detailed postcard from France in the turn of the twentieth century is an icon among anti-Semitic postcards of the Golden Era. The card is a microcosmic statement of the anti-Semitic sentiment that emerged in France in the late nineteenth century. Following a string of national difficulties beginning with its 1871 loss to the Germans in the Franco-Prussian War and ending with several financial crises and political upheavals following the Dreyfus Affair, this card names the nation's scapegoat: the Jews. The image begins at the left, where there are five women: the first three are peasants holding an axe, a sickle, and a rake; the fourth woman, representing the Church, is lifting a shining cross up high; on a protruding cliff, there is an allegorical figure with the tricolor flag wrapped around her, representing the French Republic, one that is righteous and militant. Further right is a Gaulish warrior raising his arm and pointing eastward and, while looking at the five women, he exclaims: "Frenchmen! The Jew! He is the Enemy!" The Jew/Judaism in this postcard is depicted as a demonic dragon dangling long tentacles: one grasps a fortress-like building resting on the map of France; another one a calf, perhaps representing food and agriculture; a third one surrounds and protects a building with the words *Palais des Voleurs*, or "Palace of Thieves," where the Jews live. Other, smaller tentacles point to Berlin, Frankfurt, and Hamburg, indicating that the "Jewish enemy" is in league with Germany; others hold on to scrolls that say "justice" and "the press," as if the Jews control both. The dragon's head, with the word "Talmud" (books of Jewish law and teachings, which were falsely accused of being an anti-Christian text[2]) written on top, emits something out of its mouth at the church at the bottom, which fights back with rays of light emanating from the building. Sitting on the demon is a bearded, king-like figure, a Jew, holding and surrounded by bags of money, each with the number 100,000. Each bag is captioned, indicating where the Jew collected the money, such as by controlling natural resources—*Mines d'or* (gold mines), *Cuivre* (copper), *Petrole* (petroleum), *Blé* (wheat); and dominating financial institutions—*Credit Provincial* (provincial credit), *Comptoir d'Escompte* (discount bank), *Reassurance* (reinsurance); and by causing and profiting from scandals and fraud—*Union Generale*, *Panama*, and *Watana* (see captions to the left and right of the dragon). One bag summarizes everything by calling the Jews a "Coven of Scoundrels." "Union Generale" refers to the collapse in 1882 of the Union Générale Bank that led to a stock market crash and a severe economic crisis. Paul Eugene Bontoux, the bank's founder and president, publicly blamed "Jewish finance" for his bank's collapse. The failure led to an anti-Semitic outcry and accusations that the Jewish-owned Rothschild banking firm engineered the failure of the "Christian" bank. A judicial investigation later found that Union Générale Bank had caused its own demise through speculation and the squandering of its reserves (Bontoux was sentenced to five years in prison, but fled to Spain).[3] *Panama* refers to the Panama Canal scandal that erupted ten years later in 1892. The Panama Canal Company raised much of the capital necessary to complete the construction of the proposed canal by selling shares to ordinary French citizens, nearly 500,000, according to one estimate. The company was not able to complete its work, and it eventually went bankrupt, resulting in losses that cut across France. Investigations revealed extensive bribery of government officials and parliamentary members so that they would keep quiet about the company's failures. The scandal led to anti-Semitic accusations, fueled by the fact that several Jews were actively involved in the bribery scandal (the number of non-Jews involved was, of course, far greater). The anti-Semitic press, including Drumont's *La Libre Parole,* gained popularity as a result of the scandal and its "Jewish" causes, and the incident is considered a precursor to the anti-Semitic fever that characterized the Dreyfus Affair a few years later.[4] *Watana* refers to a gold mine in Thailand (known as Siam at that time) that was owned and operated by a French company. Similar to the Panama Canal project, the operators of the mine raised capital by selling shares in the enterprise to ordinary Frenchmen. And, like in the Panama Canal, the mining project proved to be a bust and shareholders lost their entire investment. Although far less prominent than the bank and canal debacles, the Watana affair offered another opportunity to blame the Jews. Finally, the events of the Dreyfus Affair and the blame assigned to Captain Dreyfus for passing secrets to the German enemy are memorialized in this postcard as well. At the lower right, standing above the curled tail of the dragon, is an image of a French army officer handing a large paper titled "Plan" to a German officer in exchange for a bag of money that the German hands over. Although the real traitor had been identified by the time this card was published, this card still assumed that Dreyfus passed military secrets for money. [Publisher: Imprimerie Speciale du G.O.F., Lyon; circa 1900.]

FIGURE 4-1. "Jewish Peril" reads the title of the public notice that several Frenchmen are reading. The warning calls for the "suppression of Jewish capital for the monopolist" and ends by stating "France for the French." This 1900-era postcard was hand drawn by an artist who signed the work at lower right and then sent the postcard, probably to a friend. This simple image captures the widespread attitude toward Jews in France at the time. This artist must have felt a strong hatred toward Jews, evidenced by the effort expended in drawing this image. Other examples of hand-drawn anti-Semitic postcards can be seen in figures 4-24 and 5-1.

FIGURE 4-3 The tiny village of Saint Saulge was well known for its comical "legends," which were quirky and humorous events that supposedly occurred in the town. These legends, which numbered at least eighty, were illustrated and placed on postcards, which proved to be popular and widely sold in France. Not surprisingly, one of the "legends" included an anti-Semitic tale, as displayed in this postcard. The title says "Legend of Saint-Saulge—The Division" and shows a group of Jews at the right (identified by their elongated noses) receiving what appears to be a bone and a group on the left (with normal noses) receiving a large fruit. The caption at the bottom says, "It is understood: One of you will have the fruit, and the other [the Jews] will have the tail, it will be the true division according to Saint-Saulge 'everything goes to one side and nothing to the other.'" The judges of Saint-Saulge are shown presiding over what is considered equitable treatment of Jews by the town. The sender makes no reference to the image, with a five-word message of greeting written on the back. [Publisher: Not provided; mailed within France in September 1910; note stamp at lower right.]

FIGURE 4-4. This postcard depicts a person with the head of a mouse or rat, a classic representation of a Jew (see figure 1-9 for another example), holding bags of money, each with the number 10,000. The sign says "Competition of Fierce Animals, Division of Misers, 1st Prize." It is clear from motifs used in the image that the target of this postcard was Jews. [Publisher: P.L., Paris; mailed within France in April 1907.]

FIGURE 4-5. Mr. Lévy Abraham, a Jew, is seen with enourmous antlers holding hats. The text reads: "Diploma of Honor to Mr. Lévy Abraham. Inventor of the horn hat-rack. Patented. This device has the advantage of growing a new branch at every misfortune. Come and see!" The myth of the Jews with horns is discussed in figure 2-29. The artist here used the stereotype to ridicule this ugly Jew, and to note that the Jewish "invention" takes advantage of other people. [Publisher: Collection Comique, Paris; circa 1920.]

FIGURES 4-6 to 4-8. These three postcards are part of a virulent multi-card set published by the *Librairie Antisémite* that specialized in anti-Jewish books, pamphlets, and postcards (also see figures 2-7 and 2-34). The first image (card No. 3 of the set) depicts a stereotypical Jew sitting on a map of Europe holding a tool that sweeps over France, turning the country black in its wake. The caption says: "If allowed to," implying that the powerful Jews would pillage the French nation if left free to do so. The next example (card No. 6 of the set) imagines a Jew, multi-armed like an octopus, grabbing and emptying the pockets of a helpless Gentile. The Jew here is a powerful and abominable creature that easily controls its victims in search of money. The caption says: "Allegorical Window Destined for the Synagogue of the Rue de la Victoire [referring to the Great Synagogue of Paris that was badly damaged and desecrated in World War II]." The last example (card No. 7 of the set) shows two grotesque Jews talking. The one at the left says: "Oh! Samuel! You have a beautiful watch! How much did it cost?" His friend (note the ridiculously oversized hand) responds: "Nothing at all, Isaac! The merchant was asleep!" [Publisher: Librairie Antisémite, Paris, France; 1st Series, Cards No. 3, 6, and 7; circa 1900.]

FIGURE 4-9. This interesting postcard is titled "The Strikes (February 10)," referring to a series of labor strikes that occurred in France in the early 1900s. In 1901, tailors and seamstresses who worked in factories began a month-long strike that received massive coverage in the press. An industry-wide coal miners' strike in 1902 led to almost 50,000 miners walking off the job, leading to intervention by the French government. The text below says: "A unique cooperation: Seamstresses and Miners." The miner at left is pictured as downtrodden while the seamstress holds his hand and pulls him as she goes forth in protest. Her protest is heaved upon the Jew, here represented as three stereotypical figures grabbing bags of money. The assertion is that while the workers of France struggle for higher wages, the Jews take the money from the common laborer. [Publisher: Not provided; mailed within France in September 1903.]

FIGURE 4-10. "Association of Cheapskates [Misers]" is the title of this elaborately designed and written anti-Semitic postcard adorned with rats and ugly images of Jews, including a rat-headed man below. This postcard is supposed to be the association's "Diploma of Honor" bestowed upon the recipient. The text reads as follows:

> Considering that Mr. _____ enjoys a well-deserved reputation as a miser; and taking into account that he would not kill a louse without the legitimate desire to keep its skin; and that furthermore he has an uncanny ability to execute the task of fleecing eggs; considering that his only enjoyment on this lowly earth is to contemplate his money that he amasses one cent at a time, of which he never gave the slightest amount to anyone as was found out by our inquiry; considering that such behavior gives this man all the rights to belong to our association, we proclaim him life member, and we give him, furthermore, this Diploma of Honor.

At the bottom, the "diploma" is signed by the "members of the committee," including the president and secretary, and names of other members. The comparison of money-obsessed Jews and rats is a common theme explored in figures 1-9 and 4-4. [Publisher: G.P., Paris; circa 1910.]

FIGURE 4-11. This remarkable and rare French postcard is a novelty card, with the tail of the tiger at the right made out of a metal spring which was affixed to the front of the postcard (and has somehow survived the last century). Novelty postcards were created by publishers to pique the interest of the buyer, much like "singing" birthday cards today. Publishers would affix a variety of materials, such as leather, real feathers, and buttons, often with moving parts (also known as "mechanical" postcards). This example carries an anti-Semitic message. The Jew at left, cornered by the tiger, seems to have no escape. But the Jew, who is selling his wares, can only say something to the effect of "a whisker fixing, if it would please you?" as if the Jew could "sell" his way out of trouble. The Jew here is shown as stupid and out of place, yet even in this setting, money and commerce are still his primary concerns. This card was printed in Germany, for use in France, by a firm called D.R.G.M., which was known for its wide varierty of novelty and mechanical postcards. [Publisher: D.R.G.M., France; circa 1905.]

FIGURE 4-12. *Le Juif Errant* or "The Wandering Jew" is the subject of this song, whose first lines are memorialized in this postcard, complete with musical notes. As explained in figure F, the Wandering Jew is a symbolic figure who represents all Jews and is condemned to forever roam the earth as punishment for supposedly killing Jesus. The song reads: "Is there anything on earth that is more gripping than the great misery of the poor wandering Jew? How his unhappy fate seems sad and unfortunate." The drawing at the top shows a sorry-looking Jew stared at by regular French people. The legend of the Wandering Jew was a popular subject in nineteenth-century France, another example of the obsessive nature of Judeophobia. *Le Juif Errant* was the title of a play performed in Paris in 1834 and of an opera produced at the Royal Academy of Music in Paris in 1852. [Publisher: Gu.L. Music, Paris; mailed within France in October 1908.]

comme est un animal "raisonnable"
(Extrait de l'histoire naturelle)

BXF ㉑ LE CHAMEAU
Victime de l'Heredité,
Sa mère, un soir, pauvre ingénue,
Souffrant de la maternité
Avait des envies biscornues !....

FIGURE 4-13. A caricature of a Jewish woman with a grotesquely large nose and ugly features. The cryptic text compares the Jew to an animal: "The Camel / Victim of Heredity, / Her mother, one night, poor ingenue, / Was suffering from her pregnancy / and she had distorted cravings." At the top, it says: "Man is a reasonable animal (that is from natural history)." The concept of the sexually deviant and vulgar Jew was a less common anti-Semitic theme, but it is seen in several postcards, such as in figure 7-4 and those of the Little Cohn described in chapter 8. [Publisher: BXF; circa 1920s.]

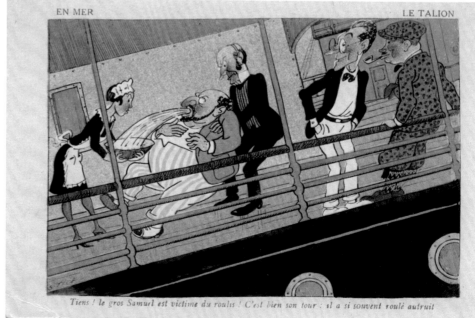

EN MER   LE TALION

Tiens ! le gros Samuel est victime du roulis ! C'est bien son tour : il a si souvent roulé autrui

FIGURE 4-14. "At Sea—Retaliation." Samuel, a Jewish passenger on the ship, is vomiting from seasickness, while the gentlemen on the right look on with smiles. They say "Well! The fat Samuel is a victim of the rolling [seasickness]! It is his turn: he frequently rolled [swindled] from someone else." The Jew's discomfort in this vignette is simply retaliation for his thieving ways. [Publisher: H. Grimaud, Marseille; circa 1927.]

ÉLECTIONS MUNICIPALES

LÉVY

Heureusement !!! les Electeurs
Comprendront, que si tu n'étais pas
Blacboulé, les chiens eux-mêmes
Deviendraient enragés.

ÉLECTIONS MUNICIPALES

À DESINFECTER

BALLOT

À DESTINATION DE

FRAGILE

GARE

LÉVY

Tu comptais nous embarquer
C'est toi qui reste au bout du quai

FIGURES 4-15 and 4-16. Two postcards from the same set titled "Municipal Elections" each showing a Jewish man, Levy, appearing dejected. Levy apparently attempted to win a certain election, but was unsuccessful, rejected by a public who understood the sinister nature of the Jew. The first card is captioned: "Fortunately!!! the voters will understand that if you were not blackballed, the dogs themselves would become enraged." The second shows Levy, with particularly grotesque devil-like ears and nose, sitting at the edge of the railroad station platform. The caption says, "You thought you could take us with you, but it is you who remains at the end of the wharf." This pair of anti-Semitic postcards suggest that the Jew attempts to take power by abusing free elections. In this case, the Jew is thwarted, attacked by dogs, and cast out. [Publisher: M.G.A.; circa 1930.]

FIGURES 4-17 and 4-18. These two postcards were part of a set published in the 1930s, when prewar anti-Semitic sentiment was on the rise. The first example shows an ugly hooked-nosed Jew below a warning message to the nation: "Frenchmen! Avoid the Jew, his lies, his good little bargains that have no backing." The second card says: "Who dominates the black market? The Jew. Crooked deals, scandalous profits, is this not seductive for Israel?" What appears to be the same man is seen holding money and surrounded by products for sale, such as the bag of rice at the top. Note the pig, a motif described in chapter 2. The Jew is prohibited from eating pork, but for profit, he will gladly handle swine. [Publisher: Not provided; 1930s era.]

Le Juif patriote

« 500.000ᶠ aux nationaux,
1 million aux marxistes juifs,
j'ai encore bien servi le peuple juif
aujourd'hui !... »

FIGURE 4-19. This postcard belongs to a series of six cards published by the Mouvement Franciste, a French Fascist and anti-Semitic league founded by Marcel Bucard in 1933. The organization reached a peak of 10,000 members and was financed by the Italian Fascist leader Benito Mussolini. The movement was banned in 1936, but Bucard was able to revive the organization after the Nazi occupation of France. In 1946, Bucard was executed for treason. This example sarcastically depicts "The Jewish Patriot" who says: "500,000 francs to the nationals, 1 million to the Jewish Marxists, I still have served the Jewish people today!" The Mouvement Franciste accused the Jews of collaborating with the enemy, in this case the Soviet Union (note the Soviet flag at top right) and the "Marxists." On the back, a small caption encourages the buyer to "read 'Le Franciste' doctrine weekly and fight against Judeo-Marxism." [Publisher: Le Franciste, Paris; circa 1934.]

CHAPTER 5

POSTCARDS FROM GREAT BRITAIN

Anti-Semitism is a relevant topic in Great Britain today: according to one member of the House of Lords, anti-Semitism is now at its worst level since 1936.[1] An inquiry on anti-Semitism commissioned by the British government in 2006 and conducted by fourteen members of Parliament (all non-Jews) concluded that: "[Anti-Semitic discourse] has contributed to an atmosphere where Jews have become more anxious and more vulnerable to abuse and attack than at any other time for a generation or longer."[2] The chairman of the parliamentary inquiry, former member of Parliament Denis MacShane, added the following comment:

> **Anti-Semitism is back. . . The conclusion is inescapable. Too many British citizens who happened to be born Jewish now face harassment, intimidation, and assault that is unacceptable in democratic Britain. . . In the 1930s, the language was of the Jewish "cabal." Today, it is the Jewish "lobby" that is all-powerful. The demonization of Jews was meant to have died in 1945. Alas it did not.[3]**

Robert Wistrich, a British-Israeli historian who in 2010 wrote a book titled *A Lethal Obsession: Anti-Semitism—From Antiquity to the Global Jihad,* stated that "in Britain, all the taboos that exist in polite society are long gone when it comes to Israel and the Jews. . . .When I look at anti-Semitism in Britain, I feel it's always been underestimated by people outside the country. Having lived with it, I would say it is structurally almost built in to British life and culture." The author added that currently, "Britain is going through one of the most anti-Jewishly tinged periods of its history."[4] Member of Parliament and Shadow Home Secretary Chris Huhne agreed with this view, noting, in July 2009, that "Britain is setting a shameful new record of anti-Semitic incidents this year."[5]

This unfortunate assessment stems from a long history of anti-Semitism in Great Britain, with some of its key "innovations" originating in this country. The blood libel was born in Great Britain in 1144 when the Jews of Norwich were accused of the ritual murder of a boy. Great Britain was the first nation to enact a widespread expulsion of its Jews, doing so in 1290, a culmination of severe persecution against Jews throughout that century. An estimated 16,000 Jews migrated primarily to mainland Europe as a result, and Great Britain was free of Jews for the next 350 years. Only in 1656, for a variety of reasons outside the scope of this book, Jews were allowed to return to England. Anti-Semitism also had a strong presence in some of the great literature produced in England, most notably by William Shakespeare. *The Merchant of Venice,* written by the playwright in the late sixteenth century, reinforced many of the negative stereotypes of Jews, regardless of Shakespeare's own intentions or feelings about Jews or his intended message in the play, all of which are still debated by scholars. Noted author and critic Harold Bloom stated: "I am hurt when I contemplate the real harm Shakespeare has done to the Jews for some four centuries now. No representation of a Jew in literature ever will surpass Shylock in power, negative eloquence, and persuasiveness." Shylock's legacy continued with Charles Dickens's portrayal of the wicked Jew Fagin in *Oliver Twist,* published in 1838, which Bloom calls "an anti-Semitic masterpiece."[6]

FIGURE 5-1. An unusual leather postcard from 1907 depicting the Jewish character Shylock from William Shakespeare's *The Merchant of Venice*. Leather postcards were novelty items popular in the United States from around 1900 to 1909, when they were banned by the post office due to the difficulty of processing the leather in the sorting machines. Leather postcards were produced both by commercial publishers and by individuals who purchased the raw leather and used burning kits to create the image. The artist in this example spared no effort in exaggerating the Jew's nose. The Shylock character reinforced many of the negative stereotypes attributed to Jews. Shakespeare's Shylock, intentionally or unintentionally, did more to perpetuate these stereotypes than the playwright could have imagined. Georg Christoph Lichtenberg (1742–1799), the famous German scientist and writer, noted in a letter after seeing a performance of the play: "When [Shylock] came out, he was greeted with three rounds of applause, with each lasting fifteen seconds. One cannot deny that to see this Jew is more than enough for all childhood prejudices to be awakened suddenly again in the most law abiding man."[7] If such sentiments of prejudice could be stirred in the soul of a leading scholar of the German Enlightenment, what could one expect from the uneducated masses? [Publisher: Not provided; mailed within the United States in 1907.]

FIGURE 5-2. The enduring influence of the Shylock character is reflected in this German postcard depicting a stereotypically ugly Jewish street vendor who is called "The Merchant of Venice." The publisher of this postcard was apparently unaware that the merchant referred to in the title of the play is actually non-Jewish. [Publisher: C.P.F., Germany; circa 1900.]

Oliver Twist & Fagin.

"The Jew stepped gently to the door, which he fastened. He then drew forth, as it seemed to Oliver, from some trap in the floor a small box."

Oliver Twist, Chap. IX

FIGURE 5-3. Fagin, the fictional Jewish character in the Charles Dickens novel *Oliver Twist,* is shown greedily admiring his treasure hidden in the floor, while Oliver, who Fagin thought was asleep, looks on in shock. Along with Shylock, Fagin ranks as one of the most infamous characters in English literature. Fagin is depicted throughout the story with all of the traditional negative traits attributed to Jews. He is greedy, dishonest, villainous, thieving, devilish, and cowardly. Perhaps worse, he exploits children and arranges for the capture and execution of unneeded members of his juvenile criminal gang. Dickens noticeably referred to Fagin throughout his novel simply as "the Jew," emphasizing the villain's religion. When Dickens replied to a letter in 1863 condemning his story for prejudice against Jews, he wrote: "Fagin, in *Oliver Twist,* is a Jew, because it unfortunately was true of the time to which that story refers, that that class of criminal was almost invariably a Jew." Thus Dickens merely confirmed his own deep prejudices. Later in his life, Dickens did not want to be seen as anti-Jewish, and in one of his acts, the author revised *Oliver Twist* by replacing many instances of the words "the Jew" with the name "Fagin." His 1864 novel *Our Mutual Friend* portrays the Jewish character Riah in a positive manner and is considered by many as Dickens's attempt to "balance out" the evil image of Fagin.[8] [Publisher: C.W. Faulkner & Co., Ltd., London; circa 1913.]

FIGURE 5-4. This scene shows a fire carriage racing to put out a blaze, and, in its haste, causing a Jewish person to fall down. The Jew angrily calls the firemen ungrateful and adds that their jobs are dependent on the Jewish people. This image contains typical anti-Semitic elements: the lazy and selfish Jew (who presumably should have moved out of the way) contrasted with the firemen risking their lives and an allusion to Jewish power and economic control. The message is from a mother writing to her daughter; there was no shame in promoting this hatred to her child. The message reads: "Dear Ethel, Thank you for the P.B. hope you are a good girl. The school board has been after you today. May Baycook has been to see me tonight. She does miss you so do I with love to all. From Mamma. Your garden is looking a.1." [Publisher: Not provided; mailed within Great Britain in July 1908.]

FIGURES 5-5 and 5-6. These two postcards are part of a set which relies on double meanings to insult Jews, clearly identified by their large noses. The first card calls the well-dressed Jew a liar. The second mocks the Jew as a "mug," which in British usage refers to a fool or a blockhead. [Publisher: Not provided; circa 1908.]

Even with widespread prejudice, Jewish life in Great Britain improved dramatically in the nineteenth century with the first Jewish member of Parliament elected in 1847, the opening of doors to Jewish immigrants fleeing Russian persecution in the late nineteenth century, and the 1868 election of Benjamin Disraeli as prime minister, the first and only Jewish prime minister in British history. The Jewish population of 300,000 in Great Britain today thrives in all aspects of society, and the government has come out forcefully against all forms of anti-Semitism. However, negative attitudes toward Jews are expressed openly by a wide cross section of the population, as highlighted in a documentary film called *The War on Britain's Jews* that was broadcast on national television in July 2007.[9]

Given the long history of British anti-Semitism, it is no surprise that the nation's prejudices would be reflected on picture postcards. Anti-Semitic postcards from Great Britain focused on the typical attributes that Jews were assumed to possess—they were greedy, conniving, deceitful, and large-nosed. Most of these postcards relied on "humor" to deliver their messages but noticeably avoided the serious depictions of Jews as animals or evil abominations that were common in German anti-Semitic postcards; nor did they depict Jews as an enemy deserving of expulsion as seen in French and other European postcards. On the scale of vileness, British anti-Semitic postcards were relatively mild, only slightly more virulent than American types.

BAMFORTH POSTCARDS

Many British anti-Semitic postcards were published by Bamforth & Co. Ltd., a Holmfirth-based postcard publisher active beginning around 1909. The company was best known for its comic postcards, most notably its "Saucy Seaside" series of off-color humor. The company was founded in the 1870s by James Bamforth, who started out by making magic lantern slides (the magic lantern was an early version of a modern slide projector) and later progressed into silent films. Producing postcards was a natural expansion of the business, and in later years, Bamforth & Co. became known exclusively for its postcards. The company continued to produce postcards into the 1980s until Bamforth's grandson died and the company was sold. The rights to its vintage postcards were sold in 2001 to a British businessman. Anti-Semitic humor was just one category of comic postcards published by Bamforth, and it did not raise any eyebrows in British society at the time. A few examples are shown below.

CHRISTIANS AWAKE.

BAMFORTH COPYRIGHT

"PLEASE MUVVER WANTS SIXPENCE ON THIS 'ERE FRYING PAN!" "HALLO! IT'S HOT!"

"YES, MUVVER'S JUST COOKED THE SOSSIDGES AN' WANTS THE MONEY FOR THE BEER!"

COPYRIGHT 1909
BAMFORTH & CO.

FIGURE 5-7 *(left).* This postcard shows a Jewish woman (note the large nose and expressive hands) looking out of the top window of her pawn shop, identified by the three globes above the doorway and the sign "W. Cohen." A group of street performers are singing a tune with the message: "Christians Awake," a warning regarding the intrusion of Jews in commerce and society. The call for Christians to act against a threatening Jewish presence is an anti-Semitic theme commonly reflected in other postcards, such as in figures 3-23 and 6-1. [Publisher: Bamforth & Co. Ltd., Holmfirth, England; Series No. 35; circa 1909.]

FIGURE 5-8 *(right).* This scene depicts a little girl standing before a Jewish pawnbroker (note the sign above the door and the three golden globes) to sell her still-hot frying pan that had just been used to cook sausages. Her family's extreme poverty is contrasted against the rich Jew with a store full of goods. The subtext is that the Jewish shopkeeper callously takes advantage of the poor to enhance his own wealth. The short note (with 114 characters, like a Twitter message) on the back reads: "Dear B. I am longing to know how hus b. is. I am writing to Lucy, this afternoon if I get time. Love to all. Ethel." [Publisher: Bamforth & Co. Ltd., Holmfirth, England; Series No. 1558; mailed within Great Britain in May 1914.]

FIGURE 5-9. The dialogue between the Jewish shopkeeper (who is mocked for speaking in a Yiddish accent, substituting "v" for "w") and the man returning silverware shows that the Jew will say anything to swindle a customer. The child seen in the doorway at the far left enhances the impact of the "money above all else" attitude attributed to Jews, for even children are acceptable victims. At the bottom of the postcard, it is revealed that the artwork was drawn by Bert Thomas for the *London Opinion*. The *London Opinion* was one of the leading weekly magazines in England from 1903 until 1954 when it merged with another periodical. The magazine was well known for its cartoons and illustrations, such as the famous 1914 drawing of Lord Kitchener that was used to boost support for the war along with the words "your country needs you." Bert Thomas was one of the *London Opinion's* leading cartoonists who began his association with the publication in 1909. Thomas rose to prominence for his 1914 cartoon titled "Arf a mo' Kaiser," showing a British private lighting his pipe. The drawing was used to raise funds to supply tobacco and cigarettes to troops. Thomas continued as a prominent wartime artist, and in 1918 he drew Britain's largest poster, an appeal to invest in war bonds, which covered the face of the National Gallery. To reward his efforts during the war, Thomas was named a Member of the Order of the British Empire (MBE), an honor indicative of outstanding service to the community. Thomas remained active for decades, drawing cartoons for various newspapers and magazines into the 1950s (he died in 1966). It is probably less well known that one of Thomas's earliest drawings for the *London Opinion,* which was then adapted for postcards, was an anti-Semitic image. The fact that one of the leading periodicals and cartoonists comfortably disseminated anti-Semitic messages, and that the government awarded this cartoonist for community service, shows that these attitudes were quite normal at the time.[10] [Publisher: Bamforth & Co. Ltd., Holmfirth, England; Series No. 50; mailed within the U.S. in September 1910.]

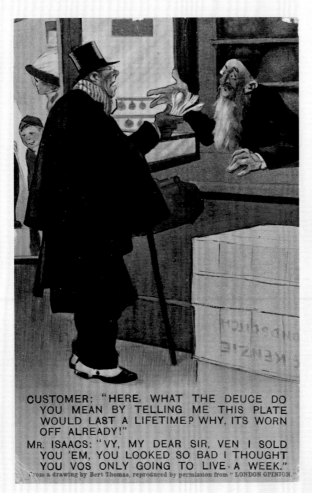

CUSTOMER: "HERE, WHAT THE DEUCE DO YOU MEAN BY TELLING ME THIS PLATE WOULD LAST A LIFETIME? WHY, ITS WORN OFF ALREADY!"
MR. ISAACS: "VY, MY DEAR SIR, VEN I SOLD YOU 'EM, YOU LOOKED SO BAD I THOUGHT YOU VOS ONLY GOING TO LIVE A WEEK."
From a drawing by Bert Thomas, reproduced by permission from " LONDON OPINION."

A BASE, VILE DECEPTION

BAMFORTH (Copyright)

FIGURE 5-10. Bamforth postcard portraying what the publisher thought of Jews: base, vile, and deceptive. The woman in this scene is horrified to encounter a Jew wearing the Scottish kilt and playing the bagpipe. The deception is that a Jew is dressed and acting like a Scotsman, an intrusion into a society in which the Jews were not welcome. The same theme is portrayed in figure 2-5. The postcard was mailed with a mostly illegible six-word message—like a text message but with a "humorous" attachment to entertain the recipient. [Publisher: Bamforth & Co. Ltd., Holmfirth, England; Series No. 2112; mailed within Great Britain in August 1913.]

FIGURE 5-11. Image of a Jewish man with a thick Yiddish accent ("ve" instead of "we" and "zee" instead of "the") proposing a fiscal policy to tax foreigners. The message is that Jews are overly concerned about money and will seek any opportunity to burden others with fees. [Publisher: The "Premier" Series, England; Series No. 2085; circa 1906.]

IKEYSTEIN: "I vant 'arf a pound of Cocoa, please, young man."

GROCER: "Vi-Cocoa, Sir?"

IKEYSTEIN: "VY NOT?"

FIGURE 5-12. The artist who drew this image, Donald McGill (1875-1962), was one of the most prolific and famous postcard illustrators in Great Britain. McGill sketched comic postcards for more than fifty years, beginning in 1904 and continuing until his death in 1962. He was most famous for Bamforth's "Saucy Seaside" postcard series, which depicted risqué comic themes. It is estimated that McGill created more than 10,000 postcard images. Less familiar to fans of McGill are his postcards mocking Jews. McGill's postcards were so widespread in England that George Orwell wrote a short essay in September 1941 titled "The Art of Donald McGill" where he analyzed the various themes depicted by the artist. Orwell's wartime essay revealed an interesting change in McGill's drawings: "A feature of the last few years is the complete absence of anti-Jew postcards. The 'Jew joke,' always somewhat more ill-natured than the 'Scotch joke,' disappeared abruptly soon after the rise of Hitler."[11] It seems that the persecution and murder of European Jewry at the time deflated the popularity of anti-Jewish jokes in Great Britain. The prominence of McGill and his postcards demonstrates that negative attitudes toward Jews were pervasive in British society at the time. This cartoon shows a large Jew, with a shining jewel on his belly, asking for cocoa. The grocer asks if he means "Vi-Cocoa," referring to "Dr. Tibbles' Vi-Cocoa," sold at the time as a medicinal drink with restorative attributes. The product was popular in Great Britain from the late 1890s through World War I, and it was even supplied to troops during the war. McGill makes fun of Ikeystein and his Yiddish accent, which mistakes a "w" for a "v"; the customer believes that he is being asked "Why cocoa?" and responds "Why not?" [Publisher: Not provided; mailed within Great Britain in September 1913.]

THIS IS THE TICKET
I CAME DOWN WITH :-

N.S.E & W. R Y COY

K12762

SUMWARE

TO

FIRST CLASS   SEE BACK

BUT THIS IS THE ONE I SHALL
HAVE TO GO BACK WITH

Pawned with
SAMUEL ISAACS
110 HIGH STREET
30 August 191_
Silver Watch
FOR THE
SUM OF £ :10:
John Smith
Marine Parade
325
HOURS 8 to 7 SATURDAY 8 to 10
CLOSE AT 1 ON WEDNESDAYS.

BUT, OH! WHAT A TIME I'VE HAD !

FIGURE 5-13. This postcard tells the story of a person who purchased a train ticket to London, but returned only with a receipt for a silver watch that they pawned with "Samuel Isaacs" for ten pounds. The customer sarcastically exclaims, "What a Time I've Had!" suggesting that he was actually taken advantage of by the Jew. [Publisher: Not provided; England; mailed within Great Britain in August 1919.]

FROM AN OLD PAL.

WHEN ALL YOUR CASH IS SPENT
AND YOU'RE ANXIOUS TO GET HOME,
JUST CALL AND SEE YOUR GOOD OLD PAL
AND RAISE A LITTLE LOAN.

FIGURE 5-14. Typical image of an ugly Jew with oversized hands and lips offering loans to the poor and desperate. This postcard features gold-colored pieces of metal affixed to the postcard to make the eyes and nose, alluding to Jewish wealth. [Publisher: The Regent Publishing Co., Ltd., London; circa 1905.]

"I'VE been poisoned, Ikey—so before I die I vant to confess that t'vas me vot s'vindled you of all that money !"
"Don't vorry, Abie !—t'vas me vot poisoned you !"

FIGURE 5-15. The publisher of this postcard, Entire British Production, was known for a wide range of comic postcards. Showing Jewish friends stealing from each other and resorting to murder was simply viewed as humor. The point of this scene is that Jews will do anything for money. Like in figures 6-14 and 6-15, these Jews speak with a foreign accent substituting a "v" for various consonants. [Publisher: Entire British Production; Series No. 6491; circa 1920s.]

"AN' WHAUR'S TH' FREE WHEEL?"

FIGURE 5-16. This postcard was published and mailed in the late 1930s, indicating that negative stereotypes of Jews persisted in Great Britain into the pre–World War II period. This cartoon is very similar to those depicted earlier in this chapter: a Jewish shopkeeper deceives a Gentile customer. In this case, the "I. Isaacs" cycle shop advertises a "free wheel" with each bicycle purchased. When the customer purchases the bicycle, he reasonably expects and asks for the free wheel; however, the shopkeeper's expression implies that he only meant the wheel that already comes with any bicycle purchase. The contrast between the properly dressed customer in the popular knickers of the day and the portly Jewish shopkeeper is clear. The note on the back does not refer to this vignette: "Dear George, Just a few lines to let you know I'll be home next Thursday. . . . Give my regards to all at home. Cheerio for now, Bill." [Publisher: Valentine & Sons. Ltd., Dundee and London; mailed within Great Britain in March 1938.]

DRIVING A HARD BARGAIN!

FIGURE 5-17. The same Jewish character as in figure 5-16 is shown here selling a "lemon" to the unsuspecting and trusting elderly Gentile. Only seconds after "Issy" sells the car, the customer is surprised by the rising smoke and loose tires. It is unclear why the shop uses the name "McPherson"; perhaps by using a name that is clearly not Jewish, customers will think that the shop is not owned by a Jew and, therefore, is trustworthy. [Publisher: Valentine & Sons. Ltd., Dundee and London; mailed within Great Britain in July 1939.]

CHAPTER 6

POSTCARDS FROM THE UNITED STATES

Anti-Semitism was brought to the New World in the sixteenth and seventeenth centuries, first by Christian European settlers, and then by successive groups of colonists. Anti-Semitism in the United States evolved in a weakened and less vitriolic form primarily because the newly formed United States did not have an official church, nor did its central government endorse anti-Semitic policies, sponsor pogroms, or unofficially sanction violence against Jews. Its elected officials, rather than speaking out openly against Jews, often came out against criticism of Jews. The overall attitude toward Jews in the United States was also much less negative compared to European attitudes. Reasons include the fact that the Pilgrims arrived in the New World to escape religious persecution from the English Church, the insights of the framers of the Constitution who envisioned a more democratic society, and a self-image of the United States as a tolerant nation versus the tyrannical rule of the former British rulers. Even so, anti-Semitism is a real part of the country's cultural heritage that negatively affected the experiences and opportunities for Jews in this country until well into the twentieth century.[1]

The first Jews recorded in America arrived in New Amsterdam (later renamed New York by the British) in 1654 under Governor Peter Stuyvesant. Stuyvesant's prejudice against Jews was quickly revealed when he tried to expel the twenty-three Jewish refugees who arrived in New Amsterdam from the Dutch colony in Brazil. The Jews were ultimately allowed to stay under orders from the Dutch West India Company that financed the settlement. When the British captured New Amsterdam in 1664, the main concern was economic growth and, therefore, there was greater tolerance for Jews and non-Protestants. By the end of the seventeenth century, Jews in New York were allowed to worship in public, purchase land, and engage in all areas of trade. Beginning in the 1720s, new Jewish communities arose in several other cities, such as Philadelphia, Pennsylvania; Newport, Rhode Island; and Charleston, South Carolina. Charleston was a leading economic center at the time, and Jews were treated almost as equals. After the American Revolution, South Carolina was one of the first states where Jews could vote and hold elected office.

Conditions for Jews in colonial America (of which there were approximately 1,000) were highly favorable, especially compared to Europe where old Christian attitudes toward Jews were still widely prevalent. But they did not lead to the much worse persecutions that Jews were subject to in Europe. For example, John Quincy Adams, the sixth president of the United States, remarked in his diary after visiting a synagogue that its Jews were "all

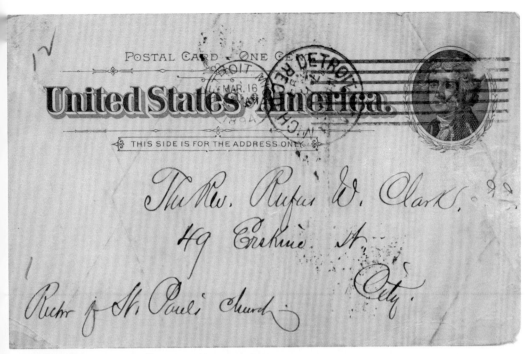

FIGURE 6-1. Postal card from 1894 mailed by the "Church Society for Promoting Christianity amongst the Jews" to a reverend as a fundraiser. The society was not simply a missionary organization promoting a message of belief. It viewed Jews as a malignant group whose rapid spread posed a threat to Christianity. The tone of the text reflected the sentiment of the populace that Jews were "taking over," as highlighted in the 1907 article in *McClure's Magazine* titled "The Great Jewish Invasion." The printed message used hatred and fear as a way to raise funds. [Official Unites States Postal Card; mailed from Detroit, Michigan, in March 1894.]

ND DEAR BROTHER :

ne Jews are among us in constantly increasing numbers, finding homes in every department of our country, and employment in every vocation. They are their families. Their children are fast coming forward to fill positions in various ranks of citizenship. They will bear an important part in moulding the destiny of our country. Shall they be Christian or anti-Christian? That is the question which God in His Providence is bringing before the Church to-day.

Leave them alone ; do nothing in their behalf, and they are sure to swell the ranks of the enemies of the Cross. But on the other hand let us come forward and meet the occasion presented to us, doing our part conscientiously, in the fear God, and we may be sure that our prayers and offerings will not be in vain.

The Church Society for Promoting Christianity amongst the Jews is in essing need of funds to meet the increasing demands for laborers to plant ions in every part of our country.

Will you not endeavor to increase your offering from Church and Sunday-School? If you have not contributed before, will you not do so this year on Palm Sunday, Good Friday, or Easter?

Please send all offerings *directly to the Treasurer,* Mr. WILLIAM G. DAVIES, 68 East Seventh Street, New York.

Yours, very truly,

Paul Ziegler

Local Secretary.

wretched creatures for I think I never saw in my life such a set of miserable looking people, and they would steal your eyes out of your head if they possibly could."[2] Adams's views reflected an acceptance of the common stereotypes of Jews as money-hungry cheats.

This mix of high levels of tolerance combined with generally negative attitudes and ambivalence toward Jews would characterize the Jewish experience in America for the eighteenth and much of the nineteenth centuries. The example of Mordecai Manuel Noah (1785–1851) was typical. Noah was one of the leading American Jews of the first half of the nineteenth century, rising to prominence as U.S. consul to Tunis and later in several prominent positions in New York City government. Throughout his career, he was taunted as "the Jew" and as "Shylock" and was never fully accepted into society. When acting as the sheriff in New York City, an outcry was raised against a Jew's hanging of a Christian. Uriah P. Levy (1792–1862), the first Jewish commodore of the U.S. Navy, was known as "the damned Jew" and wrote about his isolation due to his religion.[3]

Anti-Semitism in America witnessed an emergence in the late nineteenth century during and after the Civil War as the Jewish presence grew in the United States, primarily through immigration from Europe. Growing numbers of Jews began to fuel feelings that Jews were becoming a "menace" and were not in the nation's best interests (between 1897 and 1917, the Jewish population in the United States rose from under 1 million to over 3 million). The continued influx in the early twentieth century of lower-class Eastern European Jews, who by this time vastly outnumbered the descendants of the older Jewish population in America, transformed the negative view of Jews from simply non-believers who were crafty and greedy to unwanted aliens from inferior racial stock (hostility was also directed at Italian and other ethnic immigrants, but not to the same extent as European Jews). An article from 1907 in the popular *McClure's Magazine* titled "The Great Jewish Invasion" expressed the feelings that Jews were insidiously taking over many areas of commerce, replacing existing workers and owners. For example, while discussing sales of real estate in Manhattan, the author stated: "In real estate transfers now made, at least 75 percent of the buyers belong to this race . . . in the great Jewish quarter . . . [the Jews] now hold 70 percent of all the land. Up to 1880, when they first began to come, this was largely held by the great estates—the Astors', Stuyvesants', Rutgers', and Whitneys."[4] The 1913–1915 Leo Frank incident, in which Frank, a Jew, was wrongly accused, tried, and convicted with no evidence for murdering a thirteen-year-old girl, and then later taken from prison by a mob and lynched, stands as one of the most shocking anti-Semitic incidents in American history. The Anti-Defamation League (ADL) was formed in 1913 in response to the increasingly negative attitude held by American society toward Jews.

The World War I and postwar eras witnessed a continued rise in antagonism toward Jews. The Bolshevik Revolution in Russia led to a "Red Scare" in which Jews were considered a leading player. Rising nationalist feelings led to accusations that Jews did not consider "America first." In May 1920, an article titled "The International Jew: The World's Problem" appeared in Henry Ford's newspaper the *Dearborn Independent*. This piece was the first in a series of attacks against Jews that ran throughout the decade. The newspaper was not a fringe publication; its circulation matched the leading U.S. newspapers with 700,000 readers at its peak. It should be noted that, at the same time, articles appearing in various magazines denounced Ford and his anti-Semitic views. The growing distaste for Jews led to a rise in restrictions placed on Jews by schools, clubs, hotels, and other organizations. In 1922, Harvard University president A. Lawrence Lowell believed that the school had a "Jewish problem" due to the rise in Jewish undergraduates, and he proposed quotas limiting Jewish admissions. The school did not directly restrict Jews, but it created a system of geographical diversity that had the same effect. Harvard's actions inspired dozens of other schools such, as Princeton, Penn State, and John Hopkins as well as many medical schools, to implement their own allotments for Jews (some had already quietly implemented these restrictions before 1922). The schools also limited Jewish faculty. Restrictions against Jews could be found in the workplace as well, from advertising agencies to banks and insurance companies, with newspaper advertisements openly indicating a preference for Christian applicants. The cumulative effect of these restrictions was that a nationwide culture of discrimination against Jews was established. Even those Jews who were admitted to elite colleges were prohibited from joining most fraternities. The Gentile students in these fraternities carried this practice into the workplace and other areas of society whereby Jews were considered second-class citizens, even though legally they were considered equal. The controversial 1947 film *Gentleman's Agreement* highlighted the widespread discrimination against Jews by portraying a journalist (played by Gregory Peck) who goes undercover as a Jew to research anti-Semitism. The film won the Best Picture Oscar.

The bigotry against Jews in the 1920s set the stage for more virulent attacks in the 1930s, fueled by the stock market crash in 1929 and the Great Depression. American anti-Semitism now envisioned a Jewish conspiracy seeking to control the U.S. government. The 1930s saw the development of dozens of anti-Semitic organizations, including one spearheaded by Father Charles Coughlin, who railed against Jewish conspiracies in a highly popular weekly radio program that drew an estimated 3.5 million listeners. By 1940, anti-Semitic sentiment in the United States reached its peak and many Jews feared that European-style anti-Semitism and its devastating effects would reach the shores

FIGURE 6-2. This detailed image sums up the overall feeling that many Americans held for Jews in the early twentieth century. The flag of the Jews is a bill filled with negative motifs: gold and silver; the three ball symbol (on the corners) that represents pawnbrokers; devil imagery (at the center); unusually large hands; a love for old clothes, representing both a need to hoard and a lack of hygiene; and, finally, an image of a building on fire captioned "Our Friend" in contrast to the unharmed building captioned "Our Enemy." The suggestion is that Jews seek to undermine the economy and society in their quest for money and represent a "fifth column," a traitorous element living within the United States. [Publisher: F. W. Dunbar; mailed from New York City in December 1906.]

of America. A poll at the time showed that 60 percent of Americans had negative impressions of Jews, finding them to be greedy and dishonest. This sentiment continued with full strength into World War II. A 1943 Office of War Information report described widespread, and sometimes intense, anti-Semitism in half of the forty-two states that it surveyed. Jews in the military were also subject to both official and non-official animosity. Although President Roosevelt's ban on allowing Jewish refugees into the United States during the war has been much debated, what is not disputed is that the anti-refugee policy reflected the wishes of most of the U.S. population.

Anti-Semitism in America, from its beginnings, was always strengthened by Christian teachings that continually emphasized the deficiencies of Jews and their refusal to accept Jesus as their savior. Schoolchildren were taught Protestant views of Jews as wicked, disobedient, crafty, and greedy. One of the later verses of the original Mother Goose rhyme taught to children read: "Jack sold his egg / To a rogue of a Jew / Who cheated him out / Of half of his due."[5] This verse summed up the most basic view of Jews in America. Eventually the term "Jew" or to "Jew down" became a synonym for dishonest haggling and cheapness. These prejudices peaked at times of national stress. Even with the daily indignities, restrictions, and constant animosity directed at them, Jews were never subject to the legal segregations applied to Blacks or other official government restrictions that were common in Europe. Jews were also not subject to pogroms and other physical assaults that occurred in Europe. In fact, at about the same time that Germany destroyed thousands of Jewish homes and assaulted Jews in the great 1938 pogrom known as *Kristallnacht*, President Roosevelt nominated Felix Frankfurter as a Supreme Court justice (he was confirmed without dissent). Jews adjusted to discriminatory positions by establishing their own businesses and institutions (e.g., Jewish hospitals) and living and socializing with other Jews. In this way, Jews were able to continue to improve their standard of living. Many Jews changed their names to hide their heritage to avoid the indignities and exclusion that came with being Jewish (e.g., Tony Randall of *The Odd Couple* fame was born Arthur Leonard Rosenberg).

The postwar era saw a remarkable and sudden decline in anti-Semitism. Polls asking people if they heard talk against Jews in the last six months showed a sharp reduction in affirmative responses from the 50–60 percent range in the 1940s to 10–15 percent in the 1950s. The apprehensive wartime atmosphere was replaced with a strong feeling of optimism about the future, which lessened negative attitudes toward minorities (e.g., in 1947, Jackie

FIGURE 6-3. A cartoon drawing of a man's face that is identified as "Not a Jew," primarily due to his pug nose, colorful hat (as opposed to the black hat of the Eastern European Jews), and generally fine features. The postcard reflects the fact that Americans at the time were actively conscious of the presence of Jews and the stereotype of what they looked like (see the next figure). The written text on the back and front makes no reference to the content. The writer explains that she has been sick for three weeks and, therefore, could not write earlier. [Publisher: A.L. Jansson, 1904; mailed from Prairie Grove, Arkansas, to McAlester, Oklahoma, in September 1908.]

Robinson was the first African American allowed to play Major League Baseball). Peacetime growth and prosperity had less need for ethnic scapegoats. Many Americans, especially military veterans, also felt a need to combat intolerance and bigotry. The knowledge of the horrors of the Holocaust may have also curbed anti-Semitic attitudes. President Truman backed these changes, ending racial segregation in the military and proposing a civil rights bill. Fair employment legislation in the late 1940s and 1950s lessened exclusions for Jews in the workforce. Schools ended their quotas. Social anti-Semitism still existed in the workplace, exclusive clubs, and certain residential neighborhoods, but to a lesser extent. Catholic and Protestant organizations began to open dialogues with Jews that altered Christian perception of Judaism. Even attempts by certain groups to connect Jews with the communist scare failed to stir anti-Semitic sentiments. The national director of the ADL noted that the period between 1945 and 1965 was a "golden age" for the American Jewish community. It would be wrong to say that anti-Semitism disappeared; stereotypes persisted and prejudices remained, but they were considered less appropriate, and it was unfashionable to openly express these thoughts. (Anti-Semitic incidences also occurred in the South related to the civil rights movement, a topic beyond the scope of this book).

Today in America, Jews have never been more prosperous, secure, or accepted by society. Anti-Semitism has shrunk to the point of insignificance. In 2000, Senator Joe Lieberman, an Orthodox Jew, was the Democratic nominee for vice president running alongside Al Gore. Although the two ultimately lost the electoral vote, they won the popular election with approximately 500,000 more votes. The fact that the majority of U.S. voters chose a Jew as vice president is strong evidence that anti-Semitism has been virtually eliminated. The July 2010 marriage of President Bill Clinton's daughter, Chelsea Clinton, to Marc Mezvinsky, a Jew, was viewed by many observers as an event that marked another watershed in the acceptance of Jews in the United States.

It would still be wrong to say that anti-Semitism has been eradicated in the United States. There are scattered recent examples of prominent individuals revealing their hatred for Jews; actor Mel Gibson and White House reporter Helen Thomas are two examples. A 2009 ADL survey found that 12 percent of Americans (and 28 percent of African Americans) held anti-Semitic views, matching the lowest level ever recorded by the ADL (in 1998) and down from 29 percent in its 1964-benchmark survey. But 12 percent still means over thirty million Americans hold anti-Semitic views. The primary manifestation of anti-Semitic attitudes lies in the accusation of disproportionate Jewish power. The 2008 financial crisis and the Bernie Madoff incident brought to life negative stereotypes of the Jewish banker and his power over the economy. The influence of Jews in U.S. politics is another manifestation of current

FIGURE 6-4. This is how Jews were perceived in America—in contrast to the Gentile in the previous figure—the large nose, awkward features with bent legs and crossed arms, enlarged hands, and generally ugly appearance were all part of the stereotype. The phrase "Such a Business" was commonly used in anti-Semitic postcards, alluding to the Jew's obsession with money and commerce. [Publisher: E.B. & E.; mailed from Mansfield, Ohio to Catawba Island, Ohio, in August 1906.]

anti-Semitism, most prominently with accusations that an undefined, yet powerful "Israel Lobby" forces the United States to act in ways that are against its best interest. This conspiracy theory gained prominence in 2007 with the publication of a book called *The Israel Lobby and U.S. Foreign Policy* by Professors Stephen Walt and John Mearsheimer. As discussed in chapter 2, this book has been shown to be based on fraudulent scholarship, such as the usage of falsified quotes.[6]

Anti-Semitic postcards from the United States reflect the general feelings toward Jews from the late nineteenth century through World War II. The majority of American anti-Semitic postcards were cartoons and caricatures depicting Jews as money-hungry, greedy, cheap, and cunning businessmen who take advantage of Gentiles. Jews were shown wearing conspicuous jewelry,

lacking hygiene and table manners, and acting in either a vulgar or childish manner. The typical physical stereotypes are also prominent, including the large nose and awkward body. Other postcards emphasized the difference between the reviled Jew and the Gentile. The postcards stop short at dehumanizing Jews by portraying them as animals or by advocating physical violence or their expulsion. Relative to the vile imagery of German and other European postcards (excluding Great Britain), American anti-Semitic postcards can be considered mild. Most American postcards were intended to be humorous and lacked a certain aura of pure hatred and disgust that was palpable in German, Austrian, and some French postcards. American anti-Semitic postcards thus reflected precisely the strength of anti-Semitism in the country: ever present, but rarely leading to violence or calls for expulsion.

FIGURE 6-6. The vast majority of American anti-Semitic postcards offered a visual image, usually with the intention of being humorous. By simply printing a message, the publisher made clear that spreading hatred was the only purpose of this postcard. [Publisher: Not provided; circa 1907.]

FIGURE 6-5. "Israelite" was a common synonym for "Jew" in nineteenth and early twentieth-century America. The text is a play on words denigrating Jews. Christians in America were taught that Judaism was a failed religion since the Jews refused to accept Jesus as their savior. [Publisher: W.J. Dickson Co., Des Moines, Iowa; circa 1910.]

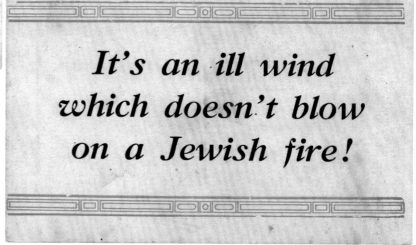

FIGURE 6-7. The greedy landlord is one of the many manifestations of the money-hungry Jew. The poem recommends that you greet this landlord with a sneer. The Jewish landlord (or, more specifically, slumlord) was a common Jewish stereotype, especially among black anti-Semites. Martin Luther King Jr. suggested that one of the causes of black anti-Semitism was the presence of Jewish landlords in black communities.[7] [Publisher: Toast Series; circa 1910.]

FIGURE 6-8. The Jewish banker charging usurious rates is a classic portrayal of the greedy Jew. The Finklestein Loan Company offers a $100 loan in return for $500 paid back. With these high rates, no questions need to be asked—the sign on the table says: "Just Sign Here." [Publisher: Southern Card Co., San Antonio; circa 1943.]

FIGURE 6-9. These three Jewish merchants are named "Cheates, Shab, and Bogus," a play on words that suggests that Jews cheat, act shabbily (also defined as playing mean tricks), and sell bogus or counterfeit merchandise. The trio exhibits the stereotypical physical features attributed to Jews. The handwritten message on the back acknowledges the image: "Dearest Jule, What do you think of my new firm? The new name of the partners is U. Ketchum and I. Kisum. Some class." [Publisher: Not provided; 1910.]

FIGURE 6-10. On this postcard, a Jewish man is being burned at the stake by an American Indian. The image of an Indian burning a Jew signifies that, according to this artist, the Jew was hated even more than the Indian. The caption is a play on the word "stake," implying that the burning of the Jew is of little consequence. [Publisher: Not provided; circa 1910.]

FIGURES 6-11 to 6-13. These three postcards (as well as figures 2-20 and 2-40) were part of a series that mocks the Yiddish language and depicts ugly images of Jews in awkward situations. The first card literally says: "You are a Matzah Face" and shows an ugly Jew with a pockmarked face like a Passover matzah. The written message notes: "This is the way I looked with the measles. Wasn't I a bird?" Robert, who clearly enjoyed this humor, ends his message by making fun of the Yiddish accent, adding, "Vell vot you dinks" for "What do you think?" The next example depicts two Jews foolishly fighting each other while the caption sarcastically says "Peace Be With You" in Yiddish. Ridiculing Jews by showing them quarreling was a common theme, as seen in figure 3-2. The third card shows a grotesque Jewish mother spanking her even uglier son. Children were not considered off-limits in anti-Semitic images. The sender comically writes at top: "Say I bet that hurts don't you? From Susie you [sic] friend" above a longer message about meeting her friend. [Publisher: J.A. & A.A.; figure 6-11, mailed from Rockville, Indiana, to Indianapolis, Indiana, in April 1907; figure 6-12, mailed within New York City in September 1905; figure 6-13, mailed within Ohio in November 1906.]

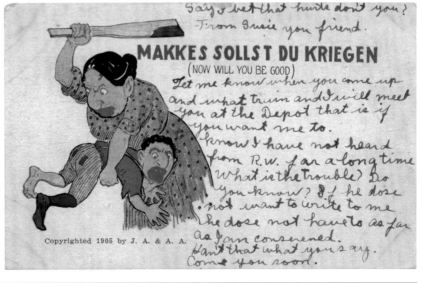

FIGURES 6-14 to 6-16. These three postcards were part of another series of cards showing ugly Jews, this time not speaking Yiddish, but Yiddish-accented English. The first card shows a horrid Jewish woman wearing an outfit with a money bag and showing off shiny jewelry. She cries: "Why not?" The sender, who clearly enjoyed the image, wrote: "Harry this is me in Trafford City." The second card shows a repulsive Jewish peddler greedily exclaiming: "What! Something for Nothing." This sender also commented on the image, writing, "I would like to see you do this for a living." On the back, the message continues: "You owe me a postal, but this was such a good one that I could not help sending it." Picking out and sending off-color ethnic humor postcards to friends was as acceptable in 1906 as mailing a funny birthday card from Hallmark is today. The last example depicts another awkward and ugly Jew, gesturing with enormous hands, intending to say "I almost smell the smoke." The alliteration provided by the "sch" sound added to the humor of this foreign-sounding Jew. [Publisher: A. Yerkes, 1905; figure 6-14, mailed from Stewart, Pennsylvania, to Brookville, Pennsylvania, in December 1905; figure 6-15, mailed within Boston, Massachusetts, in August 1906.]

 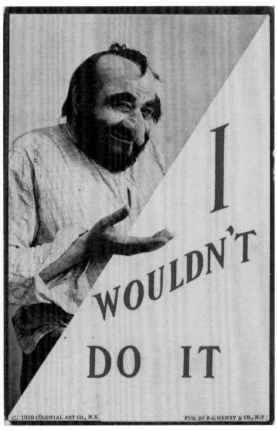 

FIGURES 6-17 to 6-19. This series of anti-Semitic postcards mocks and ridicules a man with an unusually ugly and exaggerated hooked nose. The cards have this Jew uttering foolish comments while gesticulating with his hands and smirking childishly. It is supposed to be understood from these comments that the Jew is untrustworthy. [Publisher: F.G. Henry & Co., New York; 1910; figure 6-19, mailed from Birmingham, Alabama, to Memphis, Tennessee, in November 1911.]

FIGURE 6-20. The creativity employed in mocking Jews on postcards was far-reaching. In this example, the publisher used the play on words between "cone" and the Jewish surname "Cohen" or "Cohn" to suggest that the shadow of the rare "Pine Cohen" looks like a Jewish face, distinguished by the hooked nose. [Publisher: The Mansell Art Co., Portland, Maine; 1909.]

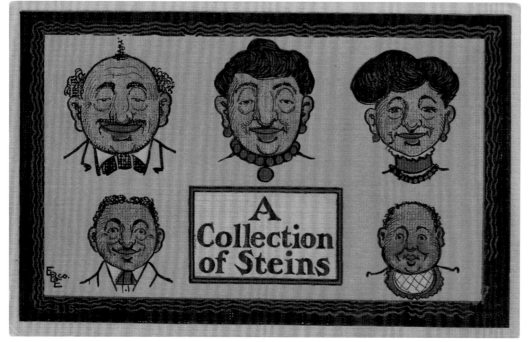

FIGURE 6-21. Making fun of Jewish names was common in anti-Semitic postcards, similar to the German postcards that played on the Jewish last names Hirsch and Löwe to depict Jews as deer and lions (see figures 3-26 to 3-28). "Stein" in English also refers to a large mug, used especially for beer; the word "mug" is also slang that refers to a face. The image does not show a collection of coffee mugs, but the faces of a family of Jews with typical features. Someone gave this postcard to a friend and wrote on the back: "These are for your new house"—again playing on the joke that, instead of new cups, he is giving this postcard. The publisher, EBE Co. of Detroit, Michigan, was known for their wide variety of comic postcards. [Publisher: EBE Co.; circa 1906.]

FIGURE 6-22. This postcard is another example of the expansive imagination postcard publishers used to mock Jews. The drawing is based on the story of Moses found in Exodus 2:5–6 when Pharaoh's daughter went down to the Nile River to bathe. She immediately spied a basket among the reeds. When she opened the basket, she saw a baby boy inside and suspected that he may be a Hebrew since the Pharaoh had decreed that all Hebrew male children be thrown into the river. According to the narrative, she had pity on the child and gave him up to a Hebrew nurse—who happened to be the child's actual mother. Pharaoh's daughter didn't reveal what she had found to anyone except her maidens. The author of this postcard jokes that perhaps Moses was not really found in the river; perhaps it was simply a story made up by Pharaoh's daughter. But then we see how "Jewish" baby Moses appears with stereotypical features, implying that, of course, he could not be a non-Jew. [Publisher: The Clever Post Card Co., Chicago; circa 1910.]

FIGURE 6-23. The myth of the Jew with horns, as explained in figure 2-29, is invoked in this postcard. The Gentile at the left mocks the Jew by holding his hands to his head and smirking. The Eastern European Jew awkwardly gestures and meekly responds that he is just a Jew—the question seems unremarkable to him. This postcard was published by Hubin's Big Post Card Store, a large retailer of postcards located on the main boardwalk in Atlantic City, New Jersey. Hubin's shop, like so many others in the Golden Era, was entirely devoted to creating and selling postcards. Open as early as 1907 and in business until the early 1920s, Hubin's shop sold its own postcards as well as those produced by other publishers; this anti-Semitic card is one of the store's own creations.[8] [Publisher: Hubin's Big Post Card Store, Atlantic City, New Jersey; circa 1910.]

THE JEWISH PAWNBROKER

A pawnbroker is an individual or business that offers loans in return for collateral that is handed over and pledged by the borrower. The borrower has the right to retrieve the pawned item if the loan is repaid within a certain contractual period of time. If the loan and all interest are not paid by the due date, the pawnbroker takes possession of the pawned item and will seek to recoup the loan by selling the item. A successful pawnbroker will earn profit either by earning interest on the loan, or if the loan is not repaid, from the excess value of the item sold versus the loan amount. Pawnbroking can be traced back to ancient China, Greece, and Rome. Pawnshops have always played an important role in providing consumer credit, especially for those who are denied traditional loans. There are still over 12,000 pawnshops in the United States today, serving an estimated 10 percent of the adult population.[9]

The Jewish connection to pawnbroking originates in eleventh and twelfth century Europe when restrictions on the ability of Jews to practice most trades, as well as Church prohibitions on the charging of interest, led many Jews to take up money lending and commerce. Pawnbroking was an extension of the money lending business. In some cases, Jews were even prohibited from money lending in order to exclude them from banking on a larger scale, and they could only offer loans as part of a pawnbroking transaction. Laws regarding pawnbroking appear as early as thirteenth-century Austria where Jews were expressly permitted to take an object as a pledge for a loan without inquiring into the right of possession of the owner. In the frequent anti-Jewish riots that occurred in medieval Europe, the mobs attacking Jewish homes and businesses often retrieved the items they had handed over as collateral for the loan—pogroms were not only ideological, but economical as well.[10]

Although it was Jews who were stereotypically associated with pawnbroking, their activity in the industry was actually overshadowed by non-Jews. The industry was dominated by the Northern Italian Lombards who spread their shops throughout Europe. Some countries even opened state-run pawnshops that offered lower interest rates to compete with the Lombards and the Jews. The universal symbol of the pawnbroker, which comprises three gold balls, is usually attributed to the coat of arms of the Medici family in Italy, who operated a banking and trading business in fifteenth-century Europe, although the three balls may have simply been a traditional symbol for money at the time.[11]

FIGURE 6-24. This typical image of a Jewish pawnbroker shows a non-Jewish customer dejectedly handing over his property in return for a loan. The insinuation is that the wealthy Jew, I. Cohen in this case, is taking advantage of the desperate Gentile in need of funds—this is how the Jew succeeds. The four-line text indicates that the customer is broke; the term "in soak" is slang for pawning an object and refers to overcharging. The sender wrote on the back: "Am feeling fine and dandy will write a letter later had some rain last night Norm." At eighty-two characters and no grammar, this note is like a typical Twitter message from 2011; Norm chose to deliver his 1911 version of a Tweet with an anti-Semitic emoticon. [Publisher: Not provided; mailed from La Junta, Colorado, to Grand Rapids, Michigan, in January 1911.]

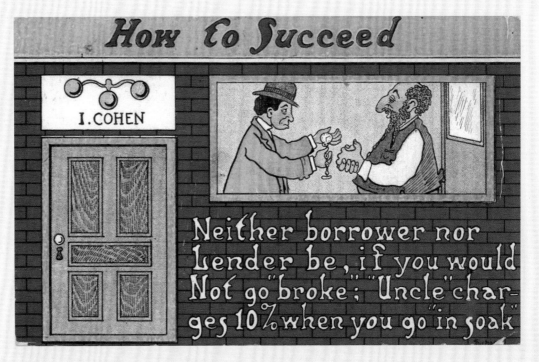

FIGURE 6-25. Another version of the ugly, hooked-nosed Jewish pawnbroker (with shiny jewel), standing under the three-ball symbol of the pawn shop. The disgust for this person is strong: a child is shown swinging a stick at the Jew. Note the text message-like note written on the front. [Publisher: Philadelphia Post Card Co.; mailed from Sauquoit, New York, to Hamilton, New York, in September 1906.]

Ironically, Nazi Germany relied on non-Jewish pawnbrokers to affect the confiscation of valuable assets held by German Jews following the November 1938 pogrom known as *Kristallnacht*. During *Kristallnacht,* German storm troopers and civilians destroyed thousands of Jewish establishments and homes, arrested tens of thousands of Jews, and imprisoned them in concentration camps. The pogrom marked the beginning of the end for Jews in Germany. In February 1939, Jews were ordered to hand in all their valuables, such as gold, silver, jewels, and artwork. Pawnbrokers were enlisted as agents for the state in this theft. For the one-week period when the confiscations occurred, it was noted that these pawnbrokers worked fifteen-hour days. Although the stereotypical Jewish pawnbroker supposedly takes unfair advantage of his non-Jewish customers, the only recorded widespread act of theft by pawnbrokers was perpetrated against Jews.[12]

The Jewish pawnbroker taking advantage of the poor Gentile was a common motif on anti-Semitic postcards from the United States. While this image can be found on postcards from other countries (e.g., figure 2-36), it is found almost exclusively on American postcards, with many dozens of cards showing the Gentile dejectedly exchanging his watch for a loan.

A QUESTION OF VALUE

POST CARD

A QUESTION OF VALUE
arises sometimes but never when Walk-Over shoes are concerned—they're worth every cent we ask for them.

WALK-OVER Boot Shop,

SMITH & CLAUSING,

Hotel Donavin Corner, Delaware, Ohio.

THIS SPACE FOR ADDRESS ONLY

FIGURE 6-26 (*above* and *below*). The Walk-Over Boot Shop in Delaware, Ohio, chose to use postcards with an anti-Semitic motif of a Jewish pawnbroker to advertise its store. A Jew with enormous hands, flat feet, hooked nose, and awkward posture gestures with his hands as a Gentile pawns his watch. The ad suggests that while the Jewish pawnbroker is unlikely to offer fair value for a pawned object, the boot shop provides full value for the price of its merchandise. [Publisher: Walk-Over Boot Shop, Delaware, Ohio; circa 1910.]

EXCLUSION FROM RESORTS AND HOTELS

In 1877, Joseph Seligman, a prominent Jewish banker and businessman, was denied entry into the Grand Union Hotel in Saratoga Springs, New York. The incident was widely reported, creating a national controversy. This event marked the first broadly publicized instance of a Jew denied entry into a hotel and highlighted that no matter how successful, refined, or assimilated a Jew became, they were socially undesirable.[13] It also brought into the open a trend that was already under way. Two years later, the president of the Manhattan Beach Corporation announced that he would not admit Jews to his exclusive hotel in Coney Island, Brooklyn, telling reporters that Jews were offensive and vulgar. Within the next decade, upper-class clubs, resorts, and private schools began to bar Jews. In the 1880s, resorts throughout New York (and about half of resorts in the Catskills, according to one report) and the New Jersey shore prohibited Jews. These exclusions from elite Gentile society were particularly hurtful to highly successful Jews. Perversely, at the same time that Jews were excluded, they were criticized for being insular and an alien part of society.[14]

Although Jews had been excluded entry into hotels for several decades, the practice accelerated in the years prior to World War I and in the 1920s. Restrictions also spread beyond the New York, New Jersey, Pennsylvania, and Florida resorts to areas in the Midwest and West, such as Arizona. The influx of lower-income Eastern European Jews, who were viewed as bizarre and unkempt, was one of the factors that strengthened the walls of discrimination. Advertisements specified "Gentiles Only," "No Hebrews Allowed," or, with more subtlety, simply the word "Restricted." Jews reacted by developing their own resorts. In the 1890s, the leading hotel in Lakewood, New Jersey, turned away Nathan Straus, a successful businessman, philanthropist, and public servant, whereupon he built a larger hotel next door. Jewish hotels became particularly well known in New York's Sullivan County (e.g., Grossingers) which became known as the "Borscht Belt" due to the large numbers of Jews who vacationed in the region. A 1956–1957 survey showed that about a quarter of resorts still restricted Jews, although the actual number was probably much higher because many hotels in the survey refused to answer. The number was particularly high in Arizona, with 45 percent barring Jews. The situation in Canada was similar, with 28 percent of resorts prohibiting Jews, although the postcard record for this practice in Canada is limited. By the early 1960s, these restrictions mostly came to an end. The need for Jewish resorts also ended, and, by the 1980s, most of the Borscht Belt establishments went out of business.[15]

THE MARINE TERRACE HOTEL   DIRECTLY ON THE OCEAN — PRIVATE BEACH   MIAMI BEACH, FLORIDA

FIGURE 6-27. Anti-Semitism in the 1930s and 1940s had a wide presence in Miami Beach. The majority of hotels forbade Jewish guests. Land covenants prohibited real estate sales to Jews to the point that Jews could only live in certain areas of the city. Nevertheless, Miami Beach became a popular winter destination for Jews from the north. Some owners who operated Jewish hotels in the New York Catskills also opened winter places in Florida (e.g., Grossinger's operated hotels of the same name in Florida and New York). In 1945, a group of Jews began a campaign to rid Miami Beach of signs restricting Jews. In large part due to this effort, the Miami Beach city council passed an ordinance in 1949 outlawing "Gentiles only" signs at hotels. A dramatic easing of prewar anti-Semitism in the United States also had a positive effect on Jewish life in Miami; at the start of World War II, only 8,000 Jews lived in the Miami area, increasing to about 140,000 by the end of the 1950s. Even so, as late as 1960, no beach or golf club in the city would accept Jewish members. The Marine Terrace Hotel was one of the restricted establishments of the 1940s. While most postcards and other advertisements were more subtle in promoting their exclusivity by using the word "restricted" or "select clientele," this hotel made it clear that they allowed only a "Strictly Gentile Clientele" (see the detail of the reverse, *left*). Like most of these types of postcards, the hotel often noted this feature first, and then the other amenities offered by the establishment.[16] [Publisher: Colourpicture Publication, Boston, Massachusetts; 1940s era.]

TROUVILLE — VILLAS APARTMENTS

ON BEAUTIFUL NORMANDY ISLE

TROUVILLE — VILLAS
1931-41 Everglades Concourse
Normandy Isle — Miami Beach, Fla.
Phone 6-3093   Eleanor T. Barnhart Mgr.
One and Two Bedroom Apartments. Hotel Rooms.
Private Porches . . . Beautiful Court . . . Near
the Ocean. Select Clientele . . . OPEN ALL
YEAR.

Surely wonderf...

FIGURE 6-28. The Trouville Villas was another one of many Miami Beach establishments that would only rent its apartments and hotel rooms to a "Select Clientele," as indicated in the back of the postcard (see scan which also shows the postmark). The sender notes in her message that it is "Surely wonderful here—weather hottest in 38 years." [Publisher: Colourpicture Publication, Cambridge, Massachusetts; mailed from Miami to Indianapolis, Indiana, in December 1948.]

Billy Boots Motel

Alt. Route 40, 2 Miles West,
FREDERICK, MD.

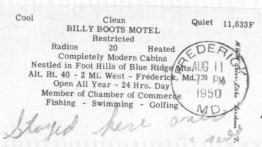

Cool   Clean   Quiet 11,633F
BILLY BOOTS MOTEL
Restricted
Radios   20   Heated
Completely Modern Cabins
Nestled in Foot Hills of Blue Ridge Mts.
Alt. Rt. 40 - 2 Mi. West - Frederick, Md.
Open All Year - 24 Hrs. Day
Member of Chamber of Commerce
Fishing - Swimming - Golfing

Stayed here one...

FIGURE 6-29. The Billy Boots Motel outside of Frederick, Maryland, was one of numerous roadside motels that sprang up around the country in the 1930s and 1940s to serve the growing number of drivers traveling the expanding highway system. This small motel was unremarkable, but still found it necessary to prohibit Jewish guests. The sender wrote: "Stayed here one nite otherwise we have been staying in a hotel. Starting on my way back, Mother, Grandma, Grandpa." The motel continued to offer postcards to its guest throughout the 1950s; a card it published later in the decade includes all of the descriptive text found in the version shown here, except it does not have the word "restricted." It seems that at some point in the 1950s, the Billy Boots Motel ended its racist policies, following a general waning of anti-Semitism in the United States in the two decades after World War II. The postcard record reflects this trend. [Publisher: MWM; mailed from Frederick, Maryland, to Mt. Clemens, Michigan, in August 1950.]

Showing part of Retlaw Concrete Dock and Steam Boat Landing.

FIGURE 6-30. W.J. Putnam was the proprietor of the Retlaw House resort with dock and boat landing on Oquaga Lake in New York near the Pennsylvania border (between Deposit, New York, and Lanesboro, Pennsylvania). Guests were offered a variety of activities from boating to tennis. This 1915-era postcard was adapted into a preprinted advertisement handed out to prospective customers. Ten lines down, the card notes: "No Hebrews need apply." Even minor establishments prohibited Jews. [Publisher: Not provided; circa 1915.]

15-Club House, Shops and Restaurants on Boardwalk, Lake Mohawk Reservation, Sparta, N.J.

LAKE MOHAWK SPARTA, N.J.
THE LARGEST RESTRICTED LAKE IN NEW JERSEY

15—The Reservation contains 2500 acres in the Sparta Mountains, 50 miles northwest of New York. Hundreds of artistic cottages surround the lake, considered the finest all year vacation playground in the East. Reached over N. J. Highway Routes 23, 31 or 6, 10 to Dover, Scenic Route 6A to Sparta.

THIS SI

FIGURE 6-31. Lake Mohawk is the largest artificial body of water in New Jersey. The lake was created with the completion of a dam on the Walkill River in August 1926. Soon after the lake was born, a private resort community was established on its shores. Houses and shops were built in a distinct style as can be seen in this postcard, which is captioned, "Club House, Shops and Restaurants on Boardwalk, Lake Mohawk Reservation, Sparta, NJ." Construction on the lake expanded in the 1930s and 1940s with the addition of many new summer homes. The vacation spot was idyllic—except that the resorts all prohibited Jewish guests. This postcard was mailed in 1954, when restrictions against Jews were on the decline, although still prevalent. Lake Mohawk today is a residential lakeside community with approximately 8,000 residents. Its racist history is likely long forgotten. [Publisher: Runca Import Company; mailed from Sparta, New Jersey, to New York City in June 1954.]

EXCLUSION FROM RESIDENTIAL NEIGHBORHOODS

Discrimination and restrictions against Jews were not only implemented at hotels and institutions, but also in apartment buildings and residential neighborhoods. While the local government did not prohibit Jews from living in certain areas, private communities restricted its residents to "select clientele," which meant white Gentiles only. Residents of exclusive neighborhoods privately agreed never to sell their properties to Jews, and some real estate deeds even had covenants that prohibited future sales to Jews and other minorities. Similarly, real estate developers who sold homes or plots of land would openly boast that their development catered to a restricted group of buyers.

These practices kept Jews out of many desirable neighborhoods in cities throughout the nation, such as Washington DC, Baltimore, Los Angeles, Denver, and Cleveland, as well as their suburbs. This type of bigotry was particularly prominent in the New York area as second-generation Jews began to move out of Manhattan tenements and into apartments in the Bronx and Brooklyn, as well as the growing suburbs in Queens and Long Island. Only in 1948 did the U.S. Supreme Court (*Shelley v. Kraemer*) hold that restrictive racial covenants on real estate could not be enforced. The postcards below document these practices.

HOLLIS TERRACE, HOLLIS, LONG ISLAND

2,400 restricted lots—On main line of Long Island R. R.—21 minutes from Broadway – Concrete sidewalks and macademized roads. For full particulars, maps and **free tickets**, apply to owner

NEW YORK & PITTSBURG REAL ESTATE CO., (Inc.)
356-358 FULTON ST., BROOKLYN, N. Y. Phone, 5330-5331 Main

CHICHESTER AVENUE, HOLLIS TERRACE

FIGURE 6-32. In the early 1900s, New York City's population was expanding into Queens, much of which was still rural. Numerous real estate developers and investors purchased land that was divided and resold for the construction of homes. The New York & Pittsburg Real Estate Company boasted of being the largest owner and operator of real estate on Long Island (which, at the time, included Queens), including a development at Hollis Terrace comprising 2,400 lots. The company heavily promoted these plots in advertisements that claimed that the land's value would triple in only two years. This postcard was another form of advertising. The first item noted by the card was that 2,400 "restricted" lots were available; proximity to the railroad and a ride twenty-one minutes to Broadway were the next features mentioned. A *New York Times* article from 1906 describing the extensive home construction in Queens noted that in only one week, 300 lots were sold in the Hollis Terrace development by the New York & Pittsburg Real Estate Company at an average price of $340. It is certain that none of these buyers were Jewish. Many Jews eventually moved into the Hollis area, and in 1948, the Jewish community founded the Hollis Hill Jewish Center synagogue.[17] [Publisher: Not provided; 1906.]

DOUGLAS MANOR, DOUGLASTON, LONG ISLAND   The Platinachrome Co N.Y. Ⓟ

2,500 restricted lots with over a mile of shore front   20 minutes from Herald Square, when Pennsylvania tunnels are completed

Send for full particulars and free tickets to see the property

RICKERT-FINLAY REALTY COMPANY, 1 WEST 34th ST., NEW YORK. TEL. 114—38 ST.

FIGURE 6-33. Similar to Hollis Terrace described in figure 6-32, Douglas Manor was a residential development project in Queens, New York, at the turn of the century; and like the developer of Hollis Terrace, the Rickert-Finlay Realty Company announced that its lots were available only to non-Jewish whites. Douglas Manor, part of the community of Douglaston, was named after George Douglas, whose son, William, sold this large family estate to the Rickert-Finlay Realty Company. The company planned to build homes for middle- and upper-middle class residents. The postcard noted that the area was "20 minutes from Herald Square, when Pennsylvania tunnels are completed." Today, Douglas Manor is an upscale neighborhood designated by the city's Landmark Preservation Commission as the Douglaston Historic District. Besides Douglas Manor, The Rickert-Finlay Realty Company developed neighborhoods in several locations in Queens, such as Westmoreland in Little Neck, Bellcourt in Bayside, Norwood in Long Island City, and parts of Flushing. By 1908, the company, headquartered at 1 West 34th Street in Manhattan, called itself the largest developer of real estate in Queens with over 10,000 lots. A large portion of Queens was thus off limits to Jews in the early years of its development. Interestingly, in researching multiple sources discussing the early development of Queens, the restrictions against Jews and blacks is not mentioned. The postcard record may be one of the few remaining documents where this fact is preserved.[18] [Publisher: The Platinachrome Co., New York; mailed within New York City in March 1906.]

THE MOORS, FALMOUTH, CAPE COD.

A Carefully Restricted
Community
With golf, tennis, boating and bathing.

Don't you love my postal?
They are free—that's why
I use them.

FALMOUTH ASSOCIATES
Falmouth, Mass.

FIGURE 6-34. A recent real estate listing in Cape Cod, Massachusetts, noted that The Moors was one of the Cape's most sought-after neighborhoods. In the 1930s the community was "carefully restricted" as the developers, Falmouth Associates, only sold to white non-Jews. The sender's written message on the back recounts how she spent a recent weekend. On the front, she writes, "Don't you love my postal? They are free—that's why I use them!" Falmouth Associates handed out these postcards free of charge as a form of advertising—and made sure to indicate the community's restricted status as its most important feature. A 1945 study titled *Falmouth, Massachusetts: Problems of a Resort Community* surveyed summer guests about their likes and dislikes of the resort; "Too many Jews" was listed among the top half of complaints.[19] [Publisher: Tichnor Quality Views; mailed from Falmouth to Brookline, Massachusetts, in August 1932.]

THE HUMOROUS ANTI-SEMITIC POSTCARDS OF TAYLOR, PLATT & CO.

Taylor, Platt & Co. was a prolific publisher of postcards during the Golden Era, active from 1906 through 1916. The company was based at 1161 Broadway in New York City. The company, commonly abbreviated as "T.P. & Co." in its logo, published cards in a wide variety of subjects, such as views of cities in America, greetings, artistic images, and novelty cards. Given its wide range of topics, it is not surprising that the company also published anti-Semitic postcards. Taylor, Platt & Co. commissioned an artist (uncredited) to draw a series of humorous postcards, each showing a scene of a Jew acting in negative stereotypical fashion, in most cases related to greed, cheapness, and love of money. The captions always have the Jewish characters speaking in broken, Yiddish-accented English. This anti-Semitic series probably comprised at least two dozen postcards. Presented below are six examples.

"SHOOT HIM IN DER PANDTS, OFFICER! DER COADT AND VEST VAS MINE!"

FIGURE 6-35. The hooked-nosed Jew at the right tells the officer to shoot the robber in the pants, so as not to harm the coat and vest which belong to the Jew. The Jew is so preoccupied with his possessions that he does not care about the policeman or his work. [Publisher: Taylor, Platt & Co., New York; mailed from Falmouth, Massachusetts, to Brookline, Massachusetts, in August 1932.]

FIGURE 6-36. The Jew in this vignette is told to leave the hotel because of a fire. Even as the smoke rolls into the room, his first concern is to be sure that he will not have to pay for a night's stay. The sender of this postcard enjoyed this image, writing: "Hello Dollie, Have a heart don't charge a guy for a room if the hotel is on fire. As ever, JMZ." It is likely that JMZ did not think about the anti-Semitic stereotype represented in this postcard; it merely provided a short moment of humor that was shared, like a Facebook posting with a friend who lives 150 miles to the east in Iowa. [Publisher: Taylor, Platt & Co., New York; mailed from Burlington, Iowa, to Humeston, Iowa, in April 1914.]

FIGURE 6-37. Isaac and his Jewish friend chuckle as to how the Gentiles, seen in automobiles in the background, have any money since the Jews take it away from them. The pair is wealthy, finely dressed, and wearing visible jewels. The message on the back is interesting: "Oct 14, 1913, Dear Father Statler, Mary & O were over at the auction sale of Campbell Hardware last night his stuff is selling awfully cheap. I bought some very pretty postcards and thought I'd send you one. Hope you will soon be able to get home. Yours lovingly Wilbur." Wilbur's belief that wealthy Jews steal from Gentiles was probably so ingrained in his mind that this postcard was unremarkable—simply "pretty." He then wanted to share this image with his priest, who no doubt subscribed to the same prejudiced thinking. [Publisher: Taylor, Platt & Co., New York; mailed from Wilmington, Ohio, to Chicago, Illinois, in October 1913.]

"HOW DO I KNOW HOW PAD I'M HURT PEFORE I SEE MEIN LAWYER?"

FIGURE 6-38. A Jew is knocked down by an automobile and the driver walks over to assist and ask if he is hurt. The Jew responds that he needs to see his lawyer first, of course implying that a lawsuit is coming—another way that the Jew is shown cheating for money. The sender appreciated this comic scene, writing, "Say Jack be careful they don't work this on you. Eddie." Eddie clearly believed that "they" were greedy and money-hungry. [Publisher: Taylor, Platt & Co., New York; mailed from Grand Rapids, Michigan, to Chicago, Illinois, in July 1914.]

"OH, VAT A PEAUTIFUL BRESENDT FOR UNCLE JACOB'S GOLDEN VEDDING!"

FIGURE 6-39. A Jew sees cheap goldfish in a store window and exclaims that the fish would make a good wedding present. The stereotype of the cheap Jew was a corollary to that of the greedy Jew. A similar postcard was published in Poland, as shown in figure 7-6. Also note the red umbrella, a theme discussed in chapter 2. The sender wrote a long message on the back about wanting to see her friend more often; but she also noted the image, writing on the front: "Some fine picture." [Publisher: Taylor, Platt & Co., New York; 1913.]

"DER NEXDT TIME DOT EMPIRE LOOKS AT ME LIKE DOT VEN HE SAYS 'THREE BALLS' I QVITS DER GAME!"

FIGURE 6-40. A Jewish baseball player is upset because the home-plate umpire keeps saying, "three balls," which is, of course, normal when calling balls and strikes. This is a play on words, as the symbol of the pawnbroker is three golden balls, as explained in an earlier sidebar. The Jew, who is portrayed idiotically since he does not understand that the umpire is merely calling balls and strikes, is annoyed that he is being mocked in this way. The sender explains this subtle joke, writing on the bottom: "Do you get on to this? 3 balls is Jew Pawnbroker sign." In fact, the symbol of the pawnbrokers is attributed to Italians from the Middle Ages who dominated the industry at the time. [Publisher: Taylor, Platt & Co., New York; 1913.]

CHAPTER 7

POSTCARDS FROM OTHER COUNTRIES

The previous four chapters highlighted the postcards from the leading publishers of anti-Semitic postcards, but many other countries participated in disseminating this unique and internationally widespread form of hatred. Some of these nations were not independent during the Golden Era, and their postcards can therefore be considered part of the controlling power at the time (e.g., Poland was controlled by Germany and Russia). However, there are examples unique to each country that allow us to gauge the virulence of anti-Semitism. Austrian and Polish cards were particularly hateful, with examples from each calling for the expulsion of Jews. This is not surprising since both countries had strong German influences and their own long legacies of anti-Semitism. Hungarian postcards were equally vile, which is not unexpected given the close alliance between the Hungarian government and the Nazis in World War II. Also surveyed in this chapter are postcards from the French-ruled countries in North Africa: Algeria, Morocco, and Tunisia. These interesting postcards reflect the different culture of Sephardic Jews compared to the Ashkenazi Jews predominant in Europe and America. These cards are less virulent, reflecting the generally more tolerant attitude toward Jews in Muslim nations at the time. This chapter will begin with Austria, Poland, Hungary, and the Ukraine, continue with North African postcards, and conclude with a few examples from several other nations that were not well known for anti-Semitic postcards.

The Jewish presence in modern-day Austria, like in Germany, can be traced back to Roman times. Austria participated fully in the persecution of Jews from the Middle Ages through the Holocaust with expulsions (e.g., from Vienna in 1431), blood libels, and basic discriminations, such as prohibitions on land ownership and exclusion from employment in civil service. In 1867, following Austria's defeat by Prussia and the joining of the Austrian monarchy with Hungary, a new constitution granted Jews emancipation and wide freedoms. However, deep-seated anti-Semitic attitudes prevailed. The German population in multi-ethnic Austria-Hungary saw itself as vulnerable to other ethnic groups, particularly the Jews. Anti-Semitic organizations thrived openly in Austria (including those described in figures 7-2 and 7-3) and were often supported by politicians. Karl Lueger, a rabid and outspoken anti-Semite, was elected multiple times as mayor of Vienna from 1897 to 1910. It was in this environment that Adolf Hitler arrived in the capital city in 1907; Lueger's ideas were later reflected in the Nazi party platform.

Even so, under Emperor Franz Joseph, the last half of the nineteenth century through World War I was a relatively prosperous time for the Jews of Austria, with Vienna becoming a leading Jewish cultural center. (Theodor Herzl, the founder of political Zionism, lived in Austria during this period.) In the 1920s and 1930s, Vienna was home to over 200,000 Jews (about 11 percent of the total population), ranking it the sixth largest Jewish city in the world after New York, Warsaw, Chicago, Philadelphia, and Budapest. The rise of Nazi Germany in the 1930s and the annexation of Austria to Germany in 1938, which was welcomed by many Austrians, spelled doom for the Jews of

FIGURE 7-1. A prosperous, secular Jew, but still with the typical misshapen body, dressed in a gray striped suit with three diamonds shining on his fingers and a fourth under his bowtie. He is holding a *conto,* or "ledger." The text reads: "I am not the morning star / And I am not the evening star / I am Isaac Stern." The poem is a play on words, as "Stern," a typical Jewish surname, also means star. Stern is shown smirking while he displays his wealth and clutches all that he cares about: his ledger. [Publisher: Leo Stainer, Innsbruck; mailed from Lake Balaton, Hungary, to Steirmark, Austria, in August 1901.]

Austria. While many managed to emigrate prior to the Nazi annihilation, tens of thousands were murdered. Austria became home to the Mauthausen-Gusen concentration camp, one of the largest camps of its kind.

Today, only about 9,000 Jews reside in Austria, as the population never recovered from its destruction in World War II. Austria's postwar record on anti-Semitism is mixed. As Karl Pfeifer, a prominent Austrian-Jewish journalist explained recently, "Anti-Semitism did not cease to exist in 1945 and continues to be part and parcel of Austrian political life and culture with its strongest hold in the political parties and the media." The Austrian government suppressed or ignored its role in the Holocaust for nearly five decades. From 1986 to 1992, Austria elected as its president Kurt Waldheim, a former intelligence officer in the German army who was previously enrolled in the SA, the paramilitary Nazi organization of storm troopers. Waldheim was banned from entering the United States during most of his presidential term. It was not until 1991 that socialist chancellor Franz

Vranitzky declared in Parliament that the Austrians were partly responsible for the suffering of Jews in World War II. Even then, Vranitzky did not do so in a special statement nor did he say that the state was responsible, but only that its citizens were partly culpable. In 1999, Jörg Haider's Freedom Party won 27 percent of the national elections in Austria, partnering with the governing coalition. Haider was considered to be a far-right-wing politician with a history of making dubious statements about Jews and praising Nazism. Israel withdrew its ambassador from Austria in 2000 over Haider's inclusion in the government, along with fourteen European Union countries, but reestablished ties in 2003.[1]

Anti-Semitic postcards from Austria are similar to those from Germany in style and content, as shown in the examples below. Also see chapter 9, which discusses anti-Semitic postcards from the spa towns of Karlsbad and Marienbad which were part of the Austro-Hungarian Empire during the Golden Era.

FIGURE 7-2. This postcard mimics the theme of the expulsion postcards shown in chapter 2. A boot is kicking a Jew out of doors marked "City of Vienna" toward the railroad station and a long caravan of Jews carry their belongings away in sacks. At the bottom, the text says: "Our greatest wish!" The postcard's significance is enhanced when we note that it was commissioned by the Schutzverein 'Antisemitenbund' Vienna, or the "'Anti-Semitic' Coalition of Vienna," a partnership between the Christian Social Party and the Greater German People's Party that was founded in 1919 during a peak in anti-Semitic activity. One of the main goals of the organization was to unite all anti-Semites in a single umbrella organization in order to protect them from what they perceived to be the powerful influence of the Jews. The group called for a legal separation of Jews and non-Jews from all facets of society and sought to expel all Jews who had immigrated since 1914. In 1921, the coalition attracted 40,000 people to its international congress in Vienna, but its influence waned in the late 1920s. A few years after Hitler took power in the 1930s, the organization established new chapters throughout Austria.[2] [Publisher: Schutzverein 'Antisemitenbund' Vienna; 1920s era.]

Homunkulus Auszug der Juden

FIGURE 7-3. This postcard is captioned "Homunculus Aussug der Juden," or "Homunculus Exodus of the Jews." In the context of this postcard, Homunculus, which refers to a miniature human, denotes a diminutive or malformed Jew, much like the Little Cohn described in chapter 8. Once again, the Austrian fantasy of Jewish emigration is evoked. This postcard was published by the Bund der Deutschen Niederösterreich (the German Association of Lower Austria), which was founded in 1880. The association's goal was to increase awareness of German literature and language in the Austro-Hungarian Empire, though it later became associated with the German National-Socialist party. [Publisher: Bund der Deutschen Niederösterreich, Vienna; circa 1910s.]

Was ein Häkchen werden will — krümmt sich bei Zeiten. Alle Rechte vorbehalten.

FIGURE 7-4. A Jewish boy is surrounded by a group of Jews who seem delighted by what the boy is showing them. The caption says: "If you want to become a little hook—there's nothing like starting young." The text seems to imply that the boy is displaying his small genitalia with pride. The boy is drawn with exaggerated bowed legs, the women are large and unattractive, and the men are poorly dressed and awkward. The point of this scene is to display Jews as ugly, deformed, and crude, like the postcards in figures 2-18 and 9-2, which depict Jews defecating. The card's publisher was Kikeriki (which means "cock-a-doodle-doo"), a conservative satirical magazine published in Vienna from 1861 through 1933; in the early twentieth century the magazine was known for being strongly anti-Semitic.[3] [Publisher: Kikeriki, Vienna; circa 1907.]

POLAND

The history of Polish Jewry is of particular importance since an estimated 70 percent of the world's Ashkenazi Jews can trace their ancestry to Poland. The Jewish presence in Poland can be traced as far back as the tenth century CE, with the earliest permanent settlements recorded in the twelfth and thirteenth centuries. Polish Jewry expanded rapidly in the fourteenth and fifteenth centuries when immigrants from Western Europe, primarily Germany, fled from persecution resulting from the Black Plague. Some Jews escaped from persecution in the East, such as from Crimea in today's Ukraine. Poland was seen as a safe haven for Jews as they were granted some basic rights that assured them security and freedom of religion. Their status began to turn for the worse in the late fifteenth century, with expulsions from Krakow and Warsaw in 1495. Over the next 150 years, the Jewish settlement of Poland, which by this time was united in a commonwealth with Lithuania, continued to grow with another wave of immigrants, this time from Germany, Italy, Austria, and Hungary. The sixteenth century is considered a Golden Age for Jews in Poland, with growth in commerce, culture, and religion. The common language was the Judeo-German dialect, Yiddish, which was brought over by the Jews of Germany.

The Jewish settlement in Poland suffered its first series of catastrophes in 1648, most notably a Cossack rebellion (known as the Chmielnicki Uprising) in the Ukrainian part of Poland and invasions by forces from Moscow and Sweden. Jews were specifically targeted in these attacks and hundreds of Jewish communities were destroyed. The Polish army, in retreat from foreign forces, also devastated the Jewish population. After these wars, Jews began to return to their villages and homes, but they lost the support and protections that they had previously. In the late eighteenth and early nineteenth centuries, most of the Polish Kingdom was divided among three of its neighbors, Russia, Austria, and Germany, and the 2 million Jews of Poland came under the rule of the three surrounding countries. These three nations treated the Jews poorly, especially Russia, which established a region where Jews were required to live (known as the "Pale of Settlement"). Throughout the period of foreign domination of Poland, Jews were viewed as foreign competitors, and Polish nationalist parties were thoroughly anti-Semitic. World War I changed the political and geographical landscape, and a newly independent Poland was resurrected from the ruins of the Russian, Austro-Hungarian, and German empires, with a Jewish population estimated at over 2.8 million.

Freedom for Poland did not translate into better conditions for Jews. Poland's independence immediately resulted in anti-Jewish pogroms and persecutions. Jews were excluded from various professions and trades, including all jobs in civil service. By the 1930s, anti-Semitic attitudes escalated dramatically, with open and active hostility to Jews in all areas of society, from religious practice to commerce. Prior to World War II, the Jewish population in Poland reached approximately 3.5 million; only 500,000 survived the Holocaust.

After the war, Jews were still subjected to deadly pogroms by Poles who feared that returning Jews would seek to reclaim property that had been taken over by other Poles. A 1968 anti-Jewish purge forced out most of the remaining survivors, and only about 10,000 Jews remain in Poland today. Anti-Semitic attitudes are still widely prevalent in Poland: 48 percent of Polish respondents in a 2009 survey agreed with common anti-Semitic stereotypes versus 20 percent in France and Germany and 10 percent in the UK.[4]

The postcards used in Poland during the Golden Era were from either Germany, Austria-Hungary, or Russia, as Polish territory was part of these three empires at the time. The postcards shown in the examples below are those that are distinctly Polish.

Nischt ahin in nischt aher.

FIGURE 7-5. "Neither here nor there" says the caption on this mean-spirited postcard that shows a family of Jews cowering on a narrow bridge comprised of one wooden plank, while a stout man (dressed like a jester, as if to further taunt the Jews) and his aggressive dog block the family's path on either side. The message is that Jews are not welcome anywhere; in every direction, they will be confined and persecuted. This postcard was published in Krakow, Poland, at the turn of the twentieth century. Krakow, which, at the time, was part of the Austro-Hungarian Empire, was a Jewish cultural center; prior to World War II there were more than 50,000 Jews in the city, comprising approximately 25 percent of its total population. This postcard foreshadowed the famous Krakow ghetto, whereby the Jews of the city and nearby areas were confined to a small area, like the bridge here, surrounded by barbed-wire fences and stone walls. Most of Krakow's Jews died in the Holocaust. [Publisher: S.M.P., Krakow; circa 1903].

Mariem!
nur dich allein
liebe ich.

FIGURE 7-6. A scene of a stingy Jew giving a pretzel to a girl as a token of his love. He says: "Miriam [a typical Jewish girl's name]! I love only you." The Jew offering a cheap gift was also the subject of the American postcard shown in figure 6-39. [Publisher: S.M.P., Krakow; 1906].

FIGURE 7-7. "Greetings from Russian Poland" refers to Polish territory that was under Russian rule until Poland gained independence after World War I. Two adult Jews in stereotypical garb scratch themselves due to bugs that bite them. The Jewish boy at right shows them the type of insect that bothers them, and in his other hand he holds a collection of bugs tied in a string. The boy is walking around gathering bugs from Jews. The printed script at the upper rights says: "A bug bites and causes itching / A Jew bends over and is bent / Here boy again we have another one / string them on a rope!" Associating Jews with dirt, torn clothes, poor hygiene, and unsanitary conditions was a common anti-Semitic trope. The sender's handwritten German message begins on the reverse and ends with two lines on the front. A simple birthday greeting from 1916 was an opportunity to send the celebrant anti-Semitic humor. The artist and publisher, Fritz Ferdinand Preiss, was also responsible for the postcard in figure 2-26, which also employs an "insect" theme. [Publisher: F. Preiss, Berlin; 1915.]

FIGURE 7-8. "Wesołych Świąt," or "Seasons Greetings," suggests that the holiday season is the perfect occasion to send a postcard with an anti-Semitic message. At the left is a Jew, dressed in Hasidic garb with a beard and long, pointed fingers in an awkward pose, either threatening or backing away from a Polish fiddler who, in contrast, stands tall and straight, swinging his fiddle. Jędrek-Mędrek, the fiddler, says: "Jew, Jew, I'll soon teach you, / On your back and on your front / You'll feel the sting of my fiddle's bow." The Jew's response: "Oy vay gevalt! Oy vay gevalt! [a Yiddish expression of alarm meaning "oh goodness" or "for heaven's sake"] / What is this pain? / What are you doing stupid peasant? / For God's sake! / La! la! la! For God's sake!" This quote represents the last lines of the first act of a nativity play called Polish Bethlehem (Betleem Polskie) written by Polish playwright Lucjan Rydel (1870–1918) and first staged in 1904. At the end of the first act the violinist, Jędrek-Mędrek, tells the Jew of the newly born Messiah and wants to take the Jew to see the Messiah. The Jew refuses by explaining that he believes in the old God— these lines in the postcard come at the end of this discussion. Neither Rydel nor his play were understood to be specifically anti-Semitic; rather, it was the postcard editor who used the words of the play to illustrate a grotesque Jew being admonished and threatened by a handsome Polish violinist.[5] [Publisher: Nakład J. Czerneckiego, Wieliczka; circa 1908.]

WESOŁYCH ŚWIĄT!

WŁ. TETMAJER.

JĘDREK-MĘDREK:

Żydzie, żydzie, wnet ja cię nauczę,
Jak cię z tyłu, jak cię z przodu
Tym smyczkiem wymłócę.

ŻYD:

Aj waj gewalt! Aj waj gewalt!
Albo to tu rozbój?
Co wyrabiasz głupi chłopie!
Pana Boga się bój!
Laj! laj! laj! Pana Boga się bój!

(Lucyan Rydel — Betleem polskie).

FIGURES 7-9 and 7-10. "Moshe don't give up!" [Mojsie is the vernacular Yiddish version of the Hebrew name Moshe or Moses] is the mocking caption of these two similarly themed cards that show a Jew being harassed by animals. This is a common motif in anti-Semitic postcards (see figures 2-20 and 3-26 for other examples); it implies that the dogs know that the Jew is an interloper and, thus, the animals are justified in going after the Jew. [Publisher: figure 7-9: S.M.P., Krakow; 1907; figure 7-10: W.k.p.–A.S., Krakow; 1907.]

HUNGARY

Jews have lived in Hungary since the Roman era, and their population expanded in the eleventh century as immigrants arrived from Germany, Bohemia, and Moravia. Hungary was considered relatively safe for Jews until 1349, when Hungary, like much of Europe, expelled and persecuted Jews as a reaction to the Black Death. Jews were eventually readmitted, but they continued to face persecutions, such as anti-Jewish riots and blood libels (e.g., in 1494, sixteen Jews were burned at the stake following the unexplained disappearance of a Christian boy). When the Ottoman Empire captured most of Hungary in the sixteenth century, the Jews came under the rule of the Turkish sultan who treated them relatively well. The Christian Hapsburg Empire captured Hungary in the late seventeenth century, leading to a revival of harsh restrictions against Jews, such as expulsions and "toleration taxes."

In 1867, Hungary joined the Austro-Hungarian monarchy, and Jews benefitted from emancipation under Emperor Franz Joseph as described in the section on Austria. Hungary became an independent nation during the 1918–1920 period after the Austro-Hungarian monarchy collapsed from being on the losing side in World War I. The new Hungarian government passed several anti-Jewish legislations and restrictions. In the 1930s, Hungary allied itself with the Fascist governments in Germany and Italy, and its attitudes and policies toward Jews became more repressive. In 1938, Hungary passed yet another series of anti-Jewish legislations based on Germany's Nuremberg Laws, which, among other things, classified people who were Jews and removed their citizenship. In 1941, Hungary entered the war allied with Nazi Germany. In March 1944, German troops occupied Hungary and installed a puppet government after Hungary sought to negotiate surrender to the Allies. Although the situation for Jews in Hungary was already awful prior to the Nazi occupation (e.g., 100,000 Jews were mobilized for forced labor, causing the death of about 40,000), Jews were not subject to mass deportation and extermination. This changed soon after the occupation; within eight weeks, more than 400,000 Hungarian Jews were deported. By the end of the war, an estimated 600,000 Hungarian Jews were murdered out of a total of approximately 825,000. The Hungarian government cooperated with the Nazis in effecting the "Final Solution" in Hungary and committed atrocities of its own.

After World War II, Hungary became a Soviet satellite state, and anti-Semitism was not openly present under the Communists, although anti-Jewish and anti-Zionist policies and attitudes widely prevailed. After the country's transition to democracy in 1989, anti-Semitism reemerged in the open almost immediately. A 2010 article published by the Institute for Global Jewish Affairs notes that more recently, traditional anti-Semitism has resurfaced, characterized by both verbal and physical aggression against Jews. This hatred for Jews has also been institutionalized with the popularity of the right-wing and anti-Semitic Jobbik political party, which earned 17 percent of the national vote in April 2010. Anti-Semitic attitudes are still popular in Hungary, especially in the right-wing media; 47 percent of Hungarian respondents in a 2009 survey agreed that common anti-Semitic stereotypes were true, similar to the 48 percent result in Poland. It should be noted, however, that the Jewish community in Hungary today, which numbers about 100,000, is relatively prosperous and flourishing, and it has been supported by the senior leadership of the country, which also maintains an excellent relationship with the Israeli government.[6]

The anti-Semitic postcards from Hungary are similar to those of Germany and Austria, depicting the worst forms of anti-Jewish sentiment. This is to be expected given Hungary's alignment with the Nazis and its historical ties with Austria. The overall postcard record of Hungary is much smaller than that of Germany, which is why fewer examples of anti-Semitic postcards from Hungary are available today. A few examples are shown below, as well as in figure 2-36.

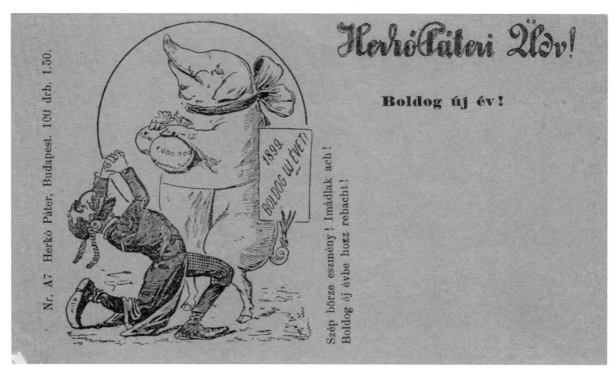

FIGURE 7-11. This Hungarian New Year's greeting postcard from 1899 offers an occasion for the sender to also provide the recipient with an anti-Semitic message. Publisher Herkó Páter offers its wishes at the top right with "Greetings from Herkó Páter / Happy New Year!" The image at left shows a grotesque Jew kneeling and pleading before a pig that is holding bags of money. The two-line vertical message says: "A great idea for the stock market! I love you! / Bring profits in the New Year!" The text plays on the word *rebacht,* Hungarian slang for profit, similar to *revach* in Hebrew. All the Jew cares for in the new year is money, and he is willing to do whatever it takes, even kneeling before an animal, to obtain profits. The choice of a pig is a deliberate choice by the artist to ridicule Jewish aversion to pork, as discussed in chapter 2. [Publisher: Herkó Páter, Budapest; 1899.]

FIGURE 7-12. "New Clothes!" exclaims the Jewish man in Yiddish, finding a pair of pants with several holes and a pair of old boots on the street. This simple anti-Semitic postcard depicts a stereotypically cheap Eastern European Jew scavenging from the street. [Publisher: TSA, Hungary; mailed within Hungary in December 1903.]

FIGURE 7-13. This postcard succinctly summarizes what was to be done with the Jews in Hungary: expulsion. The five-line caption says: "One hundred Jews in a row, / Deportation; / Nathan goes in the front, / Bundles on their backs, / bye Lueger father." Lueger refers to Austrian politician Karl Lueger, a rabid anti-Semite at the time this postcard was published. The image shows a long caravan of Jews, extending as far as the eye can see, marching into the horizon. The Jews are depicted as refugees, carrying their meager possessions on their backs, worn expressions on their faces. This postcard recalls the expulsion of Jews from Hungary in 1349 and foreshadows the rapid deportation of the majority of the Jews in Hungary to Auschwitz in 1944. The sender makes no mention of the shocking image of ethnic cleansing, casually writing at the top: "Aug. 14 901 / Many heartfelt greetings from all of us." [Publisher: Törv vévde M.J.F.B.; mailed from Lake Balaton, Hungary, to Steirmark, Austria, in August 1901.]

FIGURE 7-14. This postcard was published by the Arrow Cross Party (1935–1945), a nationalist socialist party that subscribed to the same ideology of racial purity as the Nazis. The symbol of the Arrow Cross Party was a cross with arrows at each end, a symbol of the Magyar tribes that originally settled Hungary. In this image, a typical Jew (with a Star of David in his pocket to make it clear) watches a man carry a log, suggesting that the laughing Jew watches and profits as others (non-Jews) do the work for them. However, the rising "arrow cross" in the horizon heralds the inexorable ascension of the Nationalist Socialist Party and the end of oppression by the Jews. For a brief period from October 1944 to March 1945, the Arrow Cross Party's founder and leader, Ferenc Szálasi, was the head of state and prime minister of Hungary; in close collaboration with the Nazis, he was directly responsible for murdering and deporting tens of thousands of Jews. Szálasi was hanged for war crimes in 1946. [Publisher: F.K. Hauszer, Kosice; 1920s era.]

The history of Jews in the Ukraine is complex since the territory of modern day Ukraine was dominated by various foreign powers, including Poland, Russia, and Austria-Hungary, for most of the last six hundred years. Jewish life in the Ukraine was thus dependent on the policies and politics of these controlling nations, some of which have been described in previous sections. However, Jews were also subject to persecution and a series of brutal pogroms by Ukrainian Cossacks that led to the slaughter of many thousands of Jews. The most famous of these attacks is known as the Chmielnicki Uprising, as memorialized in figure G, in which the Cossacks, led by Bohdan Chmielnicki, rose up against Polish rule in the mid-seventeenth century and massacred Jews, who were seen as an agent of foreign oppression. Similar atrocities committed by Ukrainians, known as the Haidamaky, are described in the next sidebar. Additional pogroms occurred in nineteenth- and twentieth-century Ukraine, and an estimated 1.5 million Ukrainian Jews were killed in the Holocaust. The Jewish community in Ukraine today is estimated at over 80,000 persons. Anti-Semitic discourse in this country remains widespread, with Jews blamed for the historical suffering that Ukrainians have endured.[7]

FIGURES 7-15 to 7-17. These three postcards are from a series published in Mukachevo, Ukraine, in the period before World War I. The city passed between the Austro-Hungarian Empire, Czechoslovakia, Hungary, and Russia before becoming part of Ukraine after World War II. Mukachevo had a large Jewish community; as of 1938 it was the only town in Hungary with a Jewish majority. In 1944, the Jewish population was deported to Auschwitz. The postcard publisher was thus very familiar with the Jewish community.

FIGURES 7-15 to 7-17 *(continued).* The first example depicts a Jewish merchant raising his fingers to offer a price. The woman, with a characteristic "small" nose, indicating she is not Jewish, is clearly not happy with the quote. The caption on the back of the postcard says, "Small turnover, big profit," implying that the Jew is greedily overcharging for his goods. Note the broken table propped up by large stones, contradicting the imagery of the wealthy Jew. Although Jews were often portrayed as wealthy merchants, they were simultaneously shown as unkempt and sorry looking. In the second example, the Jew is harassed by a small dog. Like figure 3-26, the Jew is attacked and mocked by dogs as if being "rooted out" by loyal pets. The caption on the back says, "Sudden Surprise." The third card has a Jewish bar owner standing before a customer who has fallen over from drinking too much. The caption on the back says, "Another one of his victims," suggesting that the Jew pumped him with alcohol. This image is a metaphor for the powerful and conniving Jew who takes advantage of Gentiles, and an allusion to historical accusations that Jews poison wells. [Publisher: Novotný and Bartošek Publishers, Mukachevo; circa 1910.]

THE HAIDAMAKY MASSACRES

The four postcards in figures 7-18 through 7-21 are part of a set published around 1905 that recounts the story of the epic poem "Haidamaky," written by the famous Ukrainian writer and poet Taras Shevchenko (1814–1861). Shevchenko protested against the oppressive rule of his native Ukraine by foreign powers, and his writings reflected this sentiment. The poem's illustrations, drawn by renowned Ukranian artist and musician Opanas Slastion (1855–1933), first appeared in an 1885 version of "Haidamaky" published in St. Petersburg, Russia. Each postcard is captioned the same at far left, with the name "T. Shevchenko" at the top and the poem title "Haidamaky" below. These postcards differ from most of the examples in this book, as they reflect an artistic depiction of a work of literature as opposed to postcards published specifically to disseminate prejudice and loathing for Jews. However, since they depict events that were part of a major anti-Semitic incident in eighteenth-century Ukraine, and represent a controversial poem with a Jew as one of the main characters, these postcards deserve to be included and studied in this book.

The Haidamaky were armed groups of Ukrainians, Cossacks, and peasants who, in the eighteenth century, initiated several popular rebellions and uprisings against Polish rule in the Western area of the Ukraine. The Haidamaky called for a Ukraine free of Catholic Poles and Jews, who were seen as agents of the Polish gentry, and for free exercise of their Greek Orthodox faith. Major Haidamaky uprisings took place in 1734 and 1750, and the Cossacks robbed and destroyed towns and estates, killing Polish nobles and Jews along the way. The most violent Haidamaky uprising, the Koliyivshchyna rebellion of 1768, is the subject of Shevchenko's poem. This rebellion is best known for the slaughter of many thousands of civilian Poles and Jews culminating in what is known as the Massacre of Uman. In one of the many atrocities committed in Uman, the Haidamaky rushed into a synagogue where 3,000 Jews had barricaded themselves, murdered most of them, and razed the building, even desecrating the Torah scrolls. The Polish and Russian armies suppressed the revolt later that same year. Even though the Haidamaky were responsible for slaughtering an estimated 20,000 civilians, they are generally viewed in a positive light in Ukrainian literature and culture since their goal was to free Ukraine from foreign domination. For the Jews, the Haidamaky were murderers; but in Ukrainian eyes, they were freedom fighters, while Jews were part of the system of oppression.[8]

Although Shevchenko glorifies the Haidamaky in his poem, and is therefore sometimes portrayed as anti-Semitic, the evidence indicates otherwise. Shevchenko, in fact, expressed sympathy for the persecution of Jews, and in 1858, was a signatory to one of the first public protests against anti-Semitism in the Russian Empire. His poem "Haidamaky" portrays Jews as both oppressors and the oppressed. The main Jewish character of the poem, an innkeeper named Leiba, is abusive to his Ukrainian servant Yarema (who later joins the Haidamaky) and his fiancé; however, the Jew is himself unjustly persecuted by the Polish nobles. In a private communication with Professor Oleh S. Ilnytzky at the University of Alberta, Canada, he wrote: "In 'Haidamaky,' Shevchenko is portraying the inhumanity of people of various nationalities, Ukrainians, Jews, and Poles. The Poles are portrayed as victimizing Jews and Ukrainians. Shevchenko's poem is a highly ethical condemnation of this inhumanity; it is a tragic investigation of how social injustice and violence by one side leads to retribution and more violence by those who have been injured."[9]

Though Shevchenko may not have intended his "Haidamaky" as an anti-Semitic work and does have a record of opposing anti-Semitism, it is clear that this poem still promotes the typical negative stereotypes of Jews as greedy and oppressive, concepts that were prevalent throughout the Ukraine and Russia at the time. The epic poem is also a glorification of an event that led to the deliberate mass slaughter of Jews. Jews were not simply in the wrong place at the wrong time during these uprisings, but they were singled out for persecution. The Russian Orthodox leadership incited hatred against Jews, who were an easy target for the Haidamaky. From the perspective of Jewish history, the Haidamaky massacres are part of a long tradition of persecution and anti-Semitism in the Ukraine.

FIGURE 7-18. At the right, Leiba, the Jew, abuses the Ukrainian peasant Yarema: "Yarema, do you hear me, you good for nothing? Go and bring the mare! Go and bring the mistress her slippers, and bring water for me!" Shevchenko portrays Leiba as a flawed character, mistreating Yarema, but, as seen in other postcards, he himself is unjustly persecuted by the Polish nobles. Ultimately, Yarema joins the Haidamaky, who rebel by slaughtering thousands of Poles and Jews. [Publisher: S. Burko, No. 4; circa 1905.]

Т. Шевченко. Гайдамаки. — „Яремо, герш ту, хамів сину? Піди кобилу приведи! Подай патинки господини, Та принеси мені води!

FIGURE 7-19. A group of Polish nobles bang on the door of Leiba, the Jew, saying, "Open the door! You hated *Zhid!* [a derogatory term for Jew, similar to the word "kike" in English] or you will be thrashed! Open up! Break down the door, before he comes the old ugly one!" In this part of the *Haidamaky* poem, the Jew is harassed by Poles who controlled a portion of the Ukraine. [Publisher: S. Burko, No. 6; circa 1905.]

Т. Шевченко. Гайдамаки. — „Одчиняй, проклятий Жиде! Бо будеш битий! Одчиняй! Ламайте двері, поки вайдэ Старий паскуда!"

FIGURE 7-20. Leiba is shown here again, this time being beaten by Polish nobles in an attempt to convert him to Christianity. The caption says: "They whistled, Christening Leiba again. They thrashed, thrashed him, until the feathers flew." In order to save himself from further whipping by the Poles, Leiba falsely sends them in search of nonexistent money at the home of the church warden. Leiba commits an act of wrongdoing, but clearly under major duress. Shevchenko's Jewish character is both victim and victimizer, a key theme of the epic poem. [Publisher: S. Burko, No. 8; circa 1905.]

Т. Шевченко.
Гайдамаки.

Засвистіли,
Хрестять Лейбу знову.

Періщили, періщили,
Аж піря летіло . . . .

Т. Шевченко.
Гайдамаки.

. . . . . . „Хоч жить?
Скажи, де гроші.“

Той мовчить.
Налигачем скрутили руки,

FIGURE 7-21. The Polish nobles torture and eventually kill the church warden, Tytar, believing, based on the word of the Jew, Leiba, that he is hiding money. The Poles say, "Do you want to live? Tell us where the money is. He doesn't say a word. With a rope his hands were bound." The victimization of innocent Ukrainians by the Poles, aided by the Jews, is an example of the cruelty that led to the Haidamaky uprisings. [Publisher: S. Burko, No. 11; circa 1905.]

FRENCH NORTH AFRICA

The recorded history of North Africa dates back to the Phoenician city of Carthage, which was founded in modern-day Tunisia in 814 BCE. The city was a major power in the Mediterranean Sea until it fell to the Romans in 146 BCE. The region later fell to the Vandals, then to the Byzantines, then to the Arabs in the seventh century CE, and in part to the Ottoman Empire in the sixteenth century. The Jewish presence can be traced to Roman Times, with the Jewish population increasing after the expulsions from Spain and Portugal in 1492. Jews living under Muslim rule were considered "protected people," or *dhimmis,* which provided them some measure of security and freedom of religion. Most scholars agree that until the mid-twentieth century, Jews in Muslim lands, including North Africa, were treated better and lived more securely than those in Christian Europe. The topic is complex, but Bernard Lewis, a leading scholar on the subject, provides this excellent summary:

> Jews have lived under Islamic rule for fourteen centuries, and in many lands, and it is therefore difficult to generalize about their experience. This much, however, may be said with reasonable certainly—that they were never free from discrimination, but only rarely subject to persecution; that their situation was never as bad as in Christendom at its worst, nor ever as good as in Christendom at its best. There is nothing in Islamic history to parallel the Spanish expulsion and Inquisition, the Russian pogroms, or the Nazi Holocaust; there is also nothing to compare with the progressive emancipation and acceptance accorded to Jews in the democratic West in the last three centuries.[10]

FIGURE 7-22. This postcard from Casablanca, Morocco, depicts a Jew drawn in the same style and manner of anti-Semitic postcards from Europe. The poor posture, ugly facial features, flat feet, and ragged clothes are all to be found here. The Jew is shown using a phone with a sign on top indicating that: "The device is being fixed. It does not work." The point of this scene is to characterize the Jew as stupid since he is trying to make a call with a phone clearly marked as broken. The caption says: "A Jew who has just been cut off." [Publisher: P. Madelaine, Casablanca, Morocco; circa 1925.]

8. - La Guerre au Maroc. — La bedide gommerce de Jacob

FIGURE 7-23. "Jacob's little business" has a Jewish merchant surrounded, taunted, and bullied by French soldiers and natives. The card is titled "The War in Morocco," which refers to the supression of ongoing Moroccan uprisings against French rule which occurred in the 1920s and 1930s. This postcard is supposed to depict a typical scene from this era. The Jew is arguing with a black African man who is also drawn in a derogatory manner. The Frenchmen are all laughing and taking things from the cart. [Publisher: Photo. Flandrin, Casablanca, Morocco; mailed from French Military Post Office to France in May 1930.]

In the nineteenth and early-twentieth century, Algeria (in 1830), Tunisia (in 1881), and part of Morocco (in 1912) became French colonies, and Jews became subjects of France. French influence in these countries was strong, especially in Algeria, which was considered to be an integral part of France Many of the postcards from these nations reflect the culture and attitudes in France. The anti-Semitic postcards from North Africa in the examples below are from these three French colonies and should be considered as extensions of French anti-Semitic postcards. A key difference is that the Sephardic Jews in these Muslim nations dressed differently than the Ashkenazi Jews of Europe—but they were mocked in exactly the same way.

Petite Retouche au Petit Z'raélite !

Humide inconvenance !...

Circoncision

FIGURES 7-24 and 7-25. These two postcards, the first from Algeria (*top*) and the second from Tunisia, ridicule the Jewish circumcision ritual. The first is mockingly titled "A Small Retouch to a Young Israelite." The *mohel*, or the person performing the circumcision, holds an exaggerated pair of scissors (the actual tool is much smaller and safer), and as he attempts to perform the ritual, the baby urinates in his face. The caption says something akin to "indecent humidity," referring to the baby's action. In the second card, the *mohel* with the enormous scissors and the Jew holding the baby are seen eagerly performing the ritual. A close inspection of the baby shows that the artist drew a large, hooked nose even for this infant. [Figure 7-24—Publisher: F. Montegut, Algiers; circa 1923. Figure 7-25—Publisher: N.S., Tunis; mailed from Tunis to Paris in August 1914.]

M'SIEU ABRAHAM

... Je crois ji viens de trouver la bonne pélite affaire...

M'AME REBECCA

Qué bon tafina ji vas préparer pour Moïse... le pôvre!..

FIGURES 7-26 and 7-27. This pair of Algerian postcards mock typically grotesque male and female Jews, Abraham and Rebecca. Abraham says in Yiddish-accented French: "I think I just found the perfect little business," alluding to the money-hungry Jew. Rebecca says: "What a good *tafina* [a stew dish often cooked by Jews for the Sabbath meal] I am going to prepare for Moses . . . the poor man!" Each card has a short message of greeting written on the back. Algeria had a large Jewish population under French rule, estimated at 140,000 at the time Algeria gained independence in 1962. However, after attaining independence, the new Muslim leadership granted Algerian citizenship only to Muslims and declared that Jews were no longer under the protection of the law. Even though the Jewish presence in Algeria pre-dated Islam, the great majority of the country's Jews were compelled to leave the country, ending the presence of an ancient community. Most moved to France, while others migrated to Israel; less than 100 Jews are estimated to reside in Algeria today. [Publisher: L. Chagny, Algiers; both postcards mailed by the same person from Algiers to Paris in April 1912.]

15 *LES MALHEURS D'ISRAEL*
Abomination, mon fils a fumé un samedi

R. Tugoz 1912

FIGURE 7-28. "The Misfortunes of Israel" shows a Jewish man throwing up his hands saying, "Abomination, my son smoked on Saturday." This postcard from Morocco ridicules the Jew for lamenting that his son violated the Jewish Sabbath observance with the lighting of fire. [Publisher: Not provided, Morocco; artist signed R. Tugotz; 1912.]

Le Maroc Illustré

FEZ. - Après l'émeute, Israélites fouillant les décombres

P. Schmitt, photo, Rabat

FIGURES 7-29 and 7-30. In March 1912, most of Morocco became a French protectorate, with a portion of the country placed under the control of Spain. A few weeks later, the Moroccan Sultan's troops in Fez revolted against the French, and local gangs took the opportunity created by the chaos to virtually destroy the Jewish quarter, known as the Mellah, that housed several thousand Jews. The pogrom resulted in the death of sixty Jews, and caused many to abandon their homes. The pillaging of Jewish property during times of upheaval, instability, and political change was common in both Muslim and Christian lands. These two postcards, part of a series titled "Illustrated Morocco," are captioned: "Fez.—After the riots, Israelites [Jews] searching the rubble." [Publisher: P. Schmitt, Rabat; 1912.]

Le Maroc Illustré

FEZ. - Après l'émeute - Exploration des décombres

P. Schmitt, photo, Rabat

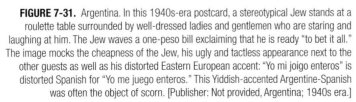

Yo mi joigo enteros

FIGURE 7-31. Argentina. In this 1940s-era postcard, a stereotypical Jew stands at a roulette table surrounded by well-dressed ladies and gentlemen who are staring and laughing at him. The Jew waves a one-peso bill exclaiming that he is ready "to bet it all." The image mocks the cheapness of the Jew, his ugly and tactless appearance next to the other guests as well as his distorted Eastern European accent: "Yo mi joigo enteros" is distorted Spanish for "Yo me juego enteros." This Yiddish-accented Argentine-Spanish was often the object of scorn. [Publisher: Not provided, Argentina; 1940s era.]

FIGURE 7-32. Belgium. This unusual World War I-era anti-Semitic postcard from Belgium revolves around the theme of Belgian resistance against the unprovoked invasion by Germany. Following the outbreak of hostilities in July 1914, Germany declared war on France. The invasion plan called for the German army to pass through neutral Belgium; prior to the attack, Germany gave Belgium an ultimatum to surrender peacefully or fight. Although vastly outmatched, Belgium chose to resist the German invasion. The Belgians fell easily to the superior German forces. This postcard accuses the Jews of controlling the levers of German power by instigating the invasion. A tiny Belgian soldier stands at guard under his country's flag, which says "Honor, Courage, Humanity," in front of a fence with the words "Passage Is Forbidden." At the left, the Germans seek to enter the tiny nation. The tall man at center is a Jew, with a hooked nose and beard, wearing a German military uniform. In one hand, he tries to hand a coin to the Belgian soldier, a bribe, while behind his back he holds a knife. The Jew says to the Belgian, in German-accented French (*see words at the top*), "I would like to get through, I won't do anything to you!" His Jewish colleague carries several bags that say: "Profits," "Support from Germany," "Gratitude of the Kaiser," "Neutrality, Respect, Freedom," and "A Bigger Belgium." The Gentile German, clearly marked with no beard and a regular-sized nose, kneels beside the Jew, ready to shine his shoes, as if the non-Jews of Germany were controlled by Jews. The Belgian responds in Flemish: "Get back! Belgium is not for sale!" The sign at the far right adds: "Notice, to avoid shameful proposals we affirm so that no one will ignore it: the honor and faith of Belgium are not for sale, signed [King] Albert." While this postcard was intended to stir Belgian patriotism, its anti-Semitic message is clear. The irony of this postcard cannot be overstated. [Publisher: Not provided; 1914.]

FIGURE 7-33. Mexico. A hooked-nosed Jew greedily counts his gold in this 1940s-era postcard that is reminiscent of the German postcards shown in figures 3-14 and 3-15. The postcard employs no text, for its message is self-explanatory. The canard of the Jewish love for money was an international phenomenon. [Publisher: FEMA, S.A., Mexico D.F.; 1940s era.]

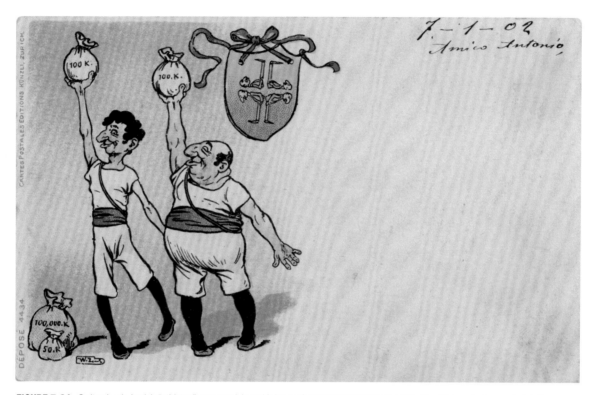

FIGURE 7-34. Switzerland. Jewish "athletes" are exercising with bags of money weighted by denomination. The coat of arms depicts four large-nosed Jews in formation. Ugly, awkward, and weak Jews obsessed with money were universal anti-Semitic themes. [Publisher: Editions Künzli, Zurich; 1902.]

CHAPTER 8

THE LITTLE COHN: AN ANTI-SEMITIC HIT SONG

In mid-1996, the dance song "Macarena" took the United States by storm, landing at the top of the charts and playing frequently at sporting events, conventions, parties, and rallies. During the Democratic National Convention that year, Vice President Al Gore played the song, standing stoically in humorous fashion while the music blasted instead of performing the catchy dance that came with the tune. "Macarena" was a true fad that even made its way overseas, charting as the number two song in the UK that same year. In 1902, a similar fad spread throughout Germany, with a song performed in theaters nationwide and its music published in large print runs and sold to a mass audience for play at home. The song was included in collections of children's songs, and it spawned a large series of postcards that added further fuel to the fad. However, the German song from the turn of the century differed significantly from the American fad of the 1990s in one major respect: the German song was not a feel-good dance song about a woman but an anti-Semitic tune whose central character was an unusually short and deformed Jew known as *Der Kleine Cohn* or "The Little Cohn."

The origin of the fad was a couplet known as *Hab'n Sie nicht den kleinen Cohn geseh'n?* or "Haven't you seen the Little Cohn?" that was played as part of a song and dance show that premiered in 1902 at the Berlin Thalia Theater, one of the leading burlesque stages in Berlin. Although the theater's most successful songs were performed elsewhere and sold in stores nationwide, the leading force for the Little Cohn craze was a popular non-Jewish comedian named Guido Thielscher, who specialized in portraying Jewish characters, particularly by exaggerating their negative cultural stereotypes. He brought the Little Cohn to the stage with his show titled *Seine Kleine* ("His Little One"). It consisted of numerous songs, including the Cohn-themed jingle, which was written by Jean Kren and Alfred Schönfeld and set to a tune composed by Julius Einödshofer. The Cohn song told the story of a husband who is about to engage in an affair with a younger woman but is frustrated by the sudden appearance of his wife. Cohn manages to escape just in time to avoid running into his spouse. The lyrics are as follows:

To a pyrotechnical performance
Goes Mr. Cohn with a young girl,
Who is very hot for Mr. Cohn,
Almost hotter than the fireworks around.
All the bigger, thus, her shock,
When Cohn all of a sudden was gone,
Because he had seen
His lovely better half pass by!

The girl is all upset and sad,
Walks up to a cop and asks:

(Chorus:)
Haven't you seen the little Cohn?
Didn't you see him pass by?
He was swallowed up by the crowd
Leaves you in a shock, now little Cohn is gone!

The popularity of "The Little Cohn" spawned souvenirs such as Little Cohn dolls and figurines that adorned children's rooms; variations and additions to the song were created. The main character's name was deliberately chosen. Cohn, at the time, was the best-known Jewish last name, and it was virtually synonymous with Judaism. In fact, the epithet "Little Cohn" was highly charged with anti-Semitism. The concept of the diminutive Cohn can be traced back to 1893 when a military pamphlet was published explaining how

Jews were congenitally unfit for service. The small Cohn was introduced as the puny, bow-legged Jew whose body was unsuitable for the military.[1] The first series of postcards depicting the Little Cohn was commissioned by the Thalia Theater itself as an advertisement (see figure 8-2). Soon, dozens of different "Little Cohn" postcards were published, some referring to the story in the song and others showing Cohn in various situations.

The purpose of the song and the postcards is clear: to make fun of the ineptness, crudeness, and virtually inhuman physical characteristics of Jews. The lyrics highlight the inability of the Jew to consummate his affair and his resulting public embarrassment. The story also alludes to a lesser-known stereotype of the Jew as hyper-virile and obscene (see figure 4-13 for another example), in contrast to Christians who are spiritually pure and who denounce sexual indulgence.[2] The Little Cohn is always shown in postcards as unusually small, at less than one meter tall, with a large nose and stereotypical features. They show Little Cohn in various awkward situations while non-Jews stare in amazement. Little Cohn is never anything but the object of mockery. He is always an outsider, and all of his efforts to fit in are met with laughter.

The song's impact is reflected in the large number of people with the Cohn surname who applied for a name change to avoid ridicule and discrimination. One Berlin lawyer who underwent a name change in 1910 explained how the word "Cohn" became a swear word, a way to offend Jews and to deride them. A newspaper in 1907 described, under a headline titled "Little Cohn," how a Jewish conscript committed suicide after constant taunting and harassment by comrades and officers. The article noted that this was not an isolated case.[3] The Little Cohn phenomenon apparently lasted for many years. The 1911 newspaper *Berliner Tageblatt,* in a critique of a show, noted that one might have by now heard enough of Cohn.[4] In popularizing *Der Kleine Cohn,* it seems that Guido Thielscher may have contributed as much to anti-Semitic culture as Shakespeare did with Shylock, except that Cohn remained mostly confined to Germany, while Shylock fed the anti-Semitic imagery of Jews throughout Europe and beyond for centuries.

The postcards of the Little Cohn highlight one of the main theses of this book: anti-Semitic postcards were reflective of an entire society's attitude toward Jews. Anti-Semitism in prewar Germany was not simply confined to a small group of rabble-rousers; it was practiced by a large segment of the population. As the "Macarena" spawned a dance craze in 1996 America, "The Little Cohn" started a fad of anti-Semitism in 1902 Germany. This national trend, like so many others, was reflected in postcards, knickknacks, and objects that were part of the daily fabric of the nation. The Little Cohn postcards described in this chapter are only a small sample of the hundreds of different cards featuring this character.

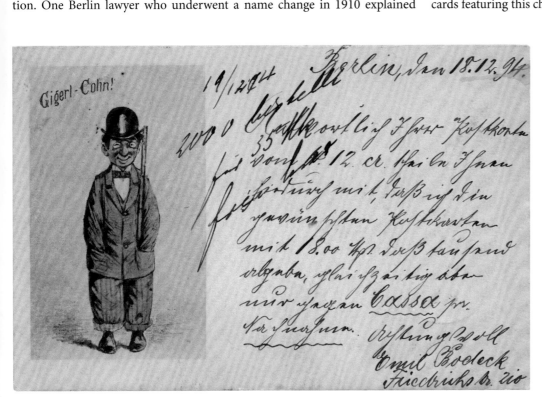

FIGURE 8-1. An 1894 postcard showing a diminutive and unattractive Jew named "Cohn." The caption says: "Dandy Cohn!" This version of Cohn, which came eight years before the phenomena of the "The Little Cohn," is depicted as small, with a bulbous nose and short pants. The handwritten message is an innocuous discussion of a business transaction. This card demonstrates the common usage of "Cohn" as a synonym for "Jew" in turn-of-the-century Germany.[5] [Publisher: Not provided; mailed within Germany in December 1894.]

FIGURE 8-2. One of the first Little Cohn cards, published on behalf of the Thalia Theater itself. The caption on top says: "Newest Hit: Haven't you seen the Little Cohn? / Sung by Guido Thielscher (Thalia-Theater)." Below is the chorus of the song: "Haven't you seen the Little Cohn? / Didn't you see him pass by? / He was swallowed up by the crowd / Leaves you in a shock, now Cohn is gone!" The small text in the left margin states: "This original couplet accompanied by music can be obtained for 1 Mark 50 Pfennigs from Max Marcus, Berlin W., Shopping Arcade 6/7." This card was an advertisement for the theater as well as the music. It did not actually show the Little Cohn or other anti-Semitic imagery, perhaps to maintain the mystery of the show. Instead, the card depicts well-dressed people at the theater. The handwritten text reads: "Greetings from a neighborhood friend [followed by many question marks, perhaps alluding to the question of where is the Little Cohn]." [Publisher: Max Marcus, Berlin; mailed within Germany in May 1902.]

No. 207. Dessin 6.

VERL.V. S.& G. SAULSOHN, BERLIN C.25.

Hab'n Sie nicht den kleinen Cohn gesehn?

Der kleine Cohn ist da!

Man munkelte schon allerhand	Die Hochbahn ward eröffnet eben	Hier im Coupé, seht deutlich hin,
Als der **kleine Cohn** verschwand,	Da sollt es ein Wunder geben,	Da sitzet er leibhaftig drin,
Aber jetzt ist er entdeckt,	Im ersten Wagen schon	freut Euch, Hurrah!
Bekannt ist, wo er steckt.	Saß der **kleine Cohn**;	**Der kleine Cohn ist da!**

FIGURE 8-3. This postcard takes the central theme of the Little Cohn song, "Haven't you seen the Little Cohn?" and provides an answer at bottom, stating, "The Little Cohn is here!" The publisher explains by providing the reader with an additional verse to the song: "There was quite a bit of gossip / When the Little Cohn disappeared, / But now he has been discovered, / And it is known where he is. / The elevated train was just opened / And miracle of miracles, / In the very first car / Sat the Little Cohn; / Here in the coupe, look closely, / There he is in person / Rejoice, hurrah! / The Little Cohn is here!" The image shows passengers sitting in the recently opened elevated trains of Berlin, but does not actually show the Little Cohn; he remains elusive, not wanting to be seen by his wife. [Publisher: V.S. & G. Saulsohn, Berlin; 1902.]

Der Cohn ist da!
Ich habe den kleinen Cohn gesehn!

Ich hab' heut' den kleinen Cohn geseh'n!
Das Suchen hat ein Ende!
Mit Cohn heut c o n versirte ich,
Er sprach mehr mit die Hände.
Können Sie das grosse Glück versteh'n?
Ich will's zusammenfassen:
„Wer Cohn und Neapel hat geseh'n,
Kann sich begraben lassen!"

Cohn hat heute doch den besten Klang,
Der Name zeugt von Rasse,
Cohn klingt schöner als wie Vogelsang,
Als Goldmann und Manasse.
Wer bis heut' ihn noch nicht sehen konnt',
Beachte, denn man irrt sich,
Der echt garantirte Cohn ist blond,
Halsweite 42.

Das hoch-komische Couplet „Ich habe den kleinen Cohn gesehn, gegen 1 Mk. zu beziehen vom Verlage Text von Alfred Schmasow, Max Marcus, Berlin W., Passage 6/7.

Nachdruck, auch des Textes, verboten.

VERLAG: MAX MARCUS, BERLIN W. No. 829

FIGURE 8-4. *Der Cohn Ist Da!* or "Cohn is Here!"—another sighting of the missing Cohn, this time by three well-dressed non-Jews pointing to and smirking at the figure in the window. The poem reads: "Cohn is here! / Today I have seen the Little Cohn! / The search had come to an end! / I conversed with Cohn today, / He talked more with his hands. / Can you understand this great fortune? / I'll sum it up: / . . . He who has seen Cohn and Naples, may let himself be buried! / Cohn sounds very good today, / The name indicates his race, / Cohn sounds lovelier than a bird's song, / And also [better] than Goldmann and Manasse. / He who hasn't been able to see so far, / Note that you could be wrong, / The real guaranteed Cohn is blond and has a neck size 42." The text on the left margin explains that "This very funny couplet, I saw the Little Cohn. Text by Alfred Schmasow, to be obtained for one Mark." The gentleman explains that he has seen the elusive Cohn, and, thus, considers himself fortunate, to the point that since he has now seen both Cohn and Naples, he can rest in peace. The speaker confirms that Cohn is a racial identifier, and that the Jew talks with his hands, a theme explained in Chapter 2. The text ends on an ironic note, explaining that maybe the ethnic traits of the Jews are not true; perhaps the real Jew is in fact large and blond, two ideal Germanic traits. The image then shows a tall, blond, and well-dressed version of Cohn in the window (the nose is still elongated)—but this fantasy image is only meant to add to the humor as, of course, the Little Cohn does not possess these traits. [Publisher: Max Marcus, Berlin; 1902.]

FIGURE 8-5. "The Great *Dreschgraf* and the Little Cohn" refers to the confrontation between the distinguished German man at the left and the Little Cohn at the right. This scene does not refer to the "The Little Cohn" song, but takes the character and places him in another demeaning setting. *Dreschgraf* is literally translated as "the thrashing count," but it was the cognomen of a well-known anti-Semitic agitator named Walter Pückler-Muskau. Pückler-Muskau was a lawyer who distinguished himself with lectures and articles advocating violence against Jews with statements like "crack their skulls," "kick them out," and "thrash them"—from the latter statement his nickname was derived. Pückler-Muskau was eventually certified as insane and institutionalized, dying in obscurity in 1924. However, during the Nazi period, he was hailed as a great National Socialist. In this image, *Dreschgraf* confronts the little Jew while spectators smirk and a policeman rushes, perhaps to intervene in case of trouble. The dialogue on the right side of the postcard reads: "The *Dreschgraf:* I am the greater, little man / The Little Cohn: Yes, big mouth and delusional / The *Dreschgraf:* I thrash and make my Germany really fly [soar] / The Little Cohn: You are and make the world 'meschügge' [Yiddish for "crazy"] / Both [something to the effect of]: We both care fully for the amusement of Germany." Although the publisher allows the Jew to respond in force, the portrayal of the Jew as unnaturally puny, while the well-known and virulent anti-Semite is shown as distinguished, reveals where the publisher's sympathies lie.[6] [Publisher: Max Marcus, Berlin; 1902.]

Der grosse Dreschgraf und der kleine Cohn.

VERLAG: MAX MARCUS, BERLIN .

Dess. No. 850

Der Dreschgraf: Ich bin der Gröss're, kleiner Mann.
Der kleine Cohn: Ja, grosser Mund und Grössenwahn.
Der Dreschgraf: Ich dresch' und mach mein Deutschland flügge.
Der kleine Cohn: Du bist und machst die Welt meschügge.
Beide: Wir Beide sorgen voller Schwung
In Deutschland für Erheiterung.

Der kleine Cohn von der Wiege bis zum Grabe.

Die Hochzeit des kleinen Cohn.

Den Cohn mit seiner Kalle	Wie ist die Braut so schön.
Die Hochzeitsgäste alle,	Jetzt macht man nun nach alter Weise
Die kann man jetzt hier seh'n,	Nach Benschen eine Hochzeitsreise.

Verlag J. Wollstein, Berlin C., Hirtenstr. 16 No. 3.

FIGURE 8-6. One of a series of cards titled "The Little Cohn from the Cradle to the Grave." The text at bottom explains that this is a scene of "The Wedding of the Little Cohn." The poem continues: "Cohn and his Kalle [Yiddish for bride] / All the invited guests, / You can all see them here, / How lovely is the bride, / And now according to old tradition / Take a honeymoon trip to Benschen." This card makes fun of the Jews as foreigners from Eastern Europe, clearly showing their appearance (see the bearded Jew at lower left), their speech (using Yiddish words), and their honeymoon destination (Benschen is a place in Poland). The sender enthusiastically embraced the ethnic humor by enlarging the Little Cohn's nose with a pen. The message is that Jews are not really part of the German nation, and although they may attempt to blend in, they cannot hide that they are *Ostjuden*. The written note says: "This card for your collection with kind regards also to mother." Helping a collector amass anti-Semitic cards was not an unusual action in Germany at this time. [Publisher: J. Wollstein, Berlin; mailed within Germany in October 1902.]

FIGURE 8-7. "The Little Cohn Widow in the Widow's Ball." The text below says: "Madam Cohn is in a good situation now,—the year of mourning is finally over, / She arranges a widow's ball,—she dances and hops in any case. / A new little Cohn'chen [a diminutive of Cohn] is what she is looking for,—should it be Meyer, that is fine with her." Here there are three Cohns, the mother dancing with her tiny son, and the daughter at right. The Little Cohn recently died, and, apparently, the family is celebrating at a Widow's Ball, even as a picture of the deceased hangs at the left. The writer pokes fun at the three Jews, showing them as ridiculously small, but still large-nosed, as regular-sized non-Jews stare at them. [Publisher: Max Marcus, Berlin; 1902.]

Die kleine Wittwe Cohn auf dem Wittwenball.

Madamchen Cohn ist schön jetzt raus,	— Das Trauerjahr ist endlich aus,
Sie arrangirt 'nen Wittwenball,	— Sie tanzt und springt auf jeden Fall.
Ein **neues** Cohn'chen sucht sie sich,	— Wenn's Meyer ist, schadt's auch ihr nich.

VERLAG MAX MARCUS, BERLIN W.   Dess. No. 860.

Berlin, Unter den Linden.

Es wird gebuddelt! — Warum? — Der kleine Cohn hat 'ne Mark verloren.

VERLAG MAX MARCUS, BERLIN W.   Dess. No. 846.

FIGURE 8-8. The title of this postcard refers to "Unter den Linden," Berlin's most famous and grandest boulevard. The Café Bauer in the background (see sign at upper left) was the most famous in Berlin, located on the corner of Unter Den Linden and Friedischstrasse. The drawing shows little Cohn at the lower center, looking down at workers who are digging the street. The caption below says: "They are digging!—Why?—Little Cohn lost a Mark." The stereotype of the Jew going to any lengths to recover the smallest amount of money is a common anti-Semitic theme. The handwritten text reads: "We are sitting comfortably here and drinking to your health." It is likely that this postcard was purchased at or near the Café Bauer and the sender thought this would be a funny card to send to a friend—like a photograph taken on an iPhone and delivered by text message. [Publisher: Max Marcus, Berlin; mailed from Berlin in March 1903.]

FIGURE 8-9. *Gruss von der Musterung* or "Greetings from the Physical," refers to the examination all those entering the army must go through. Note that this postcard was mailed in 1911, nine years after the Little Cohn song first captured the imagination of the nation; even a decade later, this anti-Semitic motif still sold postcards. At the top left is a large group of males enlisting in the army, with women waving their handkerchiefs in farewell. Among the enlistees is the Little Cohn clearly identified by his diminutive stature and bowed legs. At the top right is the conscription, and at the bottom right is the outfitting of uniforms. Little Cohn is not seen in these two images. The Jew is being ridiculed for his physical deficiencies and his silly attempt to join an important German institution: the military. The original caricature of the Little Cohn, which was first introduced in 1893, describes Cohn as possessing a body congenitally unfit for the German military. The story continues in figure 8-10. [Publisher: S. Stern, Frankfurt a/M-Sachsenhausen; mailed within Germany in March 1911.]

FIGURE 8-10. Here, Little Cohn attempts to enlist in the army. A group of German army officers has a good laugh when Little Cohn is given his examination to see if he is qualified for military service. At the top left is a small doorway where three "normal" Germans who have passed the physical also stare in amusement. As for Cohn himself, he is placed against a measuring tape reaching 1.54 meters (5 feet), but he only reaches about halfway, a puny 2 1/2 feet. Cohn is further humiliated standing naked, with a long, hooked nose, and grotesquely large feet. The text below says: "The small COHN with the out-of-proportion nose is undersized." [Publisher: S. Stern, Frankfurt a/M-Sachsenhausen; mailed within Germany in August 1907.]

FIGURE 8-11. "Greetings from the Mass Accommodations [or Barracks]" depicts a place where single men come to sleep, wash up, hang their clothing, and even exercise. While all the Gentile German men look fit and act properly, the Little Cohn sits on the "throne" with his pants down at the lower left (note the rhyme). Depicting Jews as lacking hygiene and even defecating (e.g., figures 9-2 and 9-3) was common in anti-Semitic postcards. [Publisher: S. Stern, Frankfurt a/M-Sachsenhausen; mailed within Germany in July 1905.]

FIGURE 8-12. Another view of the Little Cohn with all of the expected deformed features. Note, in particular, the bowed legs and oversized hands. The printed text recounts the tale of the "The Little Cohn" as translated earlier. The written message is enlightening as it confirms that buyers of these postcards were quite aware of the Little Cohn song and story: "Gretele here is the Little Cohn, imagine he has been found, near an oak tree in the forest, his corpse was found. Now think of the distress, Little Cohn is dead as a dodo. Greetings from Miss Bessel, her associate."[7] [Publisher: Not provided; mailed within Germany in April 1903.]

FIGURE 8-13. The immense popularity of the "The Little Cohn" inevitably led to attempts to find real-world versions of the diminutive Jew. This 1904 postcard memorializes one such instance, with a picture of Johann Behnke, the "Original Cohn!" The caption notes that this small Jew is only eighty-five centimeters tall (slightly under three feet) and thirty-five years old, yet he has a "giant full beard." The sender refers to the "Kleine Cohn" in his short message, evidence that the Little Cohn fad was long-lived and widespread. [Publisher: Graphische Kunstanstalt Mecke & Schaerf; mailed within Germany in January 1904.]

FIGURE 8-14. Although the Little Cohn fad originated in Germany, its popularity spread to other European countries later in 1902. This card, published and mailed from Hungary, shows the bow-legged, large-eared, and funny looking Little Cohn in an air balloon, no doubt escaping from his wife. The publisher also mixes in the Jewish wealth stereotype in the caption, which reads, "The Little Cohn in an air balloon. The ship even has a stirring bar, you wouldn't expect anything else, he can afford to live in this style." [Publisher: Not provided, may have been privately produced; mailed from Budapest, Hungary, to Ócsa, Hungary, in November 1902.]

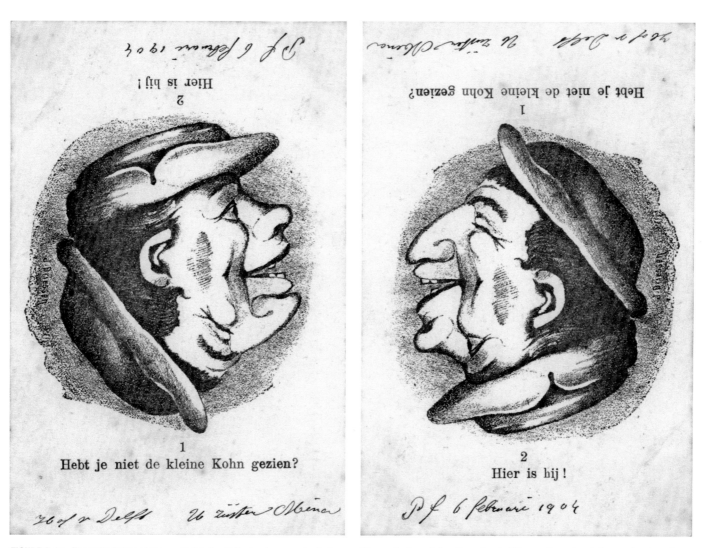

FIGURE 8-15. The Little Cohn fad also made it to the Netherlands, a country that was not known for its anti-Semitic postcards. This novelty postcard plays on the story of the "missing" Jew and the attempts to find him. Image "1" depicts a Gentile, identified by his small nose, asking, "Have you seen the Little Cohn?" When the postcard is turned over, image "2" is revealed showing the large-nosed Cohn with the caption: "Here he is!" [Publisher: Not provided; mailed within Delft, Netherlands, in February 1904.]

CHAPTER 9

THE SPA TOWNS OF KARLSBAD AND MARIENBAD

Karlsbad and Marienbad are two towns located in the Czech Republic that are famous for their numerous mineral springs, which supposedly have curative powers. During the Golden Era and through World War I, the two towns were part of the Austro-Hungarian Empire. Following Austria-Hungary's defeat in the war, the towns became part of the newly formed Czechoslovakia, and then part of the Czech Republic in 1993 when Czechoslovakia was divided into the Czech Republic and Slovakia. Karlsbad (*Karlovy Vary* in Czech) and Marienbad (*Marianske Lazne* in Czech) boomed from the mid-nineteenth century through World War I as luxury spas and resorts, attracting international nobility who came both to relax and conduct political business. Upper-middle-class visitors from around the world also arrived, following the habits of the aristocracy. Newly constructed railway lines in the early 1870s also made the towns more accessible. Jews began visiting Karlsbad and Marienbad in large numbers in the late nineteenth century as well. In 1877, an important synagogue was erected in Karlsbad, funded mostly by Jewish visitors. The spa towns offered a wide range of leisurely pursuits, such as concerts, parties, restaurants, and galleries. Jews generally stayed in the same hotels and visited locations with other Jews, while non-Jews lodged separately.

The large number of tourists visiting Karlsbad and Marienbad were an attractive audience for postcard publishers, and a large number of cards were purchased and mailed from these cities during the Golden Era. Anti-Semitic postcards sold well due to the significant Jewish tourist population that was noticed by the non-Jewish visitors. The German-speaking population also demanded these types of postcards. Both cities were part of the Sudetenland, an area bordering Germany and comprised mainly of ethnic Germans, which was annexed by Hitler in 1938.

Anti-Semitic postcards from the spa towns reflected several themes ranging from "humor" to defamation, reflecting both the physical and cultural inferiority of Jews. The key message was that while Jews may adapt to bourgeois culture and seemingly blend in with affluent society at the spa, they, in fact, ultimately fail in this endeavor. Jews will always be physically awkward, act in embarrassing ways, and remain alien entities. In 1909, an organization called the Association for the Defense against Anti-Semitism listed sixteen hotels and guesthouses in Karlsbad as anti-Semitic. It is likely that many of the anti-Semitic postcards were sold and mailed from guests in these hotels. This chapter will examine this unique subset of postcards from two multicultural cities that had German, Austrian, and Czech influences.

FIGURE 9-1. "Greetings from Karlsbad" shows a variety of tourists socializing around a plaza with a fountain. The image reflects the wide international audience that visited the exclusive spa; note the Asian man (immediately to the left of the fountain at the top), a Turkish man (to the right of the fountain at the top), and a black person. Most prominently depicted are Jews, both secular Jews (the four at the front) and Eastern European Jews in their distinct outfits (the two Jews at the far left). The Jewish men are shown in the typical fashion, either portly and gluttonous or with crooked bodies. The Jewish woman is rendered in a stereotypically unappealing manner; with a large, shapeless body and a big face and lips, she is the opposite of feminine. [Publisher: Not provided; mailed from Karlsbad to Germany in 1906.]

FIGURES 9-2 and 9-3. These two postcards, one from Karlsbad and one from Marienbad, depict visitors attending to the "urgent call of nature," which was attributed to the laxative effect of curative spa waters. Visitors from all classes of society were often caricatured waiting in front of occupied toilets (one for women and one for men), bending over and holding their stomachs in urgency. However, in anti-Semitic fashion, the ugly Jewish character in both cases is distinct from the others in that he is unable to control himself and has defecated in his pants. He is shown humiliated with his hands reaching behind in surprise while the visitors next to him hold their noses and appear horrified. In the Marienbad example, a dog is clearly shown defecating right next to the Jew—implying that the Jew and the animal are the same. In both images, the cartoonist depicted the Jew as particularly disgusting and repulsive, with poor posture, unkempt clothes, and misshapen eyes and nose. The poem in figure 9-2 says: "The water's powers are benign, / If man can tame and restrain them, / But the heavenly power wreaks havoc, / If it breaks free and is unleashed." [Figure 9-2—Publisher: Not provided; mailed from Karlsbad in 1901; Figure 9-3—Not provided; mailed from Marienbad to Kosice, Slovakia, in July 1906.]

Gruss vom Karlsbader Sprudel.

FIGURE 9-4. "Greetings from the Mineral Waters of Karlsbad" depicts a dog urinating on three misshapen Jews below. Note the properly dressed woman walking the dog. The implication here is that not only is the woman "above" the disgusting Jews, but her dog is as well. [Publisher: Leopold Weil, Karlsbad; mailed from Karlsbad to Germany in May 1907.]

Karlsbad.

Zahnpflege.

FIGURE 9-5. A stereotypical Jew at Karlsbad drinks from a straw in what the artist captions as "dental care." The message is that Jews lack in personal sanitation, in this case by neglecting their teeth. By coming to the spa at least once a year, Jews were introduced to the notion of hygiene and could attempt to imitate "respectable society." However, since they were inherently unkempt and dirty, they ultimately failed. Figure 9-6 is another postcard from this series. [Publisher: B.K.W.I., Austria; mailed from Karlovy Vary, Czechoslovakia, in August 1925.]

MARIENBAD.

Kurgäste aus Galizien.

FIGURE 9-6. Jewish "Spa Guests from Galicia" talking at Marienbad. Also note the two Jews at the right and the non-Jew at the left sneering, as if lamenting the presence of all these "interlopers." The Jews are ugly, as expected, with overly expressive hands and carrying an umbrella. Galicia is a historical region in Eastern Europe that currently comprises part of southern Poland and western Ukraine. In the period prior to World War I, Galicia was an autonomous region within the Austro-Hungarian Empire. The Jewish community of Galicia (known as *Galitzianers*) was an important one at the time, with a population exceeding 800,000, or approximately 11 percent, of the population.[1] The capital, Lviv, was a major center of Jewish study and culture. The majority of *Galitzianers* perished in the Holocaust. This postcard was published around 1925, evidence that Marienbad continued to attract Jewish guests after World War I. [Publisher: B.K.W.I., Austria; circa 1925.]

Hirsch im Moor.

Rebekka im Bade.

FIGURES 9-7 to 9-9. These three postcards, the first two captioned "Hirsch in a Mud Bath" and "Rebekka in a Bath," and the third a greeting from Marienbad (with a view of the city at bottom) captioned, "Hirsch and Rebekka in a Mud Bath," depict Jews being washed by spa attendants after a mud bath. The Jews are depicted as fat, misshapen, and ugly, with buckled postures and an emphasis on the dirt pouring off their bodies. These images follow the typical anti-Semitic motifs, which allege that Jews possess physical deformities and lack personal sanitation. In sharp contrast, the non-Jewish spa assistants are clean and stout. The Jews are shown smirking, almost like children enjoying the mud and then being washed, while the attendants are just doing their jobs. [Figure 9-7—Publisher: C.J.C.; mailed from Frankfurt, Germany, to Lyon, France, in August 1907; Figure 9-8—Publisher: C.J.C.; mailed within Germany in July 1905; Figure 9-9—Publisher: Ottmar Zieher, Munich; circa 1905.]

CHAPTER 10

NAZI-ERA POSTCARDS

Every reader is familiar with the Holocaust; therefore, they will not be surprised to see anti-Semitic postcards coming from a nation that perpetrated the destruction of more than half of European Jewry, including 90 percent of Poland's more than 3 million Jews. Nazi-era postcards merely continued a legacy of hate mail that began the moment postcards became widely used. The numerous German postcards analyzed in previous chapters are more interesting since they provide evidence of the virulent and obsessive anti-Semitic mind-set of the German population in the fifty-year period prior to the Holocaust. These postcards, and the fact that they were mailed, also prove that large segments of the population held these attitudes and that they were part of the everyday social fabric. The horrible depictions of Jews and their inhuman characteristics memorialized on postcards and other media made it easier for the German people to accept the deportation of their neighbors and their eventual destruction. The Nazis considered it their duty to destroy all Jews since they were considered a degenerate race whose goal was world control and who stood in the way of Aryan dominance. This chapter will survey only a small sample of Nazi-era anti-Semitic postcards that highlight the elaborate and enormous propaganda machine that the Nazi leadership developed. The first postcard surveyed will be the most famous and widely circulated Nazi-era postcard, that of the "Eternal Jew."

FIGURE 10-1. "The Eternal Jew, Great Political Exhibition in the Library of the German Museum in Munich—From 8 November 1937—Open Daily from 10-21 Hours [10 AM to 9 PM]." This postcard was adapted from a poster advertising an exhibition titled *Der Ewige Jude* ("The Eternal Jew"), which displayed photographs and sculptures of Jews with deformed physical features, documents and charts showing how Jews cheated in business, and warnings against the Jewish conspiracy to impose Soviet Bolshevism on Germany. The displays also blamed the Jews for Germany's loss in World War I. The exhibition was a success, attracting 412,300 visitors, or more than 5,000 per day during its nearly three-month run. In this commemorative postcard, the Jew carries coins in his right hand, demonstrating that he is motivated primarily by money. In his left hand and arm the Jew carries the hammer and sickle, symbolizing Bolshevism, stamped on a map of Germany, and a whip, which will be used to oppress the German people. "The Eternal Jew" was another version of the "Wandering Jew" described in Figures F and 4-12. [Publisher: *Der Ewige Jude* Exhibition, Munich, November 1937.]

FIGURE 10-2. *Der Ewige Jude* was not just a one-time event. Following the annexation of Austria to Nazi Germany in March 1938, the exhibition moved to Vienna, Austria, for a three-month run that began in August 1938. The Vienna show was held at an exhibition hall at the main railroad station; a 30-foot-high poster of the Jewish character (the image from figure 10-1) advertised the show on the station's façade. The impressive poster was itself memorialized in the souvenir postcard shown. Fans of the exhibit could obtain a special commemorative postmark, as seen on the reverse (*below*). The special cancel says, "Visit the Exhibition of 'The Eternal Jew'" and is dated August 30, 1938. It must have been a fun day for the entire family. [Publisher: *Der Ewige Jude* Exhibition, Vienna, August 1938.]

FIGURE 10-3. The Vienna exhibition of *Der Ewige Jude* produced several popular postcards, including this colorful example that is titled *Mander s'ischt Zeit!* or "Men, the time is now!" The phrase was a call to arms originally attributed to Andreas Hofer (1767–1810), a Tyrolean who fought for Austria against the French in 1809. (Tyrol is a region that is now divided between Austria and Italy) In this case, the postcard exhorts the nation that the time has come to expel all the enemies of the state. From left to right, are five characters fleeing from the rising tide of Nazism. The first is a Jew carrying his money box. At the center is a drawing of Kurt von Schuschnigg (1897–1977), the chancellor of Austria prior to the Nazi annexation who opposed Hitler's desire to absorb Austria. When his efforts failed, he resigned from office and was later imprisoned in concentration camps. He was liberated by American troops in 1945 and emigrated to the United States. At the bottom is a virtually deformed Jewish boy wearing the flag of Austria on his arm. The fourth character represents the aristocracy, and the last person is a monk, representing the Catholic Church. [Publisher: Leopold Stocker Verlag, Graz, August 1938.]

FIGURE 10-4. *Der Ewige Jude* was not the only propaganda exhibit that the Nazis produced. Over several years prior to World War II, the Nazi leadership railed against Bolshevism and the Soviet Union. In 1937 the Nazi Party's central propaganda office developed an anti-Bolshevist exhibit that traveled to major cities. The exhibit focused on the dangers of Bolshevism and made it clear that it was Jewish power that was behind the Communist conspiracy to take over Germany and the world. Jews were portrayed as a foreign power, an alien invader that would engulf the German nation unless someone—the Nazis—took action. After Austria fell to Nazi control in 1938, the *Gross antibolschewistische Ausstellung* ("Great Anti-Bolshevik Exhibit") made its way to Vienna from December 1938 to February 1939. This postcard, printed for the exhibition, shows a skeleton soldier carrying a rifle and a machine gun, trampling the earth and bringing fire and doom. The Star of David symbol makes clear who is ultimately behind it all: the Jews. The caption says "Bolshevism Unmasked." [Publisher: Gross antibolschewistische Ausstellung, Berlin, 1938–1939.]

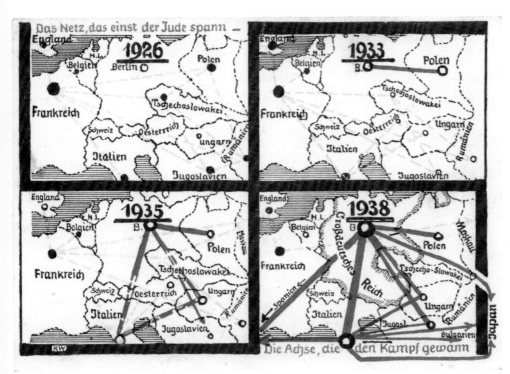

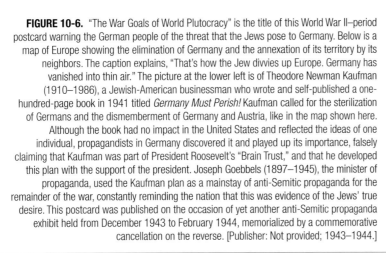

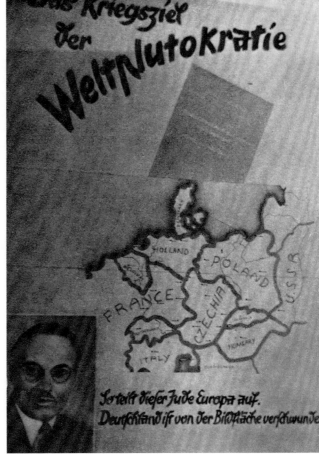

FIGURE 10-5. This prescient postcard, published in March 1939, several months before Germany invaded Poland, shows the imagined progression of Nazi influence and expansion from 1926 to 1938. In 1926, just Germany is seen. In 1933, Germany looked to expand into Poland, then into Italy and Hungary and south to Yugoslavia in 1935, and, finally, in 1938, even further to include Spain and Japan. But the text at the top and bottom reveals at whose expense the Nazi expansion will come: the Jews. It reads, "The net that once the Jew has spun / The Axis which the war has won." A printed caption on the reverse side says, "We thank our Führer! The Government Staff of the Franconia District 4 March 1939." Although the territories shown here were not yet occupied, the local government in Franconia wanted to thank Hitler for his territorial ambitions and, of course, for pushing back against what was perceived as Jewish control of Europe. [Publisher: The Government Staff of the Franconia; 1939.]

FIGURE 10-6. "The War Goals of World Plutocracy" is the title of this World War II–period postcard warning the German people of the threat that the Jews pose to Germany. Below is a map of Europe showing the elimination of Germany and the annexation of its territory by its neighbors. The caption explains, "That's how the Jew divvies up Europe. Germany has vanished into thin air." The picture at the lower left is of Theodore Newman Kaufman (1910–1986), a Jewish-American businessman who wrote and self-published a one-hundred-page book in 1941 titled *Germany Must Perish!* Kaufman called for the sterilization of Germans and the dismemberment of Germany and Austria, like in the map shown here. Although the book had no impact in the United States and reflected the ideas of one individual, propagandists in Germany discovered it and played up its importance, falsely claiming that Kaufman was part of President Roosevelt's "Brain Trust," and that he developed this plan with the support of the president. Joseph Goebbels (1897–1945), the minister of propaganda, used the Kaufman plan as a mainstay of anti-Semitic propaganda for the remainder of the war, constantly reminding the nation that this was evidence of the Jews' true desire. This postcard was published on the occasion of yet another anti-Semitic propaganda exhibit held from December 1943 to February 1944, memorialized by a commemorative cancellation on the reverse. [Publisher: Not provided; 1943–1944.]

CHAPTER 11

ANTI-ISRAEL POSTCARDS

The latest trend in anti-Semitism is substituting Israel and Zionism as a proxy for Jews. Since direct criticism of Jews is now generally seen as distasteful in Western nations (but state endorsed in Muslim nations), disproportionate and obsessive criticism of the Jewish state and Zionism has become more widely accepted. The perpetrators of these attacks on Israel claim they are simply criticizing Israeli policies, not Jewish people. This veneer of legitimate criticism makes this new form of anti-Semitism more difficult to expose. Natan Sharansky, a prominent Israeli politician and author, outlined three tests, the "3D" test, to distinguish legitimate criticism of Israel from anti-Semitism:

> The first *D* is the test of demonization. When the Jewish state is being demonized; when Israel's actions are blown out of all sensible proportion; when comparisons are made between Israelis and Nazis and between Palestinian refugee camps and Auschwitz—this is anti-Semitism, not legitimate criticism of Israel.

> The second *D* is the test of double standards. When criticism of Israel is applied selectively; when Israel is singled out by the United Nations for human rights abuses while the behavior of known and major abusers,

such as China, Iran, Cuba, and Syria, is ignored; when Israel's Magen David Adom, alone among the world's ambulance services, is denied admission to the International Red Cross—this is anti-Semitism.

> The third *D* is the test of delegitimization: when Israel's fundamental right to exist is denied—alone among all peoples in the world—this too is anti-Semitism.[1]

As described in the introduction, the European Monitoring Center on Racism and Xenophobia (EUMC) also cites these types of double standards as examples of anti-Semitism, not legitimate criticism of Israel. Examples of the new anti-Semitism are easy to find. The statistics on the UN Human Rights Council's (UNHRC) proclamations on Israel, versus the rest of the world, are absurd; they can only be explained by obsessive hatred toward the Jewish State. As U.S. Secretary of State Hillary Clinton noted in February 2011 at the opening of the UNHRC's 16th session: "The structural bias against Israel—including a standing agenda item for Israel, whereas all other countries are treated under a common item—is wrong. And it undermines the important work we are trying to do together."[2]

This new form of anti-Semitism is so common in the Muslim world that it hardly raises any eyebrows. Studies of the press in Egypt, Iran, Jordan, Lebanon, Syria, Saudi Arabia, the Gulf states, and the Palestinian Authority show that Jews and Israelis are commonly represented as poisonous snakes, bloodthirsty vampires, and as Nazis.[3] More distressing is the lack of response by Western nations to this overt anti-Semitism and the under-reporting of this story in the Western media. Postcards from the Muslim world that reflect these anti-Semitic themes are difficult to obtain as they are not sold over the Internet and are not carried by postcard dealers. But extensive evidence of anti-Semitic images in the press and other media is readily available and attests to the pervasive hatred for Jews that exists in much of the Muslim world—similar to the ingrained hatred that existed in pre-Holocaust Germany.[4] Similar to pre-Holocaust Germany, Iran has stated its goal of exterminating Israel and its Jews. The two postcards below from Iraq are typical of the types of anti-Semitic imagery used to portray Jews in many Islamic countries.

Sometimes this new form of anti-Semitism is expressed as lies whereby Israel is falsely accused of destroying holy places. The postcard shown in figure 11-3, which was published sometime around 1949, indicates that this tactic was implemented from the moment the State of Israel was born. Accusations that the Jews, even prior to Israel's formation, were seeking to destroy Muslim holy sites was used to stir up hatred and violence against Jews as early as the 1920s. Haj Amin Al-Husaini, the Mufti of Jerusalem from 1921–1948, frequently spoke of the Jewish danger to Jerusalem and warned that the Jews planned to take over the Cave of the Patriarchs in Hebron. In

— اسرائيل تزرع الأرض المقدسة . . ! !

— النابالم هي الوسيلة ! ! ! !

FIGURES 11-1 and 11-2. Two Iraqi-published postcards from the 1980s that portray Israel and the Jews as evil incarnate. The images are self-explanatory. Note both the Nazi comparisons (the swastika in the word "Israel") and the devil / angel of death motif. These types of extreme anti-Semitic depictions are unremarkable. A 2009 book titled *Cartoons and Extremism: Israel and the Jews in Arab and Western Media* reprints numerous cartoons published in recent years in the newspapers of Muslim countries, as well as some Western nations, that echo similar themes as these postcards. [Publisher: Not provided; circa 1980s era.]

1929, Arab riots against Jews were in part triggered by accusations that the Jews intended to destroy the Al-Aksa Mosque.

Another prominent example of this libel was the August 1969 fire at the Al-Aksa Mosque, which was started by a deranged Australian Protestant named Michael Dennis Rohan. Even though Rohan confessed and Israeli firefighters quickly extinguished the blaze, Muslims around the world assumed it was deliberately started by Israel. King Faisal of Saudi Arabia took advantage of these charges against Israel to rally Muslim heads of state and convened a meeting in September 1969 that led to the creation of the Organization of the Islamic Conference. The lies spread by the Muslim world over subsequent decades and the power of the libel were so pervasive that the *Wall Street Journal,* as late as November 2000, noted in an article that an Israeli Jew attempted to burn down the Mosque; two days later, the newspaper printed a correction that the arsonist was, in fact, a Christian Australian.[5]

These false accusations were used as a tool in subsequent decades to stir up the passion of the Muslim population against Israel. In 1993, Israeli authorities started to construct a certain exit tunnel more than 200 meters away from the Al-Aksa Mosque, and in 1998, the exit was completed and ready for opening. Even though the Muslim religious authorities (*Waqf*) had previously agreed to the new exit, its opening provided an opportunity for the Palestinians to accuse Jews of seeking to undermine Muslim holy sites. Yasir Arafat called the tunnel opening a "big crime against our religious and holy places" and orchestrated violent protests that led to dozens of deaths. As recently as March 2010, the Palestinian Authority leadership falsely accused Israel of planning to destroy the mosques on the Temple Mount.[6]

While Israel and the Jews have often been accused of deliberately seeking to destroy holy sites, the only cases where this type of intentional destruction has been perpertrated was against Jewish holy sites. During Jordan's nineteen-year occupation of eastern Jerusalem, all but one of the Old City's fifty-eight Jewish synagogues were destroyed, and the headstones from the ancient Jewish cemetary on the Mount of Olives were used as paving and building stones. Jews were also prohibited from visiting the Western Wall in violation of Israeli-Jordanian agreements. While Christian sites were not destroyed, Christian organizations were prohibited from expanding in Jerusalem. In October 2000, only hours after control of the area surrounding Joseph's Tomb, a holy Jewish site near Nablus, was handed over to Palestinian control, Palestinian mobs ransacked the structure and set it on fire.

FIGURE 11-3. This 1949 postcard, showing a so-called "View of Jerusalem," blamed the newly formed Israel for mutilating holy places in the Old City, presumably during the War of Independence. In this example, Christian holy sites are shown in ruins, most prominently the tower of the Lutheran Church of the Redeemer, which was built in the 1890s on order of the German Kaiser. A broken cross is shown at the lower left. Of course, Israel did not destroy these sites, and they are fully intact today. This postcard was probably printed by a publisher based in Great Britain, the colonial ruler in Palestine prior to the formation of Israel. [Publisher: Not provided; circa 1949.]

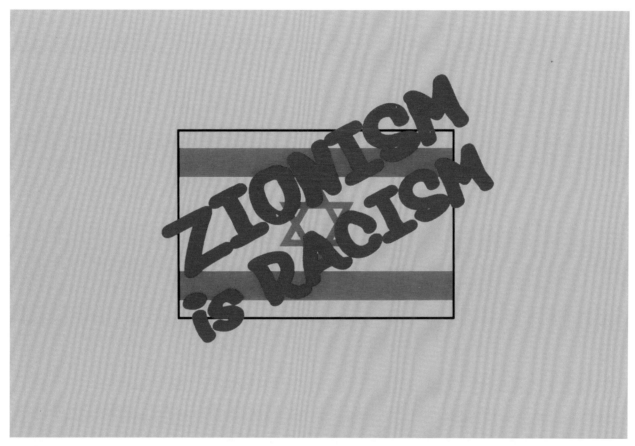

FIGURE 11-4. This postcard was purchased online by the author from an unnamed website that sells postcards. The message recalls UN General Assembly Resolution 3379, adopted in 1975 by a vote of seventy-two to thirty-five (with thirty-two abstentions), which determined that "Zionism is a form of racism and racial discrimination." Chaim Herzog responded to the resolution with an address to the General Assemby, noting that the resolution "is part of a dangerous anti-Semitic idiom which is being insinuated into every public debate. . . . Who would have believed that in this year, 1975, the malicious falsehoods of the 'Elders of Zion' would be distributed officially by Arab Governments?"[7] In 1991, the resolution was revoked. This postcard proves that this type of anti-Semitic discourse is still alive in certain segments of the population. [Publisher: Not provided; circa 1949.]

SAYINGS BY FAMOUS MEN ABOUT THE JEWS

Aussprüche berühmter Männer über die Juden.

Ich gönne den Juden alle Rechte, nur nicht das, in einem christlichen Staate ein obrigkeitliches Amt zu bekleiden. — Bismarck.

Wohin ihr faßt, ihr werdet Juden faßen / Allüberall das Lieblingsvolk des Herrn / Geht sperrt sie wieder in die alten Gaßen / Eh' sie euch in ein Christenviertel sperr'n. — Franz v. Dingelstädt.

Fast durch alle Länder von Europa verbreitet sich ein mächtiger feindseliger Staat, der mit allen anderen in beständigem Kriege lebt und fürchterlich schwer auf die Bürger drückt; es ist das Judentum. — Fichte.

Das israelitische Volk hat niemals viel getaugt, wie es ihm seine Anführer, Richter, Vorsteher, Propheten tausendmal vorgeworfen haben, es besitzt wenig Tugenden und die meisten Fehler anderer Völker. — Goethe.

Die Juden sind unser Unglück. — Prof. Heinr. von Treitschke.

Die Juden bilden einen Staat im Staate; ihren eigenen Gesetzen gehorchend, wissen sie die des Landes zu umgehen. — Graf Moltke.

Auch in der alten Welt war das Judentum ein wirksames Ferment des Kosmopolitismus und der nationalen Decomposition. — Th. Mommsen.

Die Juden sind der Abscheu des Menschengeschlechts (taedium generis humani). Alles ist ihnen verächtlich was uns heilig ist; während ihnen alles gestattet ist, was uns frevelhaft erscheint. Sie sind das niedrigste aller Völker (deterrima gens). — Tacitus.

Trau keinem Fuchs auf grüner Heid', Trau keinem Jud' auf seinen Eid. — Dr. Martin Luther.

Der Jude ist der plastische Dämon des Verfalls der Menschheit. — Rich. Wagner.

Schriften aufklärenden Inhalts über die Judenfrage sind zu beziehen durch den

Reichsverband der deutschvölkischen Partei

Hamburg 6, Karolinenstraße 16.

Hanseatische Druck- und Verlags-Anstalt, Hamburg 36.

This postcard from World War I–era Germany, like the one described in figure 3-1, has no picture; it is simply text. The postcard was not intended to entertain or offer interesting images of the world in an era when there was no television; its purpose was for the sender (who, in this case, was in the military) to tout their anti-Semitic feelings. The card, titled "Sayings by Famous Men about the Jews," reprints anti-Jewish quotes by prominent German authors, philosophers, and politicians, mostly from the eighteenth and nineteenth centuries. One might argue (weakly, in my opinion) that an anti-Semitic postcard that depicted some type of cartoon or drawing was considered humor, and, therefore, its sending was an inadvertent anti-Semitic act; but this argument crumbles with this postcard, which is nothing more than blatant anti-Semitic text. The virulence of the quotes, and the fact that they were written by prominent Germans, highlights the ingrained anti-Semitic attitudes in Germany at the time. Furthermore, their placement on a postcard provides evidence that these ideas were well known and endorsed throughout Germany. Many of these quotes and their authors were co-opted by the Nazis for their campaign against the Jews. Once again, the postcard and its usage by the public was a foreshadowing of destruction of German Jewry.

The card was published by the Reichsverband der deutschvölkischen Partei (DVP), a German nationalist party that operated between 1914 and 1918. Above all else, it was an openly anti-Semitic organization that advocated that all Jews and foreigners of non-German lineage and heredity should be expelled from Germany. During World War I, the DVP conducted a census to prove that the Jewish population was not supportive of the German war effort; when the results demonstrated the opposite, the report was not published. The text at the bottom of the postcard states that "writings of enlightenment regarding the Jewish question can be obtained from the Reichsverband der deutschvölkischen Partei," with address provided. The postcard was mailed through the military post office inside Germany in April 1915; the DVP was able to have its postcards distributed and sold to the Germany military. Several of these quotes were later included by Theodor Fritsch (1852–1933), one of the most dedicated anti-Semites of the German empire, in his *Handbuch der Judenfrage* (Guide to the Jewish Question). This book was read by millions and became the pseudo-catechism of the Nazis and their followers.[1] The translations of the quotes, in order starting at top left, are as follows:

> **I grant the Jews all the rights, except for this one, the written right to hold a higher office in a Christian state.**
> —Bismarck

Otto Von Bismarck (1815–1898) oversaw the unification of Germany in 1871 and became its first chancellor. He is credited with strengthening the power of the German Empire in the late nineteenth century. This quote was part of a speech he delivered to the Prussian Parliament.[2]

> **Wherever you reach, you will encounter Jews / Everywhere the favorite people of the Lord / Go, lock them back in again in the old alleys from where they came / Before they lock you up in a Christian quarter.**
> —Franz v. Dingelstädt

Franz Von Dingelstädt (1814–1881) was a German poet and theater administator. This quote is the last stanza of his poem "The Frankfurt Ghetto," first published in 1841. The poem specifically targets the Rothschild family, which was headquatered in Frankfurt at the time.

> **A powerful enemy state, which lives in constant war with all other states and oppresses its citizens horribly, is spreading out in almost all the lands of Europe; this state is the Jews.**
> —Fichte

Johann Gottlieb Fichte (1762–1814) was a German philosopher and promoter of German Nationalism. In his defense of the ideals of the French Revolution,

he singled out the Jews as constituting a "state-within-a-state" that was "predicated on the hatred of the entire human race." In subsequent years, anti-Jewish writers frequently invoked Fichte's authority to deny Jews rights.[3]

> **The Israelite nation has never been worth much, as it has been a thousand times reproached by its leaders, judges, principal men and prophets; it possess few of the virtues and most of the flaws of other nations.**
> —Goethe

Johann Wolfgang von Goethe (1749–1832) is considered by many to be the most important German writer and scholar. His most famous work is the tragic play *Faust*. Interestingly, the words on the postcard are only the first part of a longer paragraph. His thought continues as follows: "But in self-reliance, constancy, bravery, and . . . in tenacity, it has no equal. It is the most persistent people on earth; it is, it was, and it shall be, that it may glorify the name of Jehovah through the ages. That is why we have presented it here as a model, as the central subject, which the others only serve to frame." Thus, the first part of the quote is worthy to be included among anti-Semitic sayings by renowned Germans, while the second one concludes with some backhanded compliments. These and other excerpts in Goethe's works reflect an ambivalent relationship to the Jews of his time. Like several of his contemporaries, Goethe admired the Jews of the Jewish Bible, but he couldn't connect them with the Jews of his time. He opposed the efforts for Jewish emancipation and became especially active against granting permission for mixed marriages between Christians and Jews. In spite of these views, Goethe cannot be seen as endorsing any of the racial and discriminatory laws that Nazi Germany would come to impose upon Jews. But Hitler, in his *Mein Kampf*, would employ Goethe as a principal witness for his racial ideology.[4]

> **The Jews are our misfortune.**
> —Prof. Heinr. Von Treitschke

Professor Heinrich von Treitschke (1834–1896) was a prominent German historian and writer, best known for his five-volume *History of Germany in the Nineteenth Century* and for the famous quote from 1879 cited in this postcard. Treitschke argued that Jews clung to their identity instead of joining the Germany nation, an act that harmed the state. Given his prominent position at the University of Berlin, his statements helped legitimize anti-Semitism in academia. His quote later adorned the masthead of the Nazi newspaper, *Der Stürmer*.

> **The Jews form a state within the state; they obey their own laws, and know how to evade the laws of the land.**
> —Graf Moltke

Helmuth Karl Bernhard Graf von Moltke (1800–1891) was a German general who served as chief of staff of the Prussian army for thirty years. Moltke's statement on the postcard is paraphrased from an essay he wrote and published in 1832. The statement was later reprinted numerous times in anti-Semitic publications, including one published in Hitler's hometown in 1907 and said to have been read by him.[5]

> In the ancient world, too, the Jews were an effective ferment of cosmo-politanism and national decomposition.
>
> —Th. Mommsen

Christian Matthias Theodor Mommsen (1817–1903) was a German classical scholar and politician who received the Nobel Prize in Literature in 1902. His most famous work is *History of Rome,* which he wrote in three volumes in the 1850s. This quote from that work is quoted out of context, as it merely describes some of the elements that led to the breakdown of the Roman state. Anti-Semites often misused this sentence. Mommsen was actually a stated opponent of anti-Semitism and, in 1880, signed a public declaration of German notables against anti-Semitism. Despite his opposition to anti-Semitism, the ingrained prejudices of most Germans at the time did not escape Mommsen. He called on Jews to abandon their separate culture and assimilate, blaming Jews for the negative feelings Christians had for them; he also stated that "the Jewish usurer is no fable" and, thus, Jews could not remain outside of Christianity and "inside the [German] nation."[6]

> Jews are the abhorrence of humankind *(taedium generis humani)*. They disdain everything that is holy to us. They are the lowest of all peoples *(deterrima gens)*.
>
> —Tacitus

Publius Cornelius Tacitus (56 CE–117 CE) was a Roman historian and politician best known for his two major works, the *Annals* and the *Histories* (the quote is from this work). Although not German, Tacitus's quote was included over and over again among rabid anti-Semitic expressions by nineteenth- and twentieth-century Germans. One of Tacitus's basic premises was that Jews were only loyal to each other and expressed hostility to other peoples.[7]

> Trust no fox on his green heath, And no Jew on his oath.
>
> —Dr. Martin Luther

Martin Luther (1483–1546) played the leading role in launching the Protestant Reformation and founded the Lutheran church. Luther was also a rabid anti-Semite who wrote extensively about the Jews. His work *Von den Juden und ihren Lügen* (The Jews and Their Lies) used hate-filled terminology against Jews, calling them cursed, deranged criminals and ritual murderers as well as agents of Satan. Interestingly, although the quote in the postcard is commonly attributed to Luther, nowhere in his writings did he actually make this statement (although the sentiment expressed by the quote fits neatly with Luther's other writings). Nevertheless, both the quote and its attribution were repeated often enough to become canonized. Following the Nazi takeover of Germany, an eighteen-year-old German woman, Elvira Bauer, wrote an illustrated anti-Semitic children's book using Luther's alleged phrase about distrusting Jews as the title for her volume; 100,000 copies were printed. Needless to add, Hitler too came to hail Luther as a visionary. In 1994, the Evangelical Lutheran Church in America repudiated Luther's writings regarding the Jews.[8]

> The Jew is the graphic demon of the decline of humanity.
>
> —Richard Wagner

Richard Wagner (1813–1883) was a famous German composer well known for his strong anti-Semitic views and writings. His most famous admirer was Adolf Hitler, who was drawn to both his music and anti-Semitic writings. Wagner's anti-Semitic agenda still resonates today. Many Jews refuse to attend performances of his operas, refusing to make the distinction between Wagner, the great opera master, and Wagner, the anti-Semite admired by Hitler himself. The quote from Wagner on the postcard is paraphrased from one of his essays.

messages or in small text so as not to disturb the image. These postcards are known as "undivided back" postcards. After about 1907 (the date varied by country), all postcards were printed with the non-picture side split in two, one part for the address and stamp, and the other for messages; this "divided back" postcard style is still the norm today.

2. Parts of the section on anti-Semitism adapted from "An Abridged History of Anti-Semitism," Anti-Defamation League website, http://www.adl.org/education/holocaust/holocaust_history.asp.

3. "Contemporary Global Anti-Semitism," a report provided to the United States Congress, U.S. Department of State, 2008.

4. "Attitudes toward Jews in Seven European Countries," a report issued by the Anti-Defamation League, February 2009; "'The Passion of the Christ': Is the Movie Anti-Semitic?" ReligiousTolerance.Org website.

5. Andrea Levin, "Anatomy of a Swedish Blood Libel," *Wall Street Journal*, October 14, 2009. For a detailed overview of the multiple errors and distortions in the *Aftonbladet* article see: Andrea Levin, "Sweden's Aftonbladet Spreads Libels, Bigotry," CAMERA website, October 15, 2009, http://www.camera.org/index.asp?x_context=8&x_nameinnews=189&x_article=1105.

6. The actual video of Helen Thomas's statements can be viewed here: http://www.youtube.com/watch?v=RQcQdWBqt14.

7. Menahem Milson, "What Is Arab Antisemitism?," MEMRI website, Special Report No. 26, February 27, 2004, http://www.memri.org.

8. Also see: Alan Dershowitz, *The Case for Peace* (Hoboken NJ: John Wiley & Sons, 2005), 139–41; A statement made by Martin Luther King Jr. comparing anti-Zionism to anti-Semitism (see CAMERA alert, January 22, 2002, http://www.camera.org/index.asp?x_context=8&x_article=369).

9. Website of the Jewish Museum, Frankfurt.

10. Even so, anti-Semitism in Germany is actively present. A study published in January 2012 by an independent committee of experts appointed by the German parliament concluded that 20 percent of Germans have a "latent" hatred for Jews. The study noted that hatred of Jews is deeply rooted in the German mainstream. See Ofer Aderet, "Anti-Semitism is still flourishing throughout Germany, study shows," *Haaretz*, January 24, 2012.

11. See MEMRI website for numerous examples of Hamas's anti-Semitism. Also see "Iran's President Mahmoud Ahmadinejad in his Own Words," Anti-Defamation League website, August 26, 2011, http://www.adl.org/main_International_Affairs/ahmadinejad_words.htm.

12. Bari Weiss, "Palestinian Leaders Deny Jerusalem's Past," *Wall Street Journal*, September 25, 2009.

13. For example, see Efraim Karsh, "Arafat's Grand Strategy," *The Middle East Quarterly*, 11, no. 2 (Spring 2004).

14. "Contemporary Global Anti-Semitism," 39 (see note 3).

NOTES

INTRODUCTION

1. The telegraph was available but used primarily by businesses due to its high cost; the telephone was only in its early stages of development. Sources for the history of the postcard include: William Dûval, and Valerie Monahan, *Collecting Postcards in Colour, 1894–1914* (Poole, England: Blandford Press, 1978), 15–23; Howard Woody, "International Postcards: Their History, Production, and Distribution (circa 1895 to 1915)," in *Delivering Views: Distant Cultures in Early Postcards*, ed. Christraud M. Geary and Virginia Lee Webb (Washington DC: Smithsonian Institute Press, 1998), 13–45; Bjarne Rogan, "An Entangled Object: The Picture Postcard as Souvenir and Collectible, Exchange and Ritual Communications," *Cultural Analysis*, no. 4 (2005): 1–27; David Cook, *Picture Postcards in Australia 1898–1920* (Lilydale, Victoria BC: Pioneer Design Studio, 1986), 14–16; Rick Miller, "Postcards Offer Opportunities for Stamp Collectors," *Linn's Stamp News*, November 28, 2007. Note that the reverse side of all postcards produced through the early 1900s was reserved exclusively for the mailing address and stamp. Messages could only be written on the picture side of the postcard, forcing senders to write short

1. THE DREYFUS AFFAIR

1. According to one study, 85 percent of the approximately one hundred newspapers in Paris opposed a review of Dreyfus's conviction, often espousing a clear anti-Semitic agenda. In one example, *Le Journal de l'Aveyron* assured its readers that eventually the Jews "would come out crushed, annihilated, condemned to be loathed by the entire French population for centuries, and hunted down like wild animals." "The Press," website of Dreyfus Rehabilitated, http://www.dreyfus.culture.fr/en/the-french-and-the-dreyfus-affair/the-formation-of-public-opinion/the-Press.htm.
2. Sharif Gemie, *French Revolutions, 1815–1915* (Edinburgh, UK: Edinburgh University Press, 1999), 230; William Brustein, *Roots of Hate: Anti-Semitism in Europe Before the Holocaust* (Cambridge, UK: Cambridge University Press, 2003), 118–121.
3. Alan Riding, "One Hundred Years Later, Dreyfus Affair Still Festers," *New York Times*, February 9, 1994.
4. Zvi Mazel, "And Justice for All?" Ynetnews.com, July 18, 2010.
5. Harvey Goldberg, "Jean Jaurés and the Jewish Question: The Evolution of a Position," *Jewish Social Studies* 20, no. 2 (April 1958): 67–94.
6. John F. MacDonald, *The Amazing City* (London: Grant Richards, 1918), 218–219.
7. "The Support of Zadoc Kahn and the Reinach Brothers," website of Dreyfus Rehabilitated, http://www.dreyfus.culture.fr/en/dreyfus-and-his-family/the-support-of-family-and-friends/the-support-of-zadoc-kahn.htm.
8. "Der Ewige Jude," website of Holocaust Education & Archive Research Team, http://www.holocaustresearchproject.org/holoprelude/derewigejude.html.

2. THE MAIN STEREOTYPES AND CANARDS

1. Maurice Fishberg, *The Jews: A Study of Race and Environment* (New York: Charles Scribner's Sons, 1911), 78–85; Raphael Patai and Jennifer Patai Wing, *Myth of the Jewish Race* (New York: Scribner, 1975), 207–8; Hasdai Westbrook, "Jews and Their Noses," Something Jewish website, October 24, 2003, http://www.somethingjewish.co.uk/articles/522_jews_and_their_noses.htm; Jay Geller, "(G)nos(e)ology: The Cultural Construction of the Other," in *People of the Body: Jews and Judaism from an Embodied Perspective*, ed. Howard Eilberg-Schwartz (Albany NY: State University of New York Press, 1992), 247–248; Entry for "Nose," Jewish Encyclopedia website, http://www.jewishencyclopedia.com/view.jsp?artid=345&letter=N#1087.

2. "Glee' Star Lea Michele Loves Her 'Jewish Nose,'" PopEater website, August 13, 2010, http://www.popeater.com/2010/08/13/glee-lea-michele/.
3. Tim Nudd, "Halle Berry Apologizes for Joke on Leno," *People* website, October 23, 2007, http://www.people.com/people/article/0,20153681,00.html.
4. "Blaming the Jews: The Financial Crisis and Anti-Semitism," remarks by Abraham Foxman, Annual Meeting, Los Angeles, California, Anti-Defamation League website, November 13, 2008, http://www.adl.org/main_Anti_Semitism_International/Blaming_Jews_Financial.htm; Abraham Foxman, *Jews and Money* (New York: Palgrave Macmillan, 2010), 112; Entry for "Jew down," Wiktionary website, http://en.wiktionary.org/wiki/Jew_down.
5. Henrich Heine, *Wit, Wisdom and Pathos, from the Prose of Heinrich Heine*, selected and translated by J. Snodgrass, 2nd edition (London: Alexander Gardner, 1888), 259.
6. Karl Marx, *A World Without Jews*, translated from the original German with an introduction by Dagobert D. Runes (New York: Philosophical Library, 1959). Searchlight website, accessed September 20, 2011, http://www.searchlight.org.uk/marx/index.html; Henry Ford, *The International Jew* (Dearborn MI: Dearborn Publishing, 1920), 15.
7. "Ahmadinejad's Anti-Semitism at the UN . . . . and the 'Deafening Silence' among Western Elites," Briefing Number 239, Beyond Images website, April 18, 2009, http://www.beyondimages.info/b239.html; Nasrin Amirdesghi, "Ahmadinejad's 'Excellent' Speech at the UN," *Jerusalem Post*, October 21, 2008.
8. Karl Vick, "Why Israel Doesn't Care about Peace," *Time Magazine*, September 2, 2010, http://www.time.com/time/world/article/0,8599,2015602-2,00.html; Victor Davis Hanson, "For the Jews in Israel, Money Trumps All?" *National Review Online*, September 6, 2010, http://www.nationalreview.com/corner/245734/jews-israel-money-trumps-all-victor-davis-hanson; Additional analysis of the *Time Magazine* article by Karl Vick can be found at the CAMERA website. See Ricki Hollander, "Time Magazine Promotes Anti-Jewish Prejudice," CAMERA website, September 7, 2010, http://www.camera.org/index.asp?x_context=2&x_outlet=37&x_article=1921.
9. Isaac Fish Stone, "Selling the Talmud as a Business Guide," *Newsweek*, December 29, 2010, http://www.newsweek.com/2010/12/29/in-china-pushing-the-talmud-as-a-business-guide.html.
10. Preiss has been positively identified as the artist of the postcards in figures 2-26 and 7-7 by a comparison of his signatures to those in publicly available works of his art (the author found positive matches on the website FindArtInfo.com). A Preiss sculpture from a March 2010 auction in Italy sold for $22,000. Another Preiss sculpture sold in 2008 for $121,000.

11. Eli Barnavi, *A Historical Atlas of the Jewish People* (New York: Alfred A. Knopf, 1992), 110.

12. Craig S. Smith, "Non-Jews Reviving Poland's Jewish Culture," *New York Times*, July 11, 2007, http://www.nytimes.com/2007/07/11/world/europe/11iht-poland.4.6617269.html.

13. Monica Kingreen, *Nach der Kristallnacht* (Frankfurt Main: Campus Verlag GmbH, 1999), 7.

14. "Oliver Stone: 'Jewish Domination of the Media' Propogates Holocaust Myths," *The Huffington Post* website, July 26, 2010, http://www.huffingtonpost.com/2010/07/26/oliver-stone-jewish-domin_n_659795.html.

15. "Believe It or Not," editorial, *Financial Times* website, September 28, 2007, http://www.ft.com/cms/s/0/c0e62134–6df3–11dc-b8ab-0000779fd2ac.html#axzz19qR7Hpa2.

16. "Malaysian Prime Minister Urges Muslims to Unite against 'Jewish Domination,'" *USA Today*, October 16, 2003, http://www.usatoday.com/news/world/2003–10–16-malaysia-summit_x.htm.

17. "Roundup of the Walt and Mearsheimer 'Israel Lobby' Controversy," CAMERA website, October 23, 2007, http://www.camera.org/index.asp?x_context=8&x_nameinnews=189&x_article=1105.

18. Jeff Robbins, "Anti-Semitism and the Anti-Israel Lobby," *Wall Street Journal*, September 7, 2007, http://online.wsj.com/article/SB118912590978320145.html; Michael Gerson, "Seeds of Anti-Semitism," *Washington Post*, September 21, 2007, http://www.washingtonpost.com/wp-dyn/content/article/2007/09/20/AR2007092001959.html?hpid%3Dopinionsbox1&sub=AR.

19. Mendl Beilis (1874–1934) was the central figure of the 1911–1913 Kiev blood libel case that became known as the "Beilis Affair" throughout the world. He was raised in a small village, served in the Russian military, and settled in Kiev around 1897. In 1911, he was the superintendent of a brick factory in Kiev and was the only Jew living in the vicinity where the authorities found the body of a thirteen-year-old Christian boy, Andrei Yushchinski. Beilis was falsely accused of drawing Christian blood from the boy to perform religious practices. A thirty-seven-year-old family man with five children, Beilis was incarcerated, tortured, and interrogated for nearly two years. In reality, a criminal gang had murdered the young boy fearing that the youth would inform on them to the police. The Tsarist government was aware of the fact that the accusations against Beilis were false, but it hoped that a trial and conviction would win support for the regime. By the time the trial began in 1913, public opinion abroad and in Russia (although not in Russian Poland) turned against the government, and the whole story was revealed to be a sham. The jury acquitted Beilis due to a lack of evidence, but it made no pronouncement regarding the falseness of the blood libel. In later years, Beilis lived in Palestine and eventually immigrated to the United States. He is buried in the Mt. Carmel Cemetery in Queens, New York. He wrote his memoirs in Yiddish in 1925.

20. The word *oser* is a German word of Jewish or Hebrew etymology from the word *ossur*, which can mean "forbidden" or "not possible."

21. David Firestone, "Congressman Is Chastised for Remarks on Jews and Iraq Policy," *New York Times*, March 12, 2003, http://www.nytimes.com/2003/03/12/politics/12APOL.html. Also Ted Barrett, "Lawmaker Under Fire for Saying Jews Support Iraq War," CNN.com, March 12, 2003, http://articles.cnn.com/2003–03–11/politics/moran.jews_1_reston-connection-congressman-moran-jewish-groups?_s=PM:ALLPOLITICS.

22. David C. Kraemer, *Jewish Eating and Identity through the Ages* (New York: Routledge, 2007), 32–33.

23. Samuel Foster Damon, *A Blake Dictionary: The Ideas and Symbols of William Blake* (Hanover NH: University Press of New England, 1988), 215–216.

24. John F. Burns, "Lessons of Hate at Islamic Schools in Britain," *New York Times*, November 22, 2010, http://www.nytimes.com/2010/11/23/world/europe/23britain.html.

25. Frank Felsenstein, *Anti-Semitic Stereotypes: A Paradigm of Otherness in English Popular Culture, 1660–1830* (Baltimore: The Johns Hopkins University Press, 1995), 127–139.

26. Klaus P. Fischer, *The History of an Obsession* (New York: Continuum, 1998), 84, 101.

27. Dan Miron, *The Image of the Shtetl and Other Studies of Modern Jewish Literary Imagination* (Syracuse NY: Syracuse University Press, 2000), 24–25. Another reference to Jews carrying umbrellas is found in the Polish author Wladyslaw Ludwik Anczyc's work *Flisacy* (The raftsmen: 1855), "both of the play's Galician Jewish characters deviate from the traditional stereotype of a rural Jew. The acculturation of the more conservative of them, Chaim, is symbolized by a red umbrella that he carries while dressed in his traditional black garb." Magdalena Opalski and Israel Bartal, *Poles and Jews: A Failed Brotherhood* (Hanover NH: Brandeis University Press, 1992), 24.

3. POSTCARDS FROM GERMANY

1. Fischer, *History of an Obsession*, 81–118 (quote from p. 116).

2. Fischer, *History of an Obsession*, 109.

3. Many Jews throughout the previous centuries and to this day continue to display long beards and sidelocks. This practice is not based on some nebulous tradition, but rather on the literal understanding and observance of a verse in the Torah (Leviticus 19:27): "The Lord spoke to Moses, saying: 'You shall not round off the side-growth on your head, or destroy the side-growth of your beard.'" In Eastern European countries where Jews

lived, the black caftan, a hat, a long beard, and sidelocks became the distinguishing garb of Hassidic and Orthodox Jews of ethnic identification. Even though many other Jews were clean-shaven and dressed like everyone else, the stereotype of the beard and sidelocks became embedded in anti-Semitic iconography and writings as a mark of all Jews. Quite often in the popular non-Jewish imagination, the beard and hair of the Jew conferred upon him a demonic and grotesque appearance. Across Europe, the legendary "Wandering Jew" achieved a proverbial reputation for the length of his beard. One of the greatest pleasures that German SS officers and soldiers engaged in during World War II was to cut off, in public, the beards and sidelocks of Jews, while mocking them. Visual testimonies of these assaults remain preserved in images of the time.

4. Steven E. Aschheim, *Brothers and Strangers: The East European Jew in German and German Jewish Consciousness, 1800–1923* (Madison: University of Wisconsin Press), 3–6. Interestingly, more assimilated German Jews resented the *Ostjuden* themselves, and came to believe that if only their immigration could be stopped, the "Jewish question" could be eliminated from German thought.

5. The word *mauscheln* in German means "mumble," but in usage during this period referred to the language spoken by the Jews (Yiddish, considered a crude form of German) in a derogatory sense. It is the language that Jews try to hide when they don't want to reveal that they are Jewish. *Mauscheln* also had a second usage, meaning "mouse-like," another trait ascribed to Jews. See Sander Gilman, *Franz Kafka, the Jewish Patient* (New York: Routledge, 1995), 24–33.

6. The section of the written message on the front of the postcard surrounded by a line appears to refer to a place, and may refer to Starnberg, the location for the meeting. The last word that is translated as "Jewry" appears to say "*jüdisch*" ("Jewish"), which would not make sense grammatically. Our translator explained that this may be a grammatical mistake or a colloquial/abbreviated/regional expression that is most likely associated with Jews, Jewry, or Judaism.

7. Helmut Walser Smith, *The Butcher's Tale: Murder and Anti-Semitism in a German Town* (New York: W. W. Norton, 2002); Joshua Trachtenberg, *The Devil and the Jews* (New York: Meridian Books and JPS, 1961), 146–155; Edward H. Flannery, *The Anguish of the Jews* (New York: Macmillan, 1964), 98; the thought that Jews used the blood of a Christian child to mix in with their matzah dough was still prevalent in Polish rural communities as late as the interwar period. Alina Cala, in a study based on interviews with Poles in the provinces, reports that "The expression 'watch out or the Jews will grab you and make you into matzoth,' [was] often used . . . as a way of curbing recalcitrant children. [Such an expression] could grow to the dimensions of nightmarish reality in a child's imagination." (Cala, *The Image of the Jew in Polish Folk Culture* [Jerusalem: Magnes Press, The Hebrew University, 1995], 56);

R. Po-Chia Hsia, *The Myth of Ritual Murder: Jews and Magic in Reformation Germany* (New Haven: Yale University Press, 1988), 8–9; "Russian Court Tosses Blood Libel Case," JTA web site, July 18, 2010, http://jta.org/news/article/2010/07/18/2740091/russian-court-throws-out-blood-libel-case; "Blood Libel on Hamas's Al-Aqsa TV," MEMRI website, April 14, 2010, http://www.memri.org/report/en/0/0/0/0/0/0/4099.htm.

8. Cnaan Liphshiz, "I Saw Ariel Sharon Murder Two Palestinian Toddlers in Lebanon," *Haaretz*, November 19, 2010, http://www.haaretz.com/news/diplomacy-defense/i-saw-ariel-sharon-murder-2-palestinian-toddlers-in-lebanon-1.325540.

9. Jonathan Lis and Barak Ravid, "Israel Blasts Erdogan for 'Outrageous' Statements to CNN, Accuses Turkey of Supporting Terrorism," *Haaretz*, September 27, 2011, http://www.haaretz.com/print-edition/news/israel-blasts-erdogan-for-outrageous-statements-to-cnn-accuses-turkey-of-supporting-terrorism-1.386893.

10. Helmut Walser Smith, "Konitz, 1900: Ritual Murder and Antisemitic Violence," in *Exclusionary Violence: Antisemitic Riots in Modern German History*, ed. by Christhard Hoffman, Werner Bergman, and Helmut Walser Smith (Ann Arbor: University of Michigan Press: 2002), 93–122.

11. Some scholars attribute this postcard specifically to the Konitz blood libel. This is not the case, as this particular postcard was mailed on January 8, 1900, several months before the Konitz affair occurred.

12. The works of Friedrich Stoltze were published in 1880 in *Gedichte in Frankfurter Mundart* (Frankfurt: Heinrich Keller, 1880). We could not locate where or when exactly Adolf published his anti-Semitic poem. We checked with the National Library in Berlin, but they couldn't locate the poem's printed source either. Adolf's works were published in 1902 in a book with the same title as his father's, *Gedichte in Frankfurter Mundart* (Frankfurth: Heinriche Stoltze, 1902).

13. Jacob Borut, "Antisemitism in Tourist Facilities in Weimar Germany," *Yad Vashem Studies* 28 (Jerusalem, 2000): 7–50.

4. POSTCARDS FROM FRANCE

1. The Mohammed al-Durra case is one example. See Ricki Hollander, "More Support for Those Calling Al Dura Broadcast a Hoax," CAMERA website, June 15, 2010, http://www.camera.org/index.asp?x_context=3&x_outlet=167&x_article=1878.

2. Beginning in France in 1236, a Jewish apostate, Nicholas Donin, alleged that the Talmud included blasphemies of Jesus and Mary, attacks on the church, and hostile pronouncements against non-Jews—thus began a history of maligning the Talmud. In 1242 several wagonloads of Talmud texts were burned in Paris, and again in Tolouse in 1319.

3. R. F. Byrnes, "Edouard Drumont and *La France Juive*," *Jewish Social Studies* 10, no. 2 (April 1948): 165–84.
4. Brustein, *Roots of Hate,* 192–93.

5. POSTCARDS FROM GREAT BRITAIN

1. Richard Holt, "Anti-Semitism at 'Worst Level since 1936,'" *The Telegraph*, June 13, 2007, http://www.telegraph.co.uk/news/uknews/1554374/Anti-Semitism-at-worst-level-since-1936.html. Also see "Is British Anti-Semitism in Danger of Getting Out of Control?" Robin Shepherd Online, November 28, 2009, http://www.robinshepherdonline.com/is-british-anti-semitism-in-danger-of-getting-out-of-control/.
2. "Report of the All-Party Parliamentary Inquiry into Antisemitism," a report issued by the All-Party Parliamentary Group against Antisemitism, summary statement. London: Stationery Office Limited, September 2006.
3. Denis MacShane, "Anti-Semitism Is Back," *Guardian Unlimited*, September 7, 2006, http://commentisfree.guardian.co.uk/denis_macshane/2006/09/post_354.html.
4. Raphael Ahren, "The Holocaust Can Happen Again, Warns Top Anti-Semitism Scholar," *Haaretz*, April 12, 2010, http://www.haaretz.com/print-edition/news/the-holocaust-can-happen-again-warns-top-anti-semitism-scholar-1.284060.
5. Cnaan Liphshiz, "Watchdog: British Anti-Semitism Soubled after Gaza War," *Haaretz*, July 24, 2009, http://www.haaretz.com/print-edition/news/watchdog-british-anti-semitism-doubled-after-gaza-war-1.280635.
6. Harold Bloom, "The Jewish Question: British Anti-Semitism," *New York Times*, Sunday Book Review, May 7, 2010, http://www.nytimes.com/2010/05/09/books/review/Bloom-t.html?pagewanted=all.
7. Hsia, 1 (quoting from George Christoph Lichtenberg, *Vermischte Schriften* 3 [Göttingen, 1867]: 266).
8. Deborah Heller, "The Outcast as Villain and Victim: Jews in Dickens's *Oliver Twist* and *Our Mutual Friend*," in *Jewish Presences in English Literature*, ed. Derek Cohen and Deborah Heller (Quebec: McGill-Queen's University Press, 1990), 40–60.
9. *The War on Britain's Jews*, directed by Richard Littlejohn, broadcast on British Channel 4 television (July 9, 2007).
10. "Men's Magazines: an A to Z," Magforum.com website, http://www.magforum.com/mens/mensmagazinesatoz6.htm; "Bert Thomas, Biography," British Cartoon Archive website, http://www.cartoons.ac.uk/artists/bertthomas/biography.
11. George Orwell, "The Art of Donald McGill," *Horizon*, September 1941, http://www.orwell.ru/library/reviews/McGill/english/e_mcgill.

6. POSTCARDS FROM THE UNITED STATES

1. This chapter is primarily based on: Leonard Dinnerstein, *Anti-Semitism in America* (New York: Oxford University Press, 1994). Other key sources: John Higham, "Social Discrimination against Jews in America, 1830–1930," in *American Jewish History*, ed. Jeffrey S. Gurock (New York: Routledge, 1998); article originally published in *Publications of the American Jewish Historical Society* 47, no. 1 (September 1957); Carey McWilliams, *A Mask for Privilege: Anti-Semitism in America* (Boston: Little, Brown, 1948), 114–41.
2. "The Diaries of John Quincy Adams: A Digital Collection," Massachusetts Historical Society website, August 25, 1780, http://www.masshist.org/jqadiaries/doc.cfm?id=jqad03_60.
3. Henry Samuel Morais, *Eminent Israelites of the Nineteenth Century* (Philadelphia: Edward Stern, 1880), 257.
4. Burton J. Hendrick, "The Great Jewish Invasion," *McClure's Magazine* 28 (1906–1907): 307–21.
5. Walter Crane, *Mother Goose's Nursery Rhymes* (London: George Routledge and Sons, 1877), 11.
6. Alex Safian, "The Fraudulent Scholarship of Professors Walt and Mearsheimer," CAMERA website, February 11, 2008, http://www.camera.org/index.asp?x_context=8&x_nameinnews=190&x_article=1446.
7. Martin Luther King Jr., *A Testament of Hope: The Essential Writings and Speeches of Martin Luther King Jr.*, ed. by James Washington (San Francisco: HarperCollins, 1990), 669.
8. James D. Ristine and Allen Pergament, *Atlantic City* (Charleston SC: Arcadia, 2008), 68.
9. "Pawnbroker History," National Pawnbrokers website, http://www.natpawn.com/history.htm.
10. Entry for "Pledges," Jewish Encyclopedia website.
11. Sidney Homes and Richard Sylla, *A History of Interest Rates*, 4th ed. (Hoboken NJ: John Wiley and Sons, 2005), 70–71; Raymond De Roover, *The Rise and Decline of the Medici Bank: 1397–1494* (Washington DC: Beard Books, 1999), 14–15. De Roover explains that the three balls had nothing to do with the Medici family coat of arms, adding that the three ball symbol was simply a traditional symbol of money in art and heraldry.
12. Deborah Dwork and Robert Jan van Pelt, *Holocaust: A History* (New York: W. W. Norton, 2002), 228–29.
13. Several earlier examples are documented, such as an 1876 advertisement for a New Jersey hotel stating that Jews were not admitted, but the Seligman incident was the first incident that captured headlines. See Higham, p. 11.

14. Dinnerstein, 51–52.
15. Benjamin Epstein and Arnold Foster, *Some of My Best Friends . . .* (New York: Farrar, Straus and Cudahy, 1962), 56–59.
16. Steven S. Gaines, *Fool's Paradise: Players, Poseurs, and the Culture of Excess in South Beach* (New York: Crown, 2009), 90–92.
17. "Activity in Queens," *New York Times*, August 6, 1906, http://query.nytimes.com/mem/archive-free/pdf?res=9E04EEDD1F3EE733A25756C0A96E9C946797D6CF; *The Evening World*, Final Results Edition, May 12, 1906, 7 advertisement, http://chroniclingamerica.loc.gov/lccn/sn83030193/1906–05–12/ed-1/seq-7/.
18. Diana Shaman, "If You're Thinking of Living in Douglaston, Queens," *New York Times*, February 8, 2004, http://www.nytimes.com/2004/02/08/realestate/if-you-re-thinking-living-douglaston-queens-timeless-city-area-with-country-feel.html?pagewanted=all&src=pm.
19. Millard C. Faught, *Falmouth, Massachusetts: Problems of a Resort Community* (New York: Columbia University, 1945), 137.

7. POSTCARDS FROM OTHER COUNTRIES

1. "Austria, the Jews, and Anti-Semitism: Ambivalence and Ambiguity, an Interview with Karl Pfeifer," Jerusalem Center for Public Affairs website, December 1, 2003, http://www.jcpa.org/phas/phas-15.htm; "Joerg Haider: The Rise of an Austrian Extremist," Anti-Defamation League website, March 9, 2004, http://www.adl.org/backgrounders/joerg_haider.asp.
2. Bruce F. Pauley, *From Prejudice to Persecution: A History of Austrian Anti-Semitism* (Chapell Hill: University of North Carolina Press, 1992), 183–89.
3. "Caricature from the Antisemitic Viennese Magazine Kikeriki," U.S. Holocaust Memorial Museum website, http://digitalassets.ushmm.org/photoarchives/detail.aspx?id=1041735&search=CARTOONS%2fCARICATURES+(ANTI-JEWISH)&index=24.
4. Cnaan Liphshiz, "Anti-Semitism in Poland Shows Need for Holocaust Education," *Haaretz*, January 28, 2010, http://www.haaretz.com/jewish-world/news/anti-semitism-in-poland-shows-need-for-holocaust-education-1.262261; "Poland Urged to Combat Anti-Semitism," Ynet News, December 23, 2010, http://www.ynetnews.com/articles/0,7340,L-4003289,00.html; Craig S. Smith, "Non-Jews Reviving Poland's Jewish Culture," *New York Times*, July 11, 2007, http://www.nytimes.com/2007/07/11/world/europe/11iht-poland.4.6617269.html; Beata Pasek, "Confronting Poland's Anti-Semitic Demons,"

Time World, January 23, 2009, http://www.time.com/time/world/article/0,8599,1706315,00.html; "Attitudes toward Jews in Seven European Countries," Anti-Defamation League Report, February 2009.
5. Assistance with the explanation for this postcard was provided by Malgorzata Fus, education assistant at the Galicia Jewish Museum, Kraków, Poland.
6. Raphael Patai, *The Jews of Hungary: History, Culture, Psychology* (Detroit: Wayne University Press, 1996), 548–603; László Molnár, "Anti-Semitism in Hungary," *Institute for Global Jewish Affairs*, November 1, 2010, http://www.jcpa.org/JCPA/Templates/ShowPage.asp?DRIT=3&DBID=1&LNGID=1&TMID=111&FID=624&PID=0&IID=5229&TTL=Anti-Semitism_in_Hungary; Karl Pfeifer, "The Return of Hungarian Antisemitism," the Coordinating Forum for Countering Antisemitism, October 27, 2008, http://www.antisemitism.org.il/article/27833/return-hungarian-antisemitism-karl-pfeifer; Anti-Defamation League Report, February 2009.
7. "Mass Holocaust Grave Unearthed in Ukraine," *Associated Press*, June 5, 2007, http://www.msnbc.msn.com/id/19053913/ns/world_news-europe/; Omer Bartov, "Finding—or Erasing—Ukraine's Jews?" *Haaretz*, November 10, 2007, http://www.haaretz.com/print-edition/opinion/finding-or-erasing-ukraine-s-jews-1.230837.
8. Entry for "Haidamacks," *Jewish Encyclopedia* website; Ivan L. Rudnytsky, *Essays in Modern Ukrainian History* (Edmonton, Alberta: Canadian Institute of Ukrainian Studies, University of Alberta, 1987), 299–300; I. Michael Aronson, *The Origins of the 1881 Anti-Jewish Pogroms in Russia* (Pittsburgh: University of Pittsburgh Press, 1990), 113.
9. Israel Bartal, "On Top of a Volcano: Jewish-Ukrainian Co-Existence as Depicted in Modern East European Jewish Literature," and George G. Grabowicz, "The Jewish Theme in Nineteenth- and Early Twentieth-Century Ukrainian Literature," in *Ukrainian-Jewish Relations in Historical Perspective*, ed. Peter J. Potichnyj and Howard Aster (Edmonton, Alberta: Canadian Institute of Ukrainian Studies, University of Alberta, 1988), 306–342; Myroslav Shkandrij, *Jews in Ukrainian Literature: Representation and Identity* (New Haven: Yale University Press, 2009), 19–30; Oleh S. Ilnytzkyj, professor of Ukrainian literature, language, and culture, University of Alberta: "The Word Zyd ('Jew') in the Poetic Works of Taras Shevchenko," private copy of article provided to the author.
10. Bernard Lewis, *Semites and Anti-Semites* (New York: W. W. Norton, 1999), 121–122.

8. THE LITTLE COHN

1. Sander Gilman, *The Jew's Body* (New York: Routledge, 1991), 43. The pamphlet cited in Gilman's book was titled "Israel in the Army" and was published by H. Nordmann, writing under the pseudonym H. Naudh.

2. Fischer, 32.

3. Helmut Gold and Georg Heuberger, *Abgestempelt: Judenfeindliche Postkarten* (Heidelberg: Umschau/Braus, 1999), 235–40.

4. Marline Otte, *Jewish Identities in German Popular Entertainment, 1890–1933* (Cambridge: Cambridge University Press, 2006), 240–44.

5. Paul Lincke (1866–1946), a German composer whose march "Berliner Luft" became the unofficial Berlin anthem, is also the author of a humoristic march using the couplets of "Des Gigerl Cohn."

6. Entry for "Pückler-Muskau, Walter, Count," *Jewish Encyclopedia* website, http://www.jewishencyclopedia.com/view.jsp?letter=P&artid=598.

7. This difficult to read text was written in a poem in the style of the postcard itself, in rhymes and rhythm. The term "associate" at the end represents a formal expression for a friend who keeps company in what seems to be an upper-middle class context.

9. THE SPA TOWNS OF KARLSBAD AND MARIENBAD

1. Entry for "Galicia, Austria," *Jewish Encyclopedia* website.

11. ANTI-ISRAEL POSTCARDS

1. Natan Sharansky, "3D Test of Anti-Semitism: Demonization, Double Standards, Delegitimization," *Jewish Political Studies Review* 16, no. 3–4 (Fall 2004).

2. Tovah Lazaroff, "Clinton: UNHRC Bias against Israel Undermines Its Work," *The Jerusalem Post*, February 28, 2011, http://www.jpost.com/DiplomacyAndPolitics/Article.aspx?id=210208.

3. Sharansky, see endnote 11–1.

4. For example, see: Joël Kotek, *Cartoons and Extremism, Israel and the Jews in the Arab and Western Media* (Edgware, UK: Vallentine Mitchell, 2009).

5. "*Wall Street Journal*, and *New York Times* Correct Inaccurate Stories," CAMERA camera, November 15, 2000, http://www.camera.org/index.asp?x_context=2&x_outlet=35&x_article=116; Daniel Pipes, "Who Set Fire to Al-Aqsa Mosque in 1969," *danielpipes.org*, August 21, 2004, http://www.danielpipes.org/blog/2004/08/who-set-fire-to-al-aqsa-mosque-in-1969; Alex Safian, "The Media's Tunnel Vision," CAMERA website, November 1, 1996, http://www.camera.org/index.asp?x_context=7&x_issue=16&x_article=36.

6. Ricki Hollander and Gilead Ini, "*New York Times*, CNN Whitewash Palestinian Incitement," CAMERA website, March 17, 2010, http://www.camera.org/index.asp?x_context=3&x_outlet=14&x_article=1816, provides an overview of Palestinian accusation of Israel's desire to destroy the Al Aksa Mosque.

7. "Israeli Ambassador Herzog's Response to Zionism Is Racism Resolution," Jewish Virtual Library website, http://www.jewishvirtuallibrary.org/jsource/UN/herzogsp.html.

APPENDIX

1. Theodor Fritsch, *Handbuch der Judenfrage* (Leipzig: Hammer Verlag, 1941).

2. Paul Dehn, *Bismarck als Erzieher: In leitsätzen aus seinen Redden, Briefen, Berichten und Werten zusamengestelt und systematsch geordent* (München: I.S. Lehmans Verlag, 1903), entry for "Juden," item #2, 449.

3. Jonathan M. Hess, "Fichte, J. G. (1762–1814)," in *Antisemitism: A Historical Encyclopedia of Prejudice and Persections* 1 (Santa Barbara: ABC-CLIO, 2005), ed. Richard S. Levy, 227. The quote on the postcard is from Johann Gottrlieb Fichte, "Beitrag zur Berichtung der Urteile des Publicums ueber die Franzoeische Revolution" [1793], in *Saemtliche Werke* 6 (Berlin: Verlag von Veit, 1845), ed. J. H. Fichte, 149.

4. Johann Wolfgang Goethe, *Goethe's Collected Works 10: Wilhelm Meister's Journeyman Years* (New York: Suhrkamp, 1983–89; reprint, Princeton: Princeton University Press, 1994), 207; Klaus L. Berghahn and Jost Hermand, editors, *Goethe in German-Jewish Culture* (Rochester NY: Camden House, 2001), 3–15.

5. Brigitte Hamann, *Hitler's Vienna: A Dictator's Apprenticeship* (New York: Oxford University Press, 1999), 22.

6. Quote from Mommsen's *Römische Geschichte 3* (Leipzig: Reimer & Hirsel, 1856), 550; Stanley Zucker, "Theodor Mommsen and Anti-semitism," *Publications of the Leo Baeck Institute: Year Book* 17 (1972): 237–41.

7. Salo W. Baron, *A Social and Religious History of the Jews 1* (New York: Columbia University Press, 1952), 183; Peter Schäfer, *Judeophobia: Attitudes Toward the Jews in the Ancient World* (Cambridge: Harvard University Press, 1997), 210–11.

8. Marvin Perry and Frederick M. Schweitzer, editors, *Antisemitic Myths: A Historical and Contemporary Anthology* (Bloomington: Indiana University Press, 2008), 43–48; Luther's alleged statement was later included in 1942 in Ernst Hiemer, *Der Jude im Sprichwort der Wölker in Der Stürmer* (Nuremberg: Buchverlag), 48–51, in a variety of versions, and reprinted in Switzerland, Italy, and Poland.

BIBLIOGRAPHY

Published Works

All websites last accessed September 20, 2011.

Adams, John Quincy. Diary entry for 1780 August 25. *The Diaries of John Quincy Adams: A Digital Collection,* 60. Boston: Massachusetts Historical Society, 2005. http://www.masshist.org/jqadiaries/doc.cfm?id=jqad03_60.

Aderet, Ofer. "Anti-Semitism Is Still Flourishing throughout Germany, Study Shows." *Haaretz.* January 24, 2012. http://www.haaretz.com/jewish-world/anti-semitism-is-still-flourishing-throughout-germany-study-shows-1.408862.

Ahren, Raphael. "The Holocaust Can Happen Again, Warns Top Anti-Semitism Scholar." *Haaretz.* April 12, 2010. http://www.haaretz.com/print-edition/news/the-holocaust-can-happen-again-warns-top-anti-semitism-scholar-1.284060.

All-Party Parliamentary Group Against Antisemitism. *Report of the All-Party Parliamentary Inquiry into Antisemitism.* London: The Stationery Office Limited, 2006.

Amirdesghi, Nasrin. "Ahmadinejad's 'Excellent' Speech at the UN." *The Jerusalem Post.* October 21, 2008. http://www.jpost.com/Opinion/Op-EdContributors/Article.aspx?id=117878.

Anti-Defamation League. "An Abridged History of Anti-Semitism," http://www.adl.org/education/holocaust/holocaust_history.asp.

Anti-Defamation League. *Attitudes Toward Jews in Seven European Countries.* Prepared by First International Resources. February 2009. http://www.adl.org/Public%20ADL%20Anti-Semitism%20Presentation%20February%202009%20_3_.pdf.

Anti-Defamation League. "Blaming the Jews: The Financial Crisis and Anti-Semitism." Remarks by Abraham Foxman at the Anti-Defamation League Annual Meeting, Los Angeles, CA, November 13, 2008. http://www.adl.org/main_Anti_Semitism_International/Blaming_Jews_Financial.htm.

Anti-Defamation League. "Iran's President Mahmoud Ahmadinejad in His Own Words." August 26, 2011. http://www.adl.org/main_International_Affairs/ahmadinejad_words.htm.

Anti-Defamation League. "Joerg Haider, The Rise of an Austrian Extremist." March 9, 2004. http://www.adl.org/backgrounders/joerg_haider.asp.

Aronson, I. Michael. *The Origins of the 1881 Anti-Jewish Porgoms in Russia.* Pittsburgh: University of Pittsburgh Press, 1990.

Aschheim, Steven E. *Brothers and Strangers: The East European Jew in German and German Jewish Consciousness, 1800–1923.* Madison: University of Wisconsin Press, 1982.

Associated Press. "Mass Holocaust Grave Unearthed in the Ukraine." June 5, 2007. http://www.msnbc.msn.com/id/19053913/ns/world_news-europe/.

Barnavi, Eli. *A Historical Atlas of the Jewish People.* New York: Alfred A. Knopf, 1992.

Baron, Salo W. *A Social and Religious History of the Jews,* Vol I. New York: Columbia University Press, 1952.

Barrett, Ted. "Lawmaker under fire for saying Jews support Iraq war." *CNN.com.* March 12, 2003. http://articles.cnn.com/2003-03-11/politics/moran.jews_1_reston-connection-congressman-moran-jewish-groups?_s=PM:ALLPOLITICS.

Bartal, Israel. "On Top of a Volcano: Jewish-Ukrainian Co-Existence as Depicted in Modern East European Jewish Literature." In *Ukrainian-Jewish Relations in Historical Perspective,* edited by Peter J. Potichnyj and Howard Aster, 309–26. Edmonton: Canadian Institute of Ukrainian Studies, University of Alberta, 1988.

Bartov, Omer. "Finding—or Erasing—Ukraine's Jews?" *Haaretz.* November 10, 2007. http://www.haaretz.com/print-edition/opinion/finding-or-erasing-ukraine-s-jews-1.230837.

Berghahn, Klaus L., and Jost Hermand, eds. *Goethe in German-Jewish Culture.* Rochester, NY: Camden House, 2001.

Beyond Images. "Ahmadinejad's Anti-Semitism at the UN . . . and the 'Deafening Silence' among Western Elites." Briefing Number 239. April 18, 2009. http://www.beyondimages.info/b239.html.

Bloom, Harold. "The Jewish Question: British Anti-Semitism," *New York Times*. May 7, 2010. Sunday Book Review. http://www.nytimes.com/2010/05/09/books/review/Bloom-t.html?pagewanted=all.

Borut, Jacob. "Antisemitism in Tourist Facilities in Weimar Germany." *Yad Vashem Studies* 28 (2000): 7–50.

British Cartoon Archive. "Bert Thomas, Biography." http://www.cartoons.ac.uk/artists/bertthomas/biography.

Brustein, William I. *Roots of Hate: Anti-Semitism in Europe before the Holocaust*. Cambridge: Cambridge University Press, 2003.

Burns, John F. "Lessons of Hate at Islamic Schools in Britain." *New York Times*. November 22, 2010. http://www.nytimes.com/2010/11/23/world/europe/23britain.html.

Byrnes, R. F. "Edouard Drumont and *La France Juive*." *Jewish Social Studies* 10, no. 2 (1948): 165–84.

Cala, Alina. *The Image of the Jew in Polish Folk Culture*. Jerusalem: Magnes Press, The Hebrew University, 1995.

CAMERA. "Roundup of the Walt and Mearsheimer 'Israel Lobby' Controversy." October 23, 2007. http://www.camera.org/index.asp?x_context=8&x_nameinnews=189&x_article=1105.

CAMERA. "*Wall Street Journal* and *New York Times* Correct Inaccurate Stories." November 15, 2000. http://www.camera.org/index.asp?x_context=2&x_outlet=35&x_article=116.

Cook, David. *Picture Postcards in Australia 1898–1920*. Victoria, AU: Pioneer Design Studio, 1986.

Crane, Walter. *Mother Goose's Nursery Rhymes*. London: George Routledge and Sons, 1877.

Damon, Samuel Foster. *A Blake Dictionary: The Ideas and Symbols of William Blake*. Hanover, NH: University Press of New England, 1988.

De Roover, Raymond. *The Rise and Decline of the Medici Bank: 1397–1494*. Washington, DC: Beard Books, 1999.

Dehn, Paul. *Bismarck als Erzieher: In leitsätzen aus seinen Redden, Briefen, Berichten und Werten zusamengestelt und systematsch geordent*. Munich: I.S. Lehmans Verlag, 1903.

Dershowitz, Alan. *The Case for Peace*. Hoboken, NJ: John Wiley & Sons, 2005.

Dinnerstein, Leonard. *Anti-Semitism in America*. New York: Oxford University Press, 1994.

Dreyfus Rehabilitated. "The Press." http://www.dreyfus.culture.fr/en/the-french-and-the-dreyfus-affair/the-formation-of-public-opinion/the-Press.htm.

Dreyfus Rehabilitated. "The Support of Zadoc Kahn and the Reinach Brothers." http://www.dreyfus.culture.fr/en/dreyfus-and-his-family/the-support-of-family-and-friends/the-support-of-zadoc-kahn.htm.

Dûval, William. *Collecting Postcards in Colour, 1894–1914*. Wthe assistance of Poole, UK: Blandford Press, 1978.

Dwork, Deborah, and Robert Jan van Pelt. *Holocaust: A History*. New York: W.W. Norton & Company, 2002.

Epstein, Benjamin, and Arnold Foster. *Some of My Best Friends*. New York: Farrar, Straus and Cudahy, 1962.

The Evening World, Final Results Edition. May 12, 1906. http://chroniclingamerica.loc.gov/lccn/sn83030193/1906-05-12/ed-1/seq-7/.

Faught, Millard C. *Falmouth, Massachusetts: Problems of a Resort Community*. New York: Columbia University Press, 1945.

Felsenstein, Frank. *Anti-Semitic Stereotypes: A Paradigm of Otherness in English Popular Culture, 1660–1830*. Baltimore: The Johns Hopkins University Press, 1995.

Financial Times. "Believe It or Not." Editorial, September 28, 2007. http://www.ft.com/cms/s/0/c0e62134-6df3-11dc-b8ab-0000779fd2ac.html#axzz19qR7Hpa2.

Firestone, David. "Congressman Is Chastised for Remarks on Jews and Iraq Policy." *New York Times*. March 12, 2003. http://www.nytimes.com/2003/03/12/politics/12APOL.html.

Fischer, Klaus P. *The History of an Obsession*. New York: Continuum, 1998.

Fishberg, Maurice. *The Jews: A Study of Race and Environment*. New York: Charles Scribner's Sons, 1911.

Flannery, Edward H. *The Anguish of the Jews*. New York: The Macmillan Co., 1964.

Ford, Henry. *The International Jew*. Dearborn, MI: The Dearborn Publishing Co., 1920.

Foxman, Abraham. *Jews & Money*. New York: Palgrave Macmillan, 2010.

Fritsch, Theodor. *Handbuch der Judenfrage*. Leipzig: Hammer Verlag, 1941.

Gaines, Steven S. *Fool's Paradise: Players, Poseurs, and the Culture of Excess in South Beach*. New York: Crown Publishers, 2009.

Geller, Jay. "(G)nos(e)ology: The Cultural Construction of the Other." In *People of the Body: Jews and Judaism from an Embodied Perspective*, edited by Howard Eilberg-Schwartz, 243–82. Albany: State University of New York Press, 1992.

Gemie, Sharif. *French Revolutions, 1815–1914*. Edinburgh, UK: Edinburgh University Press, 1999.

Gerson, Michael. "Seeds of Anti-Semitism." *The Washington Post*. September 21, 2007. http://www.washingtonpost.com/wp-dyn/content/article/2007/09/20/AR2007092001959.html?hpid%3Dopinionsbox1&sub=AR.

Gilman, Sander. *Franz Kafka, the Jewish Patient*. New York: Routledge, 1995.

Gilman, Sander. *The Jew's Body*. New York: Routledge, 1991.

Goethe, Johann Wolfgang. *Goethe's Collected Works*. New York: Suhrkamp, 1983–89. Reprint, Princeton, NJ: Princeton University Press, 1994.

Gold, Helmut, and Georg Heuberger. *Abgestempelt: Judenfeindliche Postkarten*. Heidelberg: Umschau/Braus, 1999.

Goldberg, Harvey. "Jean Jaurés and the Jewish Question: The Evolution of a Position," *Jewish Social Studies* 20, no. 2 (1958): 67–94.

Grabowicz, George G. "The Jewish Theme in Nineteenth- and Early Twentieth-Century Ukrainian Literature." In *Ukrainian-Jewish Relations in Historical Perspective*, edited by Peter J. Potichnyj and Howard Aster, 327–42. Edmonton: Canadian Institute of Ukrainian Studies, University of Alberta, 1988.

Hamann, Brigitte. *Hitler's Vienna: A Dictator's Apprenticeship*. New York: Oxford University Press, 1999.

Hanson, Victor Davis. "For the Jews in Israel, Money Trumps All?" *National Review Online*. September 6, 2010. http://www.nationalreview.com/corner/245734/jews-israel-money-trumps-all-victor-davis-hanson.

Heine, Henrich. *Wit, Wisdom and Pathos, From the Prose of Heinrich Heine*. 2nd ed. Selected and translated by J. Snodgrass. London: Alexander Gardner, 1888.

Heller, Deborah. "The Outcast as Villain and Victim: Jews in Dicken's Oliver Twist and Our Mutual Friend." In *Jewish Presences in English Literature*, edited by Derek Cohen and Deborah Heller, 40–60. Montreal: McGill-Queen's University Press, 1990.

Hendrick, Burton J. "The Great Jewish Invasion." *McClure's Magazine* 28 (1907): 307–20.

Hess, Jonathan M. "Fichte, J.G. (1762–1814)." In *Antisemitism: A Historical Encyclopedia of Prejudice and Persecution,* Vol. 1, edited by Richard S. Levy, 227. Santa Barbara, CA: ABC-CLIO, 2005.

Higham, John. "Social Discrimination Against Jews in America, 1830–1930." In *American Jewish History*, edited by Jeffrey S. Gurock. New York: Routledge, 1998. Originally published in *Publications of the American Jewish Historical Society* 47, no. 1 (1957) 1–33.

Hollander, Ricki, and Gilead Ini. "*New York Times*, CNN Whitewash Palestinian Incitement." CAMERA. March 17, 2010. http://www.camera.org/index.asp?x_context=3&x_outlet=14&x_article=1816.

Hollander, Ricki. "More Support for Those Calling Al Dura Broadcast a Hoax," CAMERA. June 15, 2010. http://www.camera.org/index.asp?x_context=3&x_outlet=167&x_article=1878.

Holocaust Education & Archive Research Team. "Der Ewige Jew." http://www.holocaustresearchproject.org/holoprelude/derewigejude.html.

Holt, Richard. "Anti-Semitism at 'Worst Level since 1936.'" *The Telegraph*. June 13, 2007 http://www.telegraph.co.uk/news/uknews/1554374/Anti-Semitism-at-worst-level-since-1936.html.

Homes, Sidney, and Richard Sylla. *A History of Interest Rates*. 4th ed. Hoboken, NJ: John Wiley & Sons, 2005.

Hsia, R. Po-Chia. *The Myth of Ritual Murder: Jews and Magic in Reformation Germany*. New Haven, CT: Yale University Press, 1988.

Huffington Post. "Oliver Stone: 'Jewish Domination of the Media' Propogates Holocaust Myths." July 26, 2010. http://www.huffingtonpost.com/2010/07/26/oliver-stone-jewish-domin_n_659795.html.

Jerusalem Center for Public Affairs. "Austria, the Jews, and Anti-Semitism: Ambivalence and Ambiguity, An Interview with Karl Pfeifer." December 1, 2003. http://www.jcpa.org/phas/phas-15.htm.

Jewish Encyclopedia. "Galicia, Austria," "Nose," "Haidamacks," "Pledge," and "Pückler-Muskau, Walter, Count." http://www.jewishencyclopedia.com/.

Jewish Museum. http://juedischesmuseum.de/148.html?&Fsize=ucrwovnpakxxy&L=1.

Jewish Virtual Library. "Israeli Ambassador Herzog's Response to Zionism is Racism Resolution." November 10, 1975. http://www.jewishvirtuallibrary.org/jsource/UN/herzogsp.html.

JTA. "Russian Court Tosses Blood Libel Case." July 18, 2010. http://jta.org/news/article/2010/07/18/2740091/russian-court-throws-out-blood-libel-case.

Karsh, Efraim. "Arafat's Grand Strategy." *Middle East Quarterly* 11, no. 2 (2004): 3–11.

King, Martin Luther, Jr. *A Testament of Hope: The Essential Writings and Speeches of Martin Luther King, Jr.* Edited by James Washington. San Francisco: HarperCollins, 1990.

Kingreen, Monica. *Nach der Kristallnacht*. Frankfurt Main: Campus Verlag GmbH, 1999.

Kraemer, David C. *Jewish Eating and Identity through the Ages*. New York: Routledge, 2007.

Lazaroff, Tovah. "Clinton: UNHRC Bias against Israel Undermines Its Work." *Jerusalem Post*. February 28, 2011. http://www.jpost.com/DiplomacyAndPolitics/Article.aspx?id=210208.

Levin, Andrea. "Anatomy of a Swedish Blood Libel." *Wall Street Journal*. October 14, 2009. http://online.wsj.com/article/SB10001424052748704107204574470712953449876.html.

Lewis, Bernard. *Semites and Anti-Semites*. New York: W.W. Norton & Company, 1999.

Liphshiz, Cnaan. "Anti-Semitism in Poland Shows Need for Holocaust Education." *Haaretz*. January 28, 2010. http://www.haaretz.com/jewish-world/news/anti-semitism-in-poland-shows-need-for-holocaust-education-1.262261.

Liphshiz, Cnaan. "I Saw Ariel Sharon Murder 2 Palestinian Toddlers in Lebanon." *Haaretz*. November 19, 2010. http://www.haaretz.com/news/diplomacy-defense/i-saw-ariel-sharon-murder-2-palestinian-toddlers-in-lebanon-1.325540.

Liphshiz, Cnaan. "Watchdog: British Anti-Semitism Doubled after Gaza War." *Haaretz*. July 24, 2009. http://www.haaretz.com/print-edition/news/watchdog-british-anti-semitism-doubled-after-gaza-war-1.280635.

Littlejohn, Richard. *The War on Britain's Jews?* Television documentary. Directed by Dimitri Collingridge. 2007. London: Atlantic Productions.

MacDonald, John F. *The Amazing City*. London: Grant Richards, 1918.

MacShane, Denis. "Anti-Semitism Is Back." *Guardian Unlimited*. September 7, 2006. http://commentisfree.guardian.co.uk/denis_macshane/2006/09/post_354.html.

Magforum.com. "Men's Magazines: An A to Z." http://www.magforum.com/mens/mensmagazinesatoz6.htm.

Marx, Karl. *A World without Jews*. Edited and with an introduction by Dagobert D. Runes. New York: Philosophical Library, 1959.

Mazel, Zvi. "And Justice for all?" *Ynetnews.com*. July 18, 2010. http://www.ynetnews.com/articles/0,7340,L-3921033,00.html.

McWilliams, Carey. *A Mask for Privilege: Anti-Semitism in America*. Boston: Little, Brown and Company, 1948.

MEMRI website. "Blood Libel on Hamas' Al-Aqsa TV." April 14, 2010. http://www.memri.org/report/en/0/0/0/0/0/0/4099.htm.

Miller, Rick. "Postcards Offer Opportunities for Stamp Collectors." *Linn's Stamp News*. November 28, 2007. http://www.linns.com/howto/refresher/postcards_20041011/refreshercourse.aspx.

Milson, Menahem. "What Is Arab Antisemitism?" *MEMRI*, Special Report No. 26. February 27, 2004. http://www.memri.org/report/en/0/0/0/0/0/0/1074.htm.

Miron, Dan. *The Image of the Shtetl and Other Studies of Modern Jewish Literary Imagination*. Syracuse, NY: Syracuse University Press, 2000.

Molnár, László. "Anti-Semitism in Hungary." Institute for Global Jewish Affairs. November 1, 2010. http://www.jcpa.org/JCPA/Templates/ShowPage.asp?DRIT=3&DBID=1&LNGID=1&TMID=111&FID=624&PID=0&IID=5229&TTL=Anti-Semitism_in_Hungary.

Morais, Henry Samuel. *Eminent Israelites of the Nineteenth Century*. Philadelphia: Edward Stern & Co., 1880.

National Pawnbrokers website. "Pawnbroker History." http://www.natpawn.com/history.htm.

Nessenhoff, David. "Helen Thomas Tells Jews to Go Back to Germany." YouTube video, posted by "rabbilive," June 3, 2010. http://www.youtube.com/watch?v=RQcQdWBqt14.

New York Times. "Activity in Queens." August 6, 1906. http://query.nytimes.com/mem/archive-free/pdf?res=9E04EEDD1F3EE733A25756C0A96E9C946797D6CF.

Nudd, Tim. "Halle Berry Apologizes for Joke on Leno." *People*. October 23, 2007. http://www.people.com/people/article/0,,20153681,00.html.

Opalski, Magdalena, and Israel Bartal. *Poles and Jews: A Failed Brotherhood*. Hanover, NH: Brandeis University Press, 1992.

Orwell, George. "The Art of Donald McGill." *Horizon*. (September 1941). http://www.orwell.ru/library/reviews/McGill/english/e_mcgill.

Otte, Marline. *Jewish Identities in German Popular Entertainment, 1890–1933*. Cambridge: Cambridge University Press, 2006.

Pasek, Beata. "Confronting Poland's Anti-Semitic Demons." *Time World*. January 23, 2009. http://www.time.com/time/world/article/0,8599,1706315,00.html.

Patai, Raphael. *The Jews of Hungary: History, Culture, Psychology*. Detroit: Wayne University Press, 1996.

Patai, Raphael, and Jennifer Patai Wing. *Myth of the Jewish Race*. New York: Scribner, 1975.

Pauley, Bruce F. *From Prejudice to Persecution: A History of Austrian Anti-Semitism*. Chapell Hill: University of North Carolina Press, 1992.

Perry, Marvin, and Frederick M. Schweitzer, eds. *Antisemitic Myths: A Historical and Contemporary Anthology*. Bloomington: Indiana University Press, 2008.

Pfeifer, Karl. "The Return of Hungarian Antisemitism." The Coordinating Forum for Countering Antisemitism. October 27, 2008. http://www.antisemitism.org.il/article/27833/return-hungarian-antisemitism-karl-pfeifer.

Pipes, Daniel. "Who Set Fire to Al-Aqsa Mosque in 1969." *danielpipes.org*. August 21, 2004. http://www.danielpipes.org/blog/2004/08/who-set-fire-to-al-aqsa-mosque-in-1969.

PopEater. "'Glee' Star Lea Michele Loves Her 'Jewish Nose.'" August 13, 2010. http://www.popeater.com/2010/08/13/glee-lea-michele/.

Riding, Alan. "100 Years Later, Dreyfus Affair Still Festers." *The New York Times*. February 9, 2004. http://www.nytimes.com/1994/02/09/world/100-years-later-dreyfus-affair-still-festers.html.

Ristine, James D., and Allen Pergament. *Atlantic City*. Charleston, SC: Arcadia Publishing, 2008.

Robbins, Jeff. "Anti-Semitism and the Anti-Israel Lobby." *The Wall Street Journal*. September 7, 2007. http://online.wsj.com/article/SB118912590978320145.html.

Robin Shepherd Online. "Is British Anti-Semitism in Danger of Getting Out of Control?" November 28, 2009. http://www.robinshepherdonline.com/is-british-anti-semitism-in-danger-of-getting-out-of-control/.

Robinson, B. A. "'The Passion of the Christ' Is the Movie Anti-Semitic?" ReligiousTolerance.Org. May 21, 2004. http://www.religioustolerance.org/chrgibson10.htm.

Rogan, Bjarne. "An Entangled Object: The Picture Postcard as Souvenir and Collectible, Exchange and Ritual Communications." *Cultural Analysis* 4 (2005): 1–27.

Rudnytsky, Ivan L. *Essays in Modern Ukrainian History*. Edmonton: Canadian Institute of Ukrainian Studies, University of Alberta, 1987.

Safian, Alex. "The Fraudulent Scholarship of Professors Walt and Mearsheimer." CAMERA. February 11, 2008. http://www.camera.org/index.asp?x_context=8&x_nameinnews=190&x_article=1446.

Safian, Alex. "The Media's Tunnel Vision." CAMERA. November 1, 1996. http://www.camera.org/index.asp?x_context=7&x_issue=16&x_article=36.

Schäfer, Peter. *Judeophobia: Attitudes toward the Jews in the Ancient World.* Cambridge, MA: Harvard University Press, 1997.

Shaman, Diana. "If You're Thinking of Living in Douglaston, Queens." *New York Times.* February 8, 2004. http://www.nytimes.com/2004/02/08/realestate/if-you-re-thinking-living-douglaston-queens-timeless-city-area-with-country-feel.html?pagewanted=all&src=pm.

Sharansky, Natan. "3D Test of Anti-Semitism: Demonization, Double Standards, Delegitimization." *Jewish Political Studies Review* 16 (Fall 2004): 3–4.

Shkandrij, Myroslav. *Jews in Ukrainian Literature: Representation and Identity.* New Haven, CT: Yale University Press, 2009.

Smith, Craig S. "Non-Jews reviving Poland's Jewish Culture." *New York Times.* July 11, 2007. http://www.nytimes.com/2007/07/11/world/europe/11iht-poland.4.6617269.html.

Smith, Helmut Walser. *The Butcher's Tale: Murder and Anti-Semitism in a German Town.* New York: W.W. Norton & Company, 2002.

Smith, Helmut Walser. "Konitz, 1900: Ritual Murder and Antisemitic Violence." In *Exclusionary Violence: Antisemitic Riots in Modern German History*, edited by Christhard Hoffman, Werner Bergman, and Helmut Walser Smith, 93–122. Ann Arbor: University of Michigan Press, 2002.

Stone, Isaac Fish. "Selling the Talmud as a Business Guide." *Newsweek.* December 29, 2010. http://www.newsweek.com/2010/12/29/in-china-pushing-the-talmud-as-a-business-guide.html.

Trachtenberg, Joshua. *The Devil and the Jews.* New York: Meridian Books and JPS, 1961.

U.S. Department of State. *Contemporary Global Anti-Semitism: A ReportProvided to the United States Congress.* 2008. http://www.state.gov/documents/organization/102301.pdf.

U.S. Holocaust Memorial Museum. "Caricature from the Antisemitic Viennese Magazine Kikeriki.0" http://digitalassets.ushmm.org/photoarchives/detail.aspx?id=1041735&search=CARTOONS%2fCARICATURES+(ANTI-JEWISH)&index=24.

USA Today. "Malaysian Prime Minister Urges Muslims to Unite against 'Jewish Domination.'" October 16, 2003. http://www.usatoday.com/news/world/2003-10-16-malaysia-summit_x.htm.

Vick, Karl. "Why Israel Doesn't Care About Peace." *Time Magazine.* September 2, 2010. http://www.time.com/time/world/article/0,8599,2015602-2,00.html.

Weiss, Barry. "Palestinian Leaders Deny Jerusalem's Past." *Wall Street Journal.* September 25, 2009. http://online.wsj.com/article/SB10001424052970203917304574413811883589676.html.

Westbrook, Hasdai. "Jews and Their Noses." *SomethingJewish.* October 24, 2003. http://www.somethingjewish.co.uk/articles/522_jews_and_their_noses.htm.

Wiktionary. "Jew down." http://en.wiktionary.org/wiki/Jew_down.

Woody, Howard. "International Postcards: Their History, Production, and Distribution (circa 1895 to 1915)." In *Delivering Views: Distant Cultures in Early Postcards*, edited by Christraud M. Geary and Virginia Lee Webb, 13–45. Washington, DC: Smithsonian Institute Press, 1998.

Ynet News. "Poland Urged to Combat Anti-Semitism." December 23, 2010. http://www.ynetnews.com/articles/0,7340,L-4003289,00.html.

Zucker, Stanley. "Theodor Mommsen and Antisemitism." *The Leo Baeck Institute Year Book* 17, no. 1 (1972): 237–41.

Manuscripts and Archives

Ilnytzkyj, Oleh S. "The Word Zyd ('Jew') in the Poetic Works of Taras Shevchenko." Private copy of article provided to the author.

Wittenberg town church, 65
women, 52, 116, 201
world domination, 63
World's Columbian Exposition (1893), 4, 5
World War I, 6, 9, 74, 78, 109, 132, 164, 187
World War II, 109, 134

X

xenophobia, 76

Y

Yiddish language, 80, 164
   accent, mocking of, 46, 51, 52, 68, 125, 126, 128,
     140, 156, 186
   development of, 76
   mocking of, 76, 82, 139

Z

Zionism, 11, 16, 23, 161, 212–15
Zola, Emile, 21, 24, 27, 30, 31, 35